Let's Pretend
This Never Happened

(A Mostly True Memoir)

Jenny Lawson

THE BLOGGESS

PICADOR

First published 2012 by Amy Einhorn Books,
part of the Penguin Group (USA) Inc., New York

First published in Great Britain in paperback 2012 by Picador
an imprint of Pan Macmillan, a division of Macmillan Publishers Limited
Pan Macmillan, 20 New Wharf Road, London N1 9RR
Basingstoke and Oxford
Associated companies throughout the world
www.panmacmillan.com

ISBN 978-1-4472-2344-3

Although the incidents in this book are substantially as I remember them,
the names and certain identifying features of some people portrayed in it
have been changed to protect their privacy – *Jenny Lawson*

1 3 5 7 9 8 6 4 2

A CIP catalogue record for this book is available from
the British Library.

Printed and bound by CPI Group (UK) Ltd, Croydon, CR0 4YY

Visit **www.picador.com** to read more about all our books
and to buy them. You will also find features, author interviews and
news of any author events, and you can sign up for e-newsletters
so that you're always first to hear about our new releases.

This book is a love letter to my family. It's about the surprising discovery that the most terribly human moments—the ones we want to pretend never happened—are the very same moments that make us who we are today. I've reserved the very best stories of my life for this book . . . to celebrate the strange, and to give thanks for the bizarre. Because you are defined not by life's imperfect moments, but by your reaction to them. And because there is joy in embracing—rather than running screaming from—the utter absurdity of life. I thank my family for teaching me that lesson. In spades.

I want to thank everyone who helped me create this book, except for that guy who yelled at me in Kmart when I was eight because he thought I was being "too rowdy."

You're an asshole, sir.

Why, Yes, There *Is* a Method to My Madness

Contents

Introduction

This book is totally true, except for the parts that aren't. It's basically like *Little House on the Prairie* but with more cursing. And I know, you're thinking, *"But* Little House on the Prairie *was totally true!"* and no, I'm sorry, but it wasn't. Laura Ingalls was a compulsive liar with no fact-checker, and probably if she was still alive today her mom would be saying, "I don't know *how* Laura came up with this whole *'I'm-a-small-girl-on-the-prairie'* story. We lived in New Jersey with her aunt Frieda and our dog, Mary, who was blinded when Laura tried to bleach a lightning bolt on her forehead. I have no idea where she got the *'and we lived in a dugout'* thing, although we did take her to Carlsbad Caverns once."

And that's why *I'm* better than Laura Ingalls. Because my story is ninety percent accurate, *and* I really did live in a dugout.[1] The reason this memoir is only *mostly* true instead of *totally* true is that I relish not getting sued. Also, I want my family to be able to say, "Oh, *that* never happened. *Of course* we never actually tossed her out of a moving car when she was eight. That's one of those *crazy* things that isn't quite the truth." (And they're right, because the truth is that I was nine. I was sitting on my mom's

---

1. I never actually lived in a dugout. But I did totally go to Carlsbad Caverns once.

lap when my dad made a hard left, the door popped open, and I was tossed out like a sack full of kittens. My mom managed to grab my arm, which would have been helpful if my father had actually *stopped* the car, but apparently he didn't notice or possibly thought I'd just catch up, and so my legs were dragged through a parking lot that I'm pretty sure was paved with broken glass and used syringes. (I learned three lessons from this experience: *One:* that vehicle safety in the late seventies was not exceptional for children. *Two:* that you should always leave before the officials arrive, as the orangeish sting of the medicinal acid applied by a sadistic ambulance driver will hurt far worse than any injury you can sustain being dragged behind a car. *And three:* that "Don't make me come back there" is an empty threat, unless your father has been driving four hours with two screaming kids and he suddenly gets very quiet, in which case you should lock your door or at least remember to tuck and roll. I'm not saying he *intentionally* threw me out of a moving car, just that an opportunity presented itself and that my father is a dangerous man who shouldn't be trusted.)[2]

Did you notice how, like, *half* of this introduction was a rambling parenthetical? That shit is going to happen *all the time.* I apologize in advance for that, and also for offending you, because you're going to get halfway through this book and giggle at non sequiturs about Hitler and abortions and poverty, and you'll feel superior to all the uptight, easily offended people who need to learn how to take a fucking joke, but then somewhere in here you'll read one random thing that *you're* sensitive about, and everyone else will think it's hysterical, but you'll think, "Oh, that is *way* over the line." I apologize for that one thing. Honestly, I don't know what I was thinking.

---

2. When I read these stories to friends I'm always shocked when they stop me to ask, "Wait, is that *true?*" during the most accurate of all of the stories. The things that have been changed are mainly names and dates, but the stories you think couldn't possibly have happened? *Those are the real ones.* As in real life, the most horrible stories are the ones that are the truest. And, as in real life, the reverse is true as well.

I Was a
Three-Year-Old
Arsonist

C all me Ishmael. I won't answer to it, because it's not my name, but it's much more agreeable than most of the things I've been called. "Call me *'that-weird-chick-who-says-"fuck"-a-lot'*" is probably more accurate, but "Ishmael" seems classier, and it makes a way more respectable beginning than the sentence I'd originally written, which was about how I'd just run into my gynecologist at Starbucks and she totally looked right past me like she didn't even know me. And so I stood there wondering whether that's something she does on purpose to make her clients feel less uncomfortable, or whether she just *genuinely* didn't recognize me without my vagina. Either way, it's very disconcerting when people who've been inside your vagina don't acknowledge your existence. Also, I just want to clarify that I don't mean "without my vagina" like I didn't have it with me at the time. I just meant that I wasn't, you know . . . *displaying it* while I was at Starbucks. That's probably understood, but I thought I should clarify, since it's the first chapter and you don't know that much about me. So just to clarify, I *always* have my vagina with me. It's like my American Express card. (In that I don't leave home without it. Not that I use it to buy stuff with.)

This book is a true story about me and my battle with leukemia, and (*spoiler alert*) in the end I die, so you *could* just read this sentence and then pretend that you read the whole book. Unfortunately, there's a secret word somewhere in this book, and if you don't read all of it you won't find out the secret word. And then the people in your book club will totally know that you stopped reading after this paragraph and will realize that you're a big, fat fake.

Okay, *fine*. The secret word is "Snausages."
  The end.

Still there? *Good*. Because the secret word is not really "Snausages," and I don't even know how to *spell* "leukemia." This is a special test that you can use to see who really read the book. If someone in your book club even *mentions* Snausages or leukemia, they are a liar and you should make them leave and probably you should frisk them as you're throwing them out, because they may have stolen some of your silverware. The real secret word is "fork."[1]

I grew up a poor black girl in New York. Except replace "black" with "white," and "New York" with "rural Texas." The "poor" part can stay. I was born in Austin, Texas, which is known for its popular "Keep Austin Weird" campaign, and since I've spent my whole life being pigeonholed as "that weird girl," I ended up fitting in there perfectly *and-lived-happily-ever-after. The-end*. This is probably what would have been the end of my book if my parents hadn't moved us away from Austin when I was three.

I have pretty much no memory of Austin, but according to my mom we lived in a walk-up apartment near the military base, and late at night I

---

1. "Fork" is not really the real secret word. There isn't actually a secret word. Because this is a book, y'all. *Not a fucking spy movie.*

would stand up in my crib, open the curtains, and attempt to wave soldiers on the street up to my room. My father was one of those soldiers at the time, and when my mom told me this story as a teenager I pointed out that perhaps she should have appreciated my getting him off the streets like that. Instead she and my father just moved my crib away from the window, because they were concerned I was "developing an aptitude for that kind of trade." Apparently I was really distraught about this whole arrangement, because the very next week I shoved a broom into the living room furnace, set it on fire, and ran through the apartment screaming and swinging the flaming torch around my head. *Allegedly.* I have no memory of this at all, but if it *did* happen I suspect I was probably waving it around like some kinda awesomely patriotic, flaming baton. To hear my mother tell it, I was viciously brandishing it at her like she was Frankenstein's monster and I was several angry villagers. My mother refers to this as my first arson episode. I refer to it as a lesson in why rearranging someone else's furniture is dangerous to everyone. We've agreed to disagree on the wording.

Shortly after that incident, we packed up and moved to the small, violently rural town of Wall, Texas. My parents claimed it was because my dad's enlistment had ended, and my mom found herself pregnant with my little sister and wanted to be closer to family, but I suspect it was because they realized there was something wrong with me and believed that growing up in the same small West Texas town that they'd grown up in might change me into a normal person. This was one of many things that they were wrong about. (Other things they were wrong about: the existence of the tooth fairy, the "timeless appeal" of fake wood paneling, the wisdom of leaving a three-year-old alone with a straw broom and a furnace.)

If you compared the Wall, Texas, of today with the Wall, Texas, of my childhood, you would hardly recognize it, because the Wall, Texas, of today has a gas station. And if you think having a gas station is not that big of a deal, then you're probably the kind of person who grew up in a town that *has* a gas station, and that doesn't encourage students to drive to school in their tractors.

Wall is basically a tiny town with . . . um . . . dirt? There's a lot of dirt. And cotton. And gin, but not the good kind. In Wall, when people refer to gin they're talking about the Cotton Gin, which is the only real business in the town and is like a factory that turns cotton into . . . something else. I honestly have no idea. *Different* cotton, maybe? I never actually bothered to learn, because I always figured that within days I would be escaping this tiny country town, and that's pretty much how my entire life went for the next twenty years.

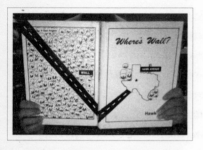

Those things on the back cover are cotton balls. No shit, y'all.

Our yearbook theme one year was simply "Where's Wall?" because it was the question you'd get asked every time you told someone you lived there. The original—*and more apt*—theme had been "Where *the fuck* is Wall?" but the yearbook teacher quickly shot down that concept, saying that age-appropriate language was important, even at the cost of journalistic accuracy.

When I was asked where Wall was, I would always answer with a vague "Oh, that direction," with a wave of my hand, and I quickly learned that if I didn't immediately change the subject to something to break their train of thought (My personal standby: "Look! *Sea monsters!*"), then they'd ask the inevitable (and often incredulous) follow-up question of *"Why Wall?"* and you were never entirely sure whether they were asking why the hell you'd choose to live there, or why anyone would choose to name a town "Wall," but it didn't actually matter, because no one seemed to have a legitimate answer for either.

Unfortunately, pointing out sea monsters was neither subtle nor believable (mostly because we were completely landlocked), so instead I began compensating for Wall's beigey blandness by making up interesting but unverifiable stories about the small town. "Oh, *Wall*?" I'd say, with what I imagined was a sophisticated sneer. "It's the city that invented the dog whistle." Or, "It's the town that *Footloose* was based on. Kevin Bacon is our national hero." Or, "I'm not surprised you've never heard of it. It was the scene of one of the most gruesome cannibalistic slaughters in American history. We don't talk about it, though. I shouldn't even be mentioning it. Let's never speak of it again." I'd hoped that the last one would give me an air of mystery and make people fascinated with our lurid history, but instead it just made them concerned about my mental health, and eventually my mother heard about my tall tales and pulled me aside to tell me that no one was buying it, and that the town was most likely named after someone whose last name happened to be Wall. I pointed out that perhaps he'd been named that because he was the man who'd *invented* walls, and she sighed impatiently, pointing out that it would be hard to believe that a man had invented walls when most of them couldn't even be bothered to close the bathroom door while they're using it. She could tell that I was disappointed at the lack of anything remotely redeeming about our town, and conceded halfheartedly that perhaps the name came from a *metaphoric* wall, designed to keep something out. Progress was my guess. My mother suggested it was more likely boll weevils.

I sometimes wonder what it would have been like to have a childhood that was *not* like mine. I have no real frame of reference, but when I question strangers I've found that their childhood generally had much less blood in it, and also that strangers seem uncomfortable when you question them about their childhood. But really, what else are you going to talk about in line at the liquor store? Childhood trauma seems like the natural choice, since it's the reason why most us are in line there to begin with. I've found, though, that people are more likely to share their personal experiences if you go first, so that's why I always keep an eleven-point list of what went wrong in my childhood to share with them. Also I usually crack open a bottle of tequila to share with them, because alcohol makes me less nervous, and also because I'm from the South, and in Texas we offer drinks to strangers even when we're waiting in line at the liquor store. In Texas we call that *"southern hospitality."* The people who own the liquor store call it "shoplifting." Probably because they're Yankees.

I'm not allowed to go back to that liquor store.[2]

---

2. Author's note: My editor informs me that this doesn't count as a chapter, because nothing relevant happens in it. I explained that that's because this is really just an introduction to the next chapter and probably should be combined with the next chapter, but I separated it because I always find it's nice to have short chapters that you can finish quickly so you can feel better about yourself. Plus, if your English teacher assigned you to read the first three chapters of this book you'll already be finished with the first two, and in another ten minutes you can go watch movies about sexy, glittery vampires, or whatever the hell you kids are into nowadays. Also, you should thank your English teacher for assigning you this book, because she sounds badass. You should probably give her a bottle from the back of your parents' liquor cabinet to thank her for having the balls to choose this book over *The Red Badge of Courage.* Something single-malt.

You're welcome, English teachers. You totally owe me.

Wait. Hang on. It just occurred to me that if English teachers assigned this book as required reading, that means that the school district just had to buy a ton of my books, so technically I owe you one, English teachers. Except that now that I think about it, my tax dollars paid for those books, so technically I'm kind of paying for people to read my own book, and now I don't know whether to be mad or not. This footnote just turned into a goddamn word problem.

You know what? Fuck it. Just send me half of the malt liquor you get from your students and we'll call it even.

Also, is this the longest footnote in the history of ever? Answer: Probably.

My Childhood:
David Copperfield Meets
Guns & Ammo Magazine

I've managed to pinpoint several key differences between my childhood and that of pretty much everyone else in the entire fucking world. I call these points, *"Eleven Things Most People Have Never Experienced or Could Have Even Possibly Imagined, but That Totally Happened to Me, Because Apparently I Did Something Awful in a Former Life That I'm Still Being Punished For."*

#1. Most people have never stood inside a dead animal, unless you count that time when Luke Skywalker crawled inside that tauntaun to keep from freezing to death, which I don't, because *Star Wars* is not a documentary. If you're easily grossed out, I recommend skipping this entire section and going straight to chapter five. Or maybe getting another book that's less disturbing than this one. Like one about kittens. Or genocide.

Still there? Good for you! Let's continue. I remember as a kid watching the Cosby family prepare dinner on TV and thinking how odd it was that no one was covered in blood, because *this* was a typical night in our house: My father, an avid bow hunter, would lumber inside the house with a deer slung over his shoulder. He'd fling it across the dining room table, and then my parents would dissect it and pull out all the useful parts, like some sort of terrible piñata. It was disgusting, but it was the only life I knew, so I assumed that everyone else was just like us.

The only thing that seemed weird about it to me was that I was the only person in the whole house who gagged at the smell of the deer blood. My parents tried to convince me that blood doesn't have a smell, but they are fucking liars. Also they told me that milk *does* have a smell, and that's ridiculous, and I'm shocked that their lies have spread so far. Milk doesn't have a smell. Blood does. And I think I'm so sensitive to the smell of a dead deer because of the time when I accidentally walked inside one.

I was about nine years old and I was playing chase with my sister while my father was cleaning a deer.

I'm going to interrupt here for a small educational explanation about what it means to "clean a deer":

"Cleaning a deer" for people who are sensitive members of PETA
You get some warm water and tearless shampoo and gently massage the deer. (Lather, rinse, but don't repeat, even though the bottle says to, because that's just a ploy to sell more shampoo.) Blow-dry on low heat and hot-glue a bow to his forehead. Send him back to the woods to meet a nice Jewish doe. Go to the next chapter.

"Cleaning a deer" for curious, nonjudgmental readers who really want to know how it's done (and who aren't PETA members who are just pretending to be curious, nonjudgmental readers, but who really want to throw blood on me at book signings)
Cleaning a deer consists of tying up the arms and legs of the deer to a clothesline-like contraption, making it look as if the dead deer is a cheerleader doing the "Give me an X!" move. Then you slice open the stomach, and all the stuff you don't want falls out. Like the genitals. And the poop rope.

"Cleaning a deer" for people who clean deer all the time
I know, right? Can you believe there are people who don't know this
shit? *Weird.* These are probably the same people who call the poop
rope "the intestines." *We all know it's a poop rope, people.* Saying it
in French doesn't make it any less disgusting.

Anyway, my dad had just finished cleaning the deer when I made a reck-
lessly fast, ninja-like U-turn to avoid getting tagged by my sister, and that's
when I ran. Right. The fuck. Inside of the deer. It took me a moment to
realize what had happened, and I stood there, kind of paralyzed and not
ninja-like at all. The best way I can describe it is that it was kind of like I
was wearing a deer sweater. Sometimes people laugh at that, but it's not
an amused laugh. It's more of an involuntary nervous giggle of *what-the-*
*fuck*ness. Probably because you aren't supposed to wear deer for sweaters.
You're not supposed to throw up inside them either, but that doesn't mean
it didn't happen.

I'd like to think that my father threw that deer away, because I'm pretty
sure you're not supposed to eat food you've worn *or* vomited into, but
while he was hosing me off he was also hosing off the deer, so my guess is
that he applied some sort of a fucked-up Grizzly Adams version of the five-
second rule. (Food on the floor is still edible as long as you pick it up within
five seconds. Unless it's peanut butter; then the five-second rule is null. Or
if it's something like dry toast, the five-second rule is extended to, like, a
week and a half, because really, what's going to get on dry toast? *Nothing*,
that's what. God, I could write a whole book on the five-second rule. That
should totally be the follow-up book to this one: *The Five Second Rule As*
It Applies to Various Foodstuffs. Brilliant. But now I've forgotten what I
was writing about. Oh, yeah, throwing up inside a deer sweater. Right.) And
that's why I still suspect that my dad took home the horribly defiled deer
sweater to eat. Except *I* didn't eat it, because after that the smell of blood
made me gag, and to this day I can't eat any meat that I've seen or smelled

raw, which my husband complains about all the time, but until *he's* worn a deer sweater he can just shut the hell up. He says it's all in my mind, but it's totally not, and I've even offered to take some sort of blind smell test, like they did in the Pepsi challenge, where he holds bowls of blood up to my nose so that I can prove that I can smell blood, but he won't do it. Probably because he's kind of anal about our bowls. He wouldn't even let me use one for throwing up in when I was sick. He was all, "*Vomit bowl?* Who uses a vomit bowl?!" and I was all, "*I* use a vomit bowl. *Everyone* uses a vomit bowl. You keep it near you in case you can't make it to the toilet," and he was all, "*No*, you use a trash can," and I was like, "You sick fuck. *I'm not throwing up in a trash can.* That's totally barbaric." Then he yelled, "That's what normal people do!" and I screamed, "*That's how civilization breaks down!*" And then I refused to speak to him for the rest of the day, because he made me yell at him while I was vomity. Did you notice how I just skipped right to having a husband even though this paragraph is supposed to be about my childhood? *My God*, this is going to be a terrible book. But both stories have to do with blood and vomit, so that's kind of impressive, in a way that's really less "impressive" and more just kind of "sad" and "disturbing."

#2. (On the list of *"Things Most People Have Never Experienced or Could Have Even Possibly Imagined but That Totally Happened to Me,"* in case you've forgotten what we were talking about because number one was way too long and needs to be edited or possibly burned.) **Most people don't have poisonous tap water in their house.** *Most people* don't get letters from the government telling them not to drink their poisonous tap water because dangerous radon has leaked into their well. In fact, *most people* don't get their poisonous tap water from a well at all.

Concerned relatives would question my mother about the risks of my sister and me being exposed to all that radon, but she waved them off, saying, "Oh, they couldn't swallow it even if they *wanted* to. They'd throw it up immediately. It's *that* toxic. So, you know, *no worries.*" Then she'd send us off to brush our teeth with it and bathe in it. My mom was a big proponent of the *"What doesn't kill you makes you stronger"* theory, almost to the point where she seemed to be *daring* the world to kill us. This theory worked well for my sister, who has never been sick a day in her life, and is one of those Amazonian women who could squat in a field to have a baby and then pick the baby up and keep on hoeing, except also the field would be on fire, and she'd be all, "Fuck you, fire!" and walk through it like that scary robot in *The Terminator.* And also her baby would be fire-resistant, and would be karate-chopping the flames like a tiny badass. I've tried to have this same level of pioneer toughness, but every couple of months I have a total breakdown or catch some kind of weird disease that only animals get. Like the time I got human parvo, which totally exists *and is no fucking picnic.* Or the time when I was brushing my hair and heard a pop in my neck, and I could barely even breathe it hurt so much. Then I drove myself to work and I almost passed out from a combination of the pain and the not-breathing, and when I got there I hurt so much I couldn't even move my mouth to talk, so I wrote, "I HAVE BROKEN MY NECK," on a Post-it, and my bewildered office mate drove me to the hospital. Turns out I'd herniated a disc, and the doctor gave me a pamphlet on domestic abuse and kept asking me whether someone was hurting me at home, because apparently most people don't herniate their discs simply from brushing their hair too hard. I prefer to think that most people just don't brush their hair as enthusiastically as I do.

#3. **Most people have running water**. I mean, we *mostly* had running water, except when we didn't, which was often. As my sister and I would always say to each other, "You know, you never really appreciate your poisonous well water until it's gone." In the summer the water would occasionally stop for no reason whatsoever, and in the winter the pipes would freeze, and we'd be forced to fill up pots of water from our cistern, and then warm the icy water on the stove to bathe in. It's even *less* glamorous than it sounds. I once pointed out to my mother that the water from the cistern was slightly brown, and that it didn't really seem like the cleanest way to wash your hair, but she sighed at me in disappointment, saying, "It's pronounced '*beige*.'" As if the pronunciation somehow made it fancier.

"*Okay,*" I capitulated grudgingly, "the cistern water seems slightly more *beige* than the water from the tap," but my mom just shrugged it off, because apparently she didn't trust water she couldn't see.

#4. **Most people don't have a cistern *or even know what a cistern is*.** Some of them *say* that they have a cistern, and then they politely add that the word is actually pronounced "*sister,*" and then I just

The back of this photo says,
"1975—Jenny & her chickens.
A dog killed them not long afterward."
Funny, I feel fine.

nod, because I really don't want to have to explain that a cistern is actually an enormous metal can that catches rainwater, sort of like an aboveground well for people who can't actually afford a well. But no one wants to explain that, because *honestly? Who's going to admit they can't afford a well?* Not me, obviously, because we *had* a well. One that was filled with poisonous radon.

#5. **Most people don't have live raccoons in the house.** My dad was always rescuing animals, and by "rescuing animals" I mean "killing the mother, and then discovering she had babies, and bringing the babies

home to raise them in the bathtub."
Once, he brought home eight newborn
raccoons in a bucket for us to raise.
When the orphaned raccoons were little, my mom sewed tiny Jams for them
to wear (because this was the eighties,
and Jams were quite popular then),
and they were adorable, but then the
raccoons got big enough to climb out
of the bathtub and pretty much destroyed the entire house. Raccoons
are totally OCD and they are driven to
wash everything that they see, which
you'd think would make them smell
better, but it doesn't, because they
smell all musky and vaguely sour, like
one-night stands.

When the raccoons were old
enough, we returned them all to the
woods, except for one raccoon that
we kept as a pet. His name was Rambo,
and he'd learned how to turn on the
bathroom sink and would wash ran-

*Photographic proof of Rambo in his
Jams. Also pictured:* Teen Beat *magazine
with Kirk Cameron on the cover, records,
and VHS tapes. It's like the eighties
threw up all over this raccoon. I couldn't
even make this shit up, people.*

dom things in it all the time, like it was his own private river. If I'd have
been thinking I would have left some Woolite and my delicates by the sink
for him to rinse out, but you never think to turn your pet raccoon into a
tiny butler until it's too late. Once, we came home to find Rambo in the
sink, washing a tiny sliver of soap that had been a new bath-size bar
that morning. He looked exhausted, and like he wanted someone to stop
him and put him to bed, but when we tried to take away the last bit of soap
he growled at us, and so we let him finish, because at that point I guess it
was like a vendetta, if raccoons had vendettas. Sometimes when I'm work-

ing on an impossible project that I know I should just give up on and someone tries to take it away, I growl and scream, "THERE CAN BE ONLY ONE!" (which is both weird and inappropriate) but I think that that's probably exactly how Rambo was feeling, with his soap sliver and puckered little fingers covered in radon water, and it makes me sad. But then I laugh, because it reminds me that right after the soap incident my mom insisted that Rambo needed to live outside in a chicken cage "to protect him from himself." I had placed him on top of the cage to pet him when my little sister, Lisa, who was about seven then, whacked him in the nose (because she was kind of a dick at the time), and then Rambo *flipped the fuck out*, stood up on his hind legs, grimaced, and jumped directly onto my sister's face. He grabbed on to her ears like he was some kinda horrible raccoon mask, and he was hissing and looking right into her eyes like, "I WILL BRING YOU DOWN, BITCH," and my sister was screaming and flailing her arms *and it was totally awesome.*

The next day my dad took Rambo to the farm, which I'd thought meant that he actually took him to my grandfather's farm to live, but now that I think about it, it probably had less to do with *going* to a farm than *buying* one. And now I'm sad again. But then I think about the fact that my dad was probably pointing the gun at Rambo, and Rambo was probably wearing his little Jams and was all, "Hi there, mister!" and my dad probably sighed defeatedly,[1] saying something like "Aw, fuck. Just go on, then. Here's ten dollars and some soap." Because deep down my father is a total softy. Unless he's inadvertently killing the mother of a bunch of baby raccoons. Then you'd better stand the fuck back, because you're totally going to get blood on you.

---

1. Is "defeatedly" a real word? As in, "She sighed defeatedly as spell-check implied that 'defeatedly' isn't a real word." Fuck it. It's going in the book, and I'm pretty sure that *makes* it a real word. Me and Shakespeare. *Making shit up as we go along.*

#6. Most people don't go out into the woods to catch armadillos so that their father can race them professionally. Also, when you find one and pull it out by its tail, *most* girls' fathers won't scream out, *"Mind the teeth! That one looks like a biter!"* Probably because most fathers don't love their daughters as much as my father loves me. Or maybe because they didn't make their daughters pull live armadillos out of tree stumps. Hard to tell. Honestly, though, those girls are missing out, because there is nothing like seeing your father down on his hands and knees with five other grown men, screaming and slapping at the ground to scare their respective armadillos into crossing the finish line first. And when I say, "There's nothing like it," what I mean is, "Holy shit, *these people are fucking insane.*"

Usually when I tell people my dad was a Texas armadillo racing champion, they assume I'm exaggerating, but then I pull out his silver armadillo championship ring (which is, *of course,* shaped like an armadillo), and then they're all, "Crap on a crap cracker, *you're actually serious.*" And then they usually leave quickly. The *gold* armadillo championship ring would be more impressive to show off, but we don't have it anymore because my father traded it for a Victorian funeral carriage. And no, I'm not joking, because why the fuck would I joke about that? But I do have photographic proof:

Why, yes, that is the shining winner's ring of the Armadillo Glitterati. Also pictured: My father during an unfortunate Magnum P.I. phase, confused spectators, unnamed armadillo.

#7. Most people don't have a professional taxidermist for a father. When I was little, my father used to sell guns and ammo at a sporting goods store, but I always told everyone he was an arms dealer, because it sounded more exciting. Eventually, though, he saved up enough money to quit his job and build a taxidermy shop next to our house (which was tiny and built out of asbestos back when people still thought that was a good thing). My dad built the taxidermy shop himself out of old wood from abandoned barns and did a remarkable job, fashioning it to look exactly like a Wild West saloon, complete with swinging doors and gaslights and a hitching post for horses. Then he hired a bunch of guys to work for him, many of whom looked to me as if they were fresh from prison or just about to go back in. I can't help feeling sorry for the confused strangers who would wander into my father's taxidermy shop, expecting to find a bar and a stiff drink, and who instead found several rough-looking men my father had hired, covered in blood and elbow deep in animal carcasses. I suspect, though, that the blood-covered taxidermists probably shared their personal flasks with the baffled stranger, because although they seemed slightly dangerous, they also were invariably good-hearted, and I'm fairly certain they recognized that anyone stumbling onto that kind of scene would probably need a strong drink even more than when they'd first set out looking for a bar to begin with.

#8. Most people don't have their childhood pets eaten by homeless people. When I was five, my dad won a duckling for me at the carnival. We named him Daffodil, and he lived in the backyard in an inflatable raft that we filled with water. He was awesome. Then he got too big to live comfortably in the raft, so we set him loose under the nearby town bridge so he could be with all the other ducks. We sang "Born Free," and he seemed very happy as he waddled away. A month later the local news ran a story on the fact that all of the ducks in the river had gone missing and had been eaten by homeless people living under the bridge. It was apparently a bad neighborhood for ducks. I stared, wide-eyed, at my mom as I stammered out, *"HOBOS. ATE. MY DAFFODIL."* My mom stared back with a tightened jaw, wondering whether she should just lie to me, but instead she decided it was time to stop protecting me from real life, and sighed, saying, "It sounds nicer if you call them *'transients,'* dear." I nodded mechanically. I was traumatized, but my vocabulary was improving.

From the back of the photo: "Jenny & Daffodil. Later he was eaten by homeless people."

#9. Most people don't share a swimming pool with pigs. We lived downwind from the (locally) famous Schwartzes' pig farm, which is something some people might be embarrassed about, but these were "show pigs," so yeah, *it was pretty fucking impressive.* When the wind was blowing from the west it would smell so strong that we'd have to close the windows, but that was less because of the pigs, and more because of the nearby rendering plant. In fact, the first time my husband caught a whiff he nearly gagged, and my mom nonchalantly said, "Oh, that? That's just the rendering plant," in the same way other people might say, "Oh, that's just our gardener." Then he gave me this look like *"What the fuck is a rendering plant?"* and I quietly explained that a rendering plant is a factory where they compost old flowers, because that sounds much more whimsical than, "It's like a slaughterhouse, but way less classy."

The Schwartzes had an enormous open-air cistern that they used to water the pigs, and on special occasions we'd get invited over to swim in the pig's water. This is all true, people.

Right here is when people begin to say, "I don't believe any of this," and I have to show them pictures or get my mom on the phone to confirm it, and then they get very quiet. Probably out of respect. Or possibly pity. This is why I always have to clarify that although my childhood *was* fucked up, it was also kind of awesome.

When you're surrounded by other people who are just as poor as you are, life doesn't seem all that weird. For instance, one of my friends grew up in a house with a dirt floor, and it's hard to feel too bad about your tiny asbestos house when you have the privilege of owning carpet. Also, in my parents' defense, I never really realized we were that poor, because my parents never said we couldn't afford things, just that we didn't need them. Things like ballet lessons. And ponies. And tap water that won't kill you.

#10. Most people don't file wild animals. When I was about six my parents decided to raise chickens, but we couldn't afford a real henhouse. Instead we put some filing cabinets in the garage, and opened the drawers like stair steps so the chickens could nest in them. Once, when I went out to gather the eggs, I stretched onto my tiptoes to reach into the top drawer and I felt what seemed like a misshapen egg, and that's because *it was in the belly of a gigantic fucking rattlesnake that was attempting to swallow another one of the eggs*. This is when I ran screaming back into the house, and my mom grabbed a rifle from the gun cabinet, and (as the escaping snake writhed down the driveway) she shot it right in the lumpy part where the egg still was, and egg exploded everywhere like some sort of terrible fireworks display. We found out later that it was actually a bull snake just *pretending* to be a rattlesnake, and my mother felt a little bad about killing it, but pretending to be a rattlesnake in front of an armed mother is basically like waving a fake gun in front of a cop. Either way, you're totally going to get shot. Also, whenever I read this paragraph to people who don't live in the South, they get hung up on the fact that we had furniture devoted to just guns, but in rural Texas pretty much everyone has a gun cabinet. Unless they're gay. Then they have gun armoires.

#11. Most people don't have to devote an entire year of therapy to a single ten-minute episode from their childhood. Three words: Stanley, the Magical Squirrel. Actually that's four words, but I don't think you're supposed to count the word "the," since it isn't important enough to be capitalized. All of this will be fixed by my editor by the time you read this anyway, so really I could write anything here. Like, did you know that Angelina Jolie hates Jewish people? True story. (*Editor's note: Angelina Jolie does not hate Jewish people at all, and this is a total fabrication. We apologize to Ms. Jolie and to the Jewish community.*)

I was going to write about Stanley the Magical Squirrel right here on number eleven, but it's way too convoluted, so instead I made it into the whole next chapter, because I'm pretty sure when you sell a book you get paid by the chapter. I could be wrong about that, though, because I *am* often wrong. Except about the Angelina-Jolie-hating-Jews thing, which is probably totally true. (*No, that's not true at all. Shut up, Jenny.—Ed.*)

Stanley, the Magical Talking Squirrel

When I tell people that my father is kind of a total lunatic, they laugh and nod knowingly. They assure me that theirs is too, and that he's just a "typical father."

And they're probably right, if the typical father runs a full-time taxidermy business out of the house, and shows up at the local bar with a miniature donkey and a Teddy Roosevelt impersonator, and thinks *other* people are weird for making such a big deal out of it. If the typical father says things like "Happy birthday! Here's a bathtub of raccoons!" or "We'll have to take your car. Mine has too much blood in it," then yeah, he's *totally* normal. Still, I don't remember any of the kids from *Charles in Charge* feeling around the deep freeze for the Popsicles and instead pulling out an enormous frozen rattlesnake that Charles had thrown in while it was still alive. Maybe I missed that episode. We didn't watch a lot of TV.

That's why whenever people try to tell me how *their* "insane father" would sometimes fall asleep on the toilet, or occasionally catch the house on fire, I put my finger to their lips and whisper, "Hush, little rabbit. Let me give you perspective."

And then I tell them this story:

It was close to midnight when I heard my father rumbling down the hall, and then suddenly the light switched on in my bedroom. My mom unsuccessfully tried to convince him to go to bed. "Let the girls sleep," she mumbled from their bedroom across the hall. My mother had learned that my father could not be dissuaded when a "great thought" hit him, but she went through the motions of arguing with him (mainly to point out what was normal and what was crazy, so that my sister and I would be able to recognize it as we got older).

I was eight, and my sister, Lisa, was six. My father, a giant bohemian man who looked like a dangerous Zach Galifianakis, lumbered into our tiny bedroom. Lisa and I shared a room most of our lives. Our bedroom was so small that there wasn't much room for anything other than the bed we shared, and a dresser. The closet doors had been removed long ago to give the illusion of more space. The illusion had failed. I'd spent hours trying to create small bastions of privacy. I'd construct forts with old quilts, and beg my mom to let me live in the garage with the chickens. I'd shut myself in the bathroom (the only room with a lock), but with one bathroom for four people, and a father with irritable bowel syndrome, this was not a good long-term solution. Occasionally I would empty my wooden toy box, curl up inside, and shut the lid, preferring the leg cramps and quiet darkness of the pine box to the outside world . . . much like a sensory deprivation chamber, but for orphans. My mom was concerned, but not concerned enough to actually do anything about it. There are few advantages to growing up poor, and not having money for therapy is the biggest.

My father crouched on the edge of our bed, and Lisa and I blinked, our eyes slowly adjusting to the bright light. "Wake up, girls," my dad boomed, his face flushed with excitement, cold, or hysteria. He was dressed in his usual camouflage hunting clothes, and the scent of deer urine wafted around the room. Hunters often use animal pee to cover their scent, and my father splashed it on like other men used Old Spice. Texas is a state that had once outlawed sodomy and fellatio, but is totally cool with men giving themselves golden showers in the name of deer hunting.

My dad held a Ritz cracker box, which was weird, because we never had brand-name food in the house, so I was all, "Hell, yeah, this is *totally* worth waking me up for," but then I realized that there was something alive and moving in the cracker box, which was disturbing; less because my father had brought some live animal in a cracker box into our room, and more because whatever was in there was ruining some perfectly good crackers.

Let me preface this by saying that my dad was always bringing home crazy-ass shit. Rabbit skulls, rocks shaped like vegetables, angry possums, glass eyes, strange drifters he picked up on the road, a live porcupine in a rubber tire. My mother (a patient and stoic lunch lady) seemed secretly convinced that she must've committed some terrible act in a former life to deserve this lot in life, and so she forced a smile and set another place for the drifter/junkie at the dinner table with the quiet dignity usually reserved for saints or catatonics.

Daddy leaned toward us and told us rather conspiratorially that this box held our newest pet. This is the same man who once brought home a baby bobcat, let it loose in the house, and forgot to mention it because he "didn't think it was important," so for him to be excited I assumed the box had to contain something truly amazing, like a two-headed lizard, or a baby chupacabra. He opened the box and whispered excitedly, "Come out and meet your new owners, Pickle."

Almost as if on cue, a tiny head poked out of the cracker box. It was a smallish, visibly frightened squirrel, its eyes glazed over from fright. My sister squealed with delight and the squirrel disappeared back into the box. "Hey now, you've gotta be quiet or you'll scare it," my father warned. And yeah, Lisa's squeal might have been jarring, but more likely it was just freaked the fuck out by our house. My taxidermist father had decorated practically every spare wall in our home with wide-eyed foxes, leering giant elk, snarling bear heads, and wild boars complete with bloody fangs from eating slow villagers. If I was that squirrel I would have totally shit myself.

Lisa and I were silent, and the tiny squirrel tentatively peeked over the top of the box. It was cute, as far as squirrels go, but all I could think was, "*Really?* A fucking squirrel? *This* is what you got me out of bed for?" And true, I may not have said "fucking" in my head, because I was eight, but the sentiment was totally there. This is a man who throws his kids in the car to chase after tornadoes for fun, and who once gave me a five-foot-long ball python when he forgot my birthday, so the whole squirrel-in-a-box thing seemed kinda anticlimactic.

My father noticed the nonplussed look on my face and leaned in further, like he was telling us a secret he didn't want the squirrel to overhear. "*This*," he whispered, "is no ordinary squirrel. *This*," he said with a dramatic pause, "is a *magic* squirrel."

My sister and I stared at each other, thinking the same thing: "*This*," we thought to ourselves, "is our father clearly thinking we are idiots." Lisa and I were both well versed in our dad's storytelling abilities, and we knew that he was not a man to be trusted. Just last week he'd woken us up and asked whether we wanted to go to the movies. *Of course* we wanted to go to the movies. Money was always tight, so seeing a movie was one of those rare glimpses into the lives of the wealthy few who could splurge on such luxuries as matinees and central heating. These people in the audience, I felt sure, were the same people who could afford real winter shoes instead of bread sacks stuffed with newspapers.

Lisa and me in the front yard in our (barely visible) bread-sack shoes.

When Lisa and I were practically bouncing off the walls from the sheer excitement of seeing a movie, he'd send us off to call both movie theaters in the nearby town and have us write down every showing so we could decide what to see. We'd listen to the recording of the movies over and over to get it all down, and after thirty minutes of intense labor we'd compiled the list, and multiple reasons why *The Mup-*

pet Movie was the only logical choice. Then my father would merrily agree and we would all cheer, and he would bend down and say, "So. Do you have any money?" My sister and I looked at each other. Of course we didn't have any money. We were wearing bread-sack shoes. "Well," said my father, with a big grin spreading across his face, "I don't have any money either. But it sure was fun when we *thought* we were going, huh?"

Some people might read this and think that my father was a sadistic asshole, but he was not. He honestly thought that the time that Lisa and I spent planning a movie date that would never happen would be a great break from what we would have been doing had he not brought it up (i.e., hot-wiring the neighbor's tractor, or playing with the family shovel). I wonder if one day my father will get as much of a kick out of this concept when Lisa and I call to tell him we're going to pick him up from the retirement home for Christmas, but then never actually show up. "But it sure was exciting when you thought you were coming home, though, right?" we'll cheerfully ask him on New Year's Eve. "Seriously, though, we'll *totally* be there to pick you up tomorrow. No enemas and heart meds for you! We're going to the circus! It's gonna be great! You should totally trust us!" *He totally shouldn't trust us.*

These were the very things running through my mind on the night my dad woke us up with the "magical" squirrel. My father seemed to sense I was plotting a nursing-home/circus-related revenge, and his eyebrows knit together as he attempted to gain back our trust. "*Seriously*, this *is* a magic squirrel," he said. "Look. I'll prove it to you." He looked into the box. "Hey, little squirrel. What's my oldest daughter's name?" The squirrel looked at my father, then at us . . . and damned if that squirrel didn't stretch up and whisper right into my father's ear.

"He said, 'Jenny,'" my dad stated quite smugly.

It was impressive, but both my sister and I were quick to point out that we didn't actually *hear* the squirrel say my name, and that it was more likely that the squirrel was just looking for food in my father's ear hair. My father sighed, clearly disappointed in his cynical children, or the ear hair comment. *"Fine,"* he said gruffly, giving us a frustrated huff and looking back into the cracker box. "Little squirrel . . . what is two plus three?"

And this amazing, magical, wonderful squirrel raised his squirrely little paw. *Five. Fucking. Times.*

Immediately I realized that this magical squirrel would be my ticket out of this tiny West Texas town. I would parlay this squirrel into money, toys, and appearances on *The Tonight Show*. I would call him Stanley, and I would hire a Cuban seamstress named Juanita to make tiny leisure suits for him. Just as I was considering whether Stanley would look more dashing in a fedora or a beret, my father smiled broadly and ripped open the box that was hiding the little squirrel.

Stanley looked . . . *strange*. I dimly realized that his stomach was huge and distended, bowing out like an enormous beer belly. "Juanita will have her work cut out for her," I thought to myself. And then I realized that Stanley's tiny back feet were swinging awfully listlessly, and that my father's hand was STUCK UP INSIDE THE BODY OF THE SQUIRREL.

"Holy fuck, you psychopath!" is what I would have said if I hadn't been eight years old. Fresh blood was drying on my father's sleeve, and my mind struggled to piece together what was happening. For a brief moment I thought that Stanley the Magical Squirrel had been alive up until only seconds before, when my father had chosen to give him some sort of bizarre colorectal exam gone horribly wrong. Then I realized that this was, more likely, a squirrel my father had found dead on the road, and that he had sliced it open and decided to use it as some sort of grotesque hand puppet culled from the very bowels of hell.

Lisa giggled and stuck her hand up the ass of the dead squirrel. The strain had been too much for her fragile little mind. At the age of only six, she had snapped. As she shoved the fresh carcass up to her elbow, I made a mental note to start checking out the backs of milk cartons, certain that my real parents, who had most likely misplaced me at a movie theater, must be very worried about me by now. I assured myself that they were probably at a PETA meeting, making large donations in the name of their long-lost daughter. "Oh, she would have *loved* this," my real mother would say consolingly to my father (the count) as they worked diligently to spread their successful prairie dog rescue mission to neighboring counties.

Many years later, my sister had a daughter named Gabi. My father (apparently misinterpreting my need to bring up the dead-squirrel story every Christmas for the rest of my life as homage to happier times, rather than the effects of post-traumatic stress disorder) decided he should bless his four-year-old granddaughter with the never-ending therapy that resulted from the talking-magic-carcass-in-a-box. He'd tanned a raccoon body, placed the stiffened corpse in a large cereal box, and had hidden it under the guest bed (apparently waiting for the perfect moment to scar Gabi for life), and then he forgot all about it. Weeks later, Gabi found the mutilated raccoon carcass under the bed and (thinking it to be a very stiff puppet) wandered around the house playing with her new friend and freaking the shit out of the cat. She crept into my father's room, where he was taking a nap, and quietly laid the dead raccoon on my father's pillow, like a message from the Godfather. The dead raccoon's shriveled paw gently grazed my father's sleeping face as Gabi moved the raccoon closer so it could give her grandfather an Eskimo kiss. "Papaw," she whispered sweetly, "wake up and say hewwo."

This is the point when my dad screamed like a little girl, and then Gabi screamed at his screaming, and she threw her hands up, and the dead raccoon went flying across the room into the kitchen and landed on my sister's foot. A normal person would have passed out or at least yelled, "What the fuck?!" but at that point in her life, flying dead raccoons and screaming people in the house were pretty much normal, so Lisa shrugged and went back to making her Pop-Tart.

Lisa called me to share the story later, and I promised to buy Gabi a pony for avenging us, but then later I felt a little sorry for my dad, because waking up to find a dead raccoon staring at you through eyeless sockets as it caresses your cheek is not something anyone with his high blood pressure should have to go through. Then again, giving me a mutilated magical squirrel in a cracker box is kinda fucked up, too, so I guess we're about even.

As an aside, I could not find a photo of Stanley the mutilated squirrel (probably because no one ever thinks to take pictures of squirrel carcasses until it's too late), but I do have a picture of my dad bottle-feeding a baby porcupine in a spare tire, and that seems somehow fitting and slightly redeeming. I did, however, just notice that my dad is holding the porcupine up with a paint stick and there are paint drops all over the tire. So it's entirely possible he's feeding the porcupine house paint. Unlikely, but stranger things have happened.

Don't Tell
Your Parents

Nearly every weekend when I was a kid, my father's Czechoslovakian parents would pick up my sister and me, and drive us away with them to their house in a nearby town. My grandmother, whom we called Grandlibby, was one of the sweetest and most patient women ever to grace the planet. I suspect most people feel that way about their grandmothers, but this was the same woman who, when pushed, would describe Hitler as a "sad little man who probably didn't get hugged enough when he was little," and would say only of Satan, "I'm not a fan."

My grandfather seemed to view the overwhelming cheerfulness of his wife as some sort of dare, and set out to balance out her effect on the world by being just generally put-out about everything. He was harmless under the gruff demeanor, but we always gave him a wide berth as he stalked through the house, muttering angrily to himself in Czech (probably about how much he wished he had a cane to hit people with). Grandlibby would always smile lovingly at him and patiently humor whatever it was he was pissed off about at the moment, as she quietly shooed us all out of the room until he had time to watch *Bonanza* and calm down. I'm not sure how much of her superhuman patience was love, and how much was simply self-preservation.

According to family legend, when my great-great-great-aunt was in her thirties, she sat down at the breakfast table and her husband drove a nail through the back of her skull and then buried her in the backyard. I've been told this was totally kosher at the time. The backyard burial, *that is*. Not the nail-through-the-head thing. Nails in the head have always been frowned on, even in Texas. There's no real proof any of this happened, but my great-great-great-uncle's alleged deathbed confession to killing his wife (and also to setting his father on fire a few years before that) was considered fact in our family. My grandfather said that after the confession, several members of our family dug up his great-aunt and found the nail still embedded in her skull. Then they buried her again, without informing the police, because this was before *CSI: Miami*. I'd pointed out that digging up a family member's corpse just to check for skull holes is almost as bizarre as murdering someone with a nail through the head, but Grampa disagreed and mumbled grumpily about "kids today not understanding family responsibilities." I sometimes wondered whether my grandmother was that inhumanly good-natured only because she was trying to avoid getting a nail in the head. I doubt it, though. Grampa wasn't that great with tools.

Deep down he was a good man. You could tell he felt uncomfortable around children, but we didn't hold it against him, as the feeling was mutual. He'd had a series of strokes in his sixties, which caused him to blink one eye involuntarily, and he became convinced that the women of their church would think he was luridly winking at them, so he began wearing dark-tinted Roy Orbison glasses, which, accompanied by his stoic demeanor, thick old-world Czech accent, and his penchant for wearing undershirts and dark suits, gave him the air of being the head of a Mafia family. Neighbors treated him with a quiet respect, perhaps fearing that he might put a hit out on them, and more than once I heard him referred to as "The Terminator."

Grampa did everything at his own pace, a speed that my sister and I referred to as *"when snails attack."* It was most obvious when he was driving. He was almost legally blind, and the dark glasses were helping no one, certainly not anyone sharing the road with him. He tempered these limitations by driving about thirty miles under the speed limit at all times. My grandparents' house was only about ten miles from ours, but the ride there would necessitate sandwiches packed for the trip, and several books to keep us occupied. Once, on a particularly slow journey, my sister realized that she needed to go to the bathroom, and I tried to convince her to hold it, but she couldn't, so Grampa turned toward a gas station. He suddenly swerved, insisting that a cougar had just darted out in front of the car. We had all seen the cougar he was referring to. It was a double-wide mobile home that had been parked by the side of the road for at least twenty years. Lisa and I calmed ourselves in the knowledge that even if Grampa *did* run into something, at this speed we'd probably just gently bounce off it. We often contemplated leaping out of the car and running the last few blocks to our grandparents' house, fairly certain that we could make it there in time to try on Grampa's spare hearing aids before they ever pulled into the driveway and realized we were missing from the backseat.

Our grandparents' house was like Caligula's palace, as my grandfather was too distracted by being indignant at the existence of cats (which he trapped in his backyard and sent home with us), and my grandmother was too sweet to say no to anything. Sharp knives, chocolates, small fires, late-night cable television . . . nothing was out of bounds here. Lunches would consist of fried eggs floating on syrup, mashed potatoes mixed with whipped cream, and homemade French fries dripping with lard. For dinner, Grandlibby would make a few pans of half-baked brownies, resulting in a mushy brownie-salmonella-pudding concoction that could only truly be enjoyed when eaten with the fingers . . . rolling the doughy mess into large chocolate speedballs.

After every bite Grandlibby would repeat her mantra: *"Now, don't tell your parents about this."* I would mumble a quick assent, too jacked up on a syrup high to do more. My sister managed a nod as she sucked down a pint of ketchup straight from the bottle. Grampa would wander in, muttering disapprovingly about our poor food choices, and my grandmother would look straight at him in wide-eyed surprise and then agree sincerely, as if she had never considered that an all-taffy breakfast would be an unhealthy idea. Then she'd sweetly thank him for his good advice, and go make him comfortable in his easy chair before returning to the kitchen to quietly suggest that we make peanut-butter-and-sugar-cube milk shakes. Inevitably, my grandfather would return a half-hour later and demand to know what the hell was going on, and my grandmother would look clueless and adorable as she pretended to understand for the first time that sugar cubes *weren't* a garnish. Her innocent face was irreproachable and he'd sigh deeply, walking away, while muttering that she was becoming senile. She wasn't. She knew *exactly* what she was doing and had perfected the art of doing whatever she wanted to do in order to make life happy, while avoiding the kinds of arguments that led to nail attacks.

As the night progressed, my grandfather would go to sleep, and we would sink further into our own childlike brand of debauchery. Our cousin Michelle, who was a year younger than me, would come over, and the night would turn full-force into the type of self-harm affair that only imaginative children with limited supervision can ever fully achieve.

In spite of the fact that the entire house was rigged with safety in mind, we were able to turn this to meet our own needs. Whereas some grandparents would lay down those plastic mats in the bathtub to keep from slipping, my grandparents had taken this a step further and had covered all usable walkways in the house with a thick yellow, plastic covering for the carpeting. We'd discovered that what kept the plastic mats so well anchored to the floor was a sea of one-inch spikes on the underside, jutting down into the gold shag carpet. Once we had reached the highest plane of thought, reserved only for yogis and children deep in the throes of a sugar overdose, we would turn the mats upside down and practice walking over our homemade bed of nails. Being younger, Michelle and Lisa were required to carry large plaster urns or heavy furniture to compensate for their smaller frames. I was allowed to walk without added weight in light of the fact that I'd had both of my big toenails sheared off by broken glass while wading barefoot in the swollen storm drains only hours earlier. *"Tell your parents you fell while I was reading you the Bible,"* Grandlibby suggested helpfully.

In the morning we would go swimming. My grandparents weren't poor, but they were the type of people to save and reuse tinfoil, always certain that another depression was looming around the corner, so they met the challenge of creating a pool for their grandchildren by salvaging three fiberglass bathtub shells that someone was throwing away. We would plug up the drain holes and fill the tubs with the garden hose outside. Grandlibby would subtly suggest that we allow the sun to warm up the frigid water in the tubs, but after a night of overindulgence and general debauchery we could not yet begin to temper ourselves. We entered the tubs, breaking the thin layer of frost that was beginning to form on the top of the water, our lips and fingers turning a faint blue, assuring one another that even if this *did* lead to pneumonia, it would most likely strike later, during the school week.

Regardless of how dangerous the activity, Grandlibby would always be standing nearby with a cherry Shasta, a first-aid kit, and a loving look of panicked resignation. As I prepared to leap off the roof of their house onto the couch pillows below, it occurred to me that this might not be a great idea, but I knew that I'd be much more likely to hurt myself climbing back down the rusty barbecue-pit chimney pipe that I'd used as an impromptu trellis. Grandlibby murmured something in Czechoslovakian that sounded suspiciously like cursing. Lisa's advice was much more helpful. "Tuck and roll!"

ONE OF OUR FAVORITE PASTIMES was to roam the neighborhood alleys, looking in trash cans and dumpsters for hidden treasures. Discarded

Christmas trees, water-damaged books, three-legged chairs, love letters from mistresses, and stained clothing: These were all our personal booty. Because I was the tallest and had the most recent tetanus shots, I felt it was my duty to dig farthest into the trash, certain that if I applied myself, one day I would find a large wad of cash, a bag of misplaced heroin, or possibly a human hand.

I knew my hard work had not been in vain the day I pulled out the stained *Playboy* magazine, its pages stuck together with (what I now hope was) dried orange juice. At age nine, this was my first real look at full nudity that didn't involve a *National Geographic* exposé. We brought the magazine back to our grandparents' lawn, and my cousin and I settled out in the yard to examine these women, who I was surprised to discover did not have breasts that sagged down to their navels, and who all seemed to have names that ended with two *e*'s. We turned to the centerfold, a well-endowed blonde called "Candee." Grandlibby tried to distract us away from the magazine with the tempting combination of a ladder and an umbrella, but we were way too sucked into the *Playboy* to listen to her suggestions that the magazine was "rubbish." My grandfather peered at us from the door and muttered loudly to himself about how little respect kids had for lawns nowadays. I have no idea whether he even noticed the torrid magazine we were engrossed in, but he continued to grumble as he stalked into the house, possibly looking for some small nails.

"Hey, Grandlibby?" I asked. "What's a 'turn-on'?"

She paled visibly, looking mildly ill. "Well," she said . . . struggling for words, "it's . . . um . . . the things that make you happy, I suppose?"

I turned to my cousin. "My turn-ons are Rainbow Brite and unicorns."

Michelle smiled back, her two front teeth missing. "My turn-ons are Monchhichis. And Tubble Gum."

Grandlibby issued a terse, strangled laugh. "Yeah. I could be wrong about that. I don't speak real great English, you know. Why don't you just *never use that phrase again*, okay?" She excused herself to go into the house. We could hear something that sounded like a prayer coming from within, but we were too fascinated with these women and their flimsy-looking (and ill-fitting) support garments to investigate any further.

Suddenly the bright, sunny day erupted into a violent hailstorm. We ran toward the porch, covering our heads with the magazine. Grandlibby stepped outside authoritatively, with one eyebrow cocked. "*So*. You see what happens when you look at dirty pictures?" she intoned knowingly. "*It hails*. And do you know where hail comes from?" she asked sweetly.

"Cumulous clouds?" I volunteered. I had recently made a B-plus in science, and I felt moderately sure this was the right answer.

"*No*," Grandlibby replied. "Hail comes from hell. The devil sent it because he's happy that you're reading evil garbage."

Michelle and I looked at each other. It *had* seemed suspicious for a hailstorm to erupt on a perfectly clear day, but we sensed that Grandlibby's logic was flawed. If the devil was happy, then why would he send hail to distract us from our newfound love of pornography? "*Certainly*," we thought, "*she must be confused.*" But what *did* worry us was the fact that the hailstorm had occurred only seconds after we'd heard Grandlibby praying in the house. It was disconcerting. *Did* my grandmother have some kind of direct line to God? Had all those years of funneling money to Jim and Tammy Faye Bakker finally paid off? We weren't sure, but felt it was better not to chance it. I placed the *Playboy* back on top of the neighbor's trash can, feeling that if *we* could no longer partake in its wonder, surely the next dumpster divers would appreciate my generosity and charity, qualities I felt sure God would admire.

Years later I realized that my grandmother had been right all along about the magazine being rubbish, and I happily bypassed the glossy but shallow *Playboy*s for her old, battered copies of *Housewife Confessions* and *True Hollywood Scandals*, which allowed for almost no nudity but a much stronger story line than *Playboy* could ever deliver. "Don't tell your parents," Grandlibby said with a sweet grin.

I smiled back. She had nothing to worry about.

Jenkins,
You Motherfucker

When I was little my mother used to say that I had "a nervous stomach." That was what we called "severe untreated anxiety disorder" back in the seventies, when everything was cured with Flintstone vitamins and threats to send me to live with my grandmother if I didn't stop hiding from people in my toy box.

By age seven I realized that there was something wrong with me, and that most children didn't hyperventilate and throw up when asked to leave the house. My mother called me "quirky." My teachers whispered "neurotic." But deep down I knew there was a better word for what I was. *Doomed.*

Doomed because every Christmas I would end up hiding under my aunt's kitchen table from the sheer panic of being around so many people. Doomed because I couldn't give a speech in class without breaking into uncontrollable hysterical laughter as the rest of my classmates looked on. Doomed because I knew, without a shadow of a doubt, that something horrible and nameless was going to happen and that I was helpless to stop it. And not just the normal terrible things that small children worry about, like your father waking you up with a bloody hand puppet. Things like nuclear holocaust. Or carbon monoxide poisoning. Or having to leave the house and interact with people who weren't my mother. It was most likely something I was just born with, but I can't help but suspect that at least some of my social anxiety could be traced back to a single episode.

WHEN I WAS in the third grade, my father rushed inside one night to tell us all to come out and look at what he had in the back of his pickup. I was young, but still well trained enough to know that nothing good could come of this.

My sister and I shared a wary look as my mother peered guardedly from the kitchen window to see whether anything large was moving in my father's truck. It was. She gave us a look that my father always seemed to interpret as "How lucky you girls are to have such an adventurous father," but which I always read as "One of you will probably not survive your father's enthusiasm. Most likely it will be Lisa, since she's smaller and can't run as fast, but she *is* quite good at hiding in small spaces, so really it's anyone's game." More likely, though, it was something like "*Christ*, why won't someone hurry up and invent Xanax?"

Usually when my father wanted us to come outside to see what was in the bed of his truck, it was only because whatever was in there was either too bloody and/or vicious for him to carry inside, so we all stayed in the relative safety of our house and asked a series of questions designed to indicate the level of danger of whatever Daddy would be exposing us to. We'd learned to interpret his answers accordingly, and had invented what we would later refer to as "The Dangerous Thesaurus of My Father."

An abridged version:

"You're really going to like this." = "I have no idea what children enjoy."

"Put your dark coat on." = "You're probably going to get blood on you."

"It's not going to hurt you." = "I hope you like Bactine."

"It's *very* excited." = "It has rabies."

"Now, don't get *too* attached." = "I got this monkey for free because it has a virus."

"It likes you!" = "This wild boar is now your responsibility."

"Now, *this* is really interesting." = "You'll still have nightmares about this when you're thirty."

"Don't scream or you'll scare it." = "You should really be running now."

"It just wants to give you a kiss." = "It's probably going to eat your face off."

My father was perpetually disappointed by our lack of trust, but I reminded him that just last week he'd brought his own mother a box he'd filled with an angry live snake that he'd found on the road on the way to her house. He tried to defend himself, but my sister and I had both been there when my father laid the box on the front yard and called his mother out to see "a surprise." Then he nudged the box open with his foot, the snake jumped out, and my grandmother and I ran inside. Lisa ran in the opposite direction and tried to jump into the bed of the truck, which was incredibly shortsighted, as that was exactly where my father stored the skinned, unidentifiable animals that he planned to boil down in order to study their bone structure. The bed of my father's pickup truck was like something that would have ended up in Dante's *Inferno*, if Dante had ever spent any time in rural Texas.

This memory was still vivid in our minds as my father pushed us all outside into the cold darkness to show us whatever horrifying booty he'd managed to capture, shoot, or run over. My sister and I hung back nervously as my mother braced herself with a deep breath and leaned forward uneasily to stare into the eyes of a dozen grim live birds, who looked as if they'd been driven through hell. A few squawked indignantly, but most huddled numbly in the corner, no doubt shell-shocked from the windblown journey, coupled with being forced to share the pickup bed with several animal carcasses my father had probably picked up for taxidermy work. To the birds, I assume it must've been very much like accepting a ride from a stranger, only to get in the back of the van to find several murdered hikers who were being made into lamp shades.

My father explained that the birds were well-behaved Wisconsin jumbo quail, and my mother countered that the birds were, in fact, rowdy *turkeys*. He explained that he'd gotten them in trade for the rusty crossbow he'd brought home a few months ago, and technically the birds seemed the lesser of the two evils, so she shook her head and went back to cleaning. My mother was a woman who knew how to pick her battles, and she probably realized that the *quails-that-were-actually-turkeys* would be less dangerous to all of us.

Those birds loved my father with a white-hot passion. They followed him around, reverently, in what I can only imagine was some sort of Patty Hearst Stockholm syndrome, no doubt strengthened by the sight of him carrying dead animals into the house every few days. My father was the only person they seemed to tolerate. As the months wore on, the turkeys grew bigger and louder and more obnoxious, and would roost on low tree branches, screaming at my mother every time she left the house. My father insisted that the quails were just eccentric, and that we were misinterpreting the loud, angry gobbling, which he maintained was simply the birds singing with joy. He implied that our response to the quail was probably just an indication of our own guilty consciences, and my mother implied that he probably needed to be stabbed repeatedly with a fork in the thigh, but she said it more with her eyes than with her mouth, and my father seldom paid enough attention to either.

As the birds grew larger and meaner, I thanked God that we had no neighbors near enough to witness the turkey's behavior. I was already plagued with insecurity and shyness, and the embarrassing angry turkey attacks were doing nothing for my already low self-confidence. My sister and I tried to ignore the whole situation, which was difficult, because my father insisted on naming the turkeys and treating them like pets. Pets who would angrily run at you in a full-out attack, nipping at your tiny ankles as you ran in circles around the yard, screaming for someone to open the door to the house and let you in.

Lisa tried to convince my father that the birds (led by an unpredictable turkey named Jenkins, for some reason) wanted to eat us, but my father assured us that "quail don't even *have* teeth, so even if they *did* manage to kill you, *they certainly wouldn't be able to eat you.*" I suppose he thought that was comforting.

"Do *turkeys* have teeth?" my sister asked him archly.

My father tried to lecture her on respecting your elders, but he got distracted trying to calm down Jenkins, who had lodged himself on the mailman's hood and was violently attacking at the windshield wiper, while gobbling accusingly at the baffled postman.

We lived on a rural route, so our mailman was fairly used to being besieged by stray dogs, but he'd been utterly unprepared for an angry turkey attack and indignantly yelled, *"You need to lock those damn turkeys up if you can't control them."*

My father lifted the large bird off the hood, with more than a little exertion, and tucked him under his arm, saying (with a surprising amount of dignity for a man with a turkey under his arm), "Sir, this bird is a *quail*. And his name is Jenkins." I was surprised at my father's elegance and poise at that moment, especially in light of the fact that Jenkins was snorting furiously at the mailman while shaking the limp rubber part of the windshield wiper blade in his beak like a whip. I was *not* surprised when we found a note in our mailbox the following day, informing us that we would no longer be allowed to tape a quarter to our letters in lieu of a stamp, and that all further packages would be left by the mailbox rather than being delivered to the door. This was upsetting to my mother, both because she hated to have to drive into town to buy stamps, and also because the mailman's idea of leaving packages at the mailbox was more like him flinging our mail in the general direction of the house without braking. The turkeys adapted to this by quickly gathering up the mail in the yard, which would have been helpful if they'd brought it to the house like a dog, but instead they'd carry the letters around proudly, as if they were important turkey documents that my mother was attempting to steal from them. She'd try to convince my sister and me that it would be a fun game to try to get the mail from the turkeys each day, but we declined, pointing out that a good game of keep-away shouldn't end with bloody ankles and the threat of bird flu.

It was far safer for our social standing and physical well-being to avoid the turkeys altogether, so my sister and I began putting together a defensive strategy to protect us from bird assault. *Flashdance* had just come out, and I tried to convince my mom to buy me leg warmers (both to help me fit in with the cool kids at school, and also to protect my legs from turkey attacks), but she refused, saying that wearing leg warmers in the Texas summer was a total waste of money. Instead I ended up just enviously staring at everyone *else's* leg warmers, who I suspected probably didn't even *have* turkeys. Lisa and I attempted to fashion ankle armor out of empty soup cans that we'd opened on both sides, but my feet were too big to fit into them, and Lisa's feet were so little that when she ran, the tin cans would clink loudly together and simply attract the attention of the vicious herd. She was basically like a tiny, pigtailed dinner bell. I considered telling her that the ankle armor wasn't helping, but that was tantamount to telling a fellow zebra that he's covered in steak sauce right before you both have to cross a parking lot full of lions. Self-preservation is a narcissistic bedfellow, and I wasn't proud of my actions, but I comforted myself in the knowledge that if Lisa did fall prey to the vicious birds I would wait a week—out of respect—before claiming her toys for my own.

Lisa had heard that turkeys were so stupid that if it rained, they would look up to see what was falling on them and drown from the rain falling into their noses, so we began to pray for rain, which was promptly answered by a full-on drought. Probably because you're not supposed to ask God to murder your pets. We often talked about spraying the water hose on them in order to weed out the stupider ones, but we could never bring ourselves to do it, both because it seemed too cruel (even in self-defense) and also because our father would probably find it suspicious if all his turkeys died in a freak rainstorm that had apparently broken out only next to the garden hose.

Occasionally the turkeys would follow us, menacingly, on our quarter-mile walk to school, lurking behind us like improbable gang members or tiny, feathered rapists. Even at age nine I was painfully self-conscious, and was aware that dysfunctional pet turkeys would not be viewed as "cool," so I would always duck inside the schoolhouse as quickly as possible and feign ignorance, conspicuously asking my classmates why the hell there were always jumbo quail on the playground. Then other students would point out that they were turkeys, and I'd shrug with indifference, saying, "Oh, are they? Well, I wouldn't know about such things." Then I'd slide into my seat and slouch over my desk, avoiding eye contact until the turkeys lost interest and wandered back home to shriek at my mother for their breakfast.

This worked perfectly until the morning when I ducked inside the school lobby a little too sluggishly, and Jenkins blithely followed me in, gobbling to himself and looking both clueless and vaguely threatening. Two other turkeys followed behind Jenkins. I quickly ran into my classroom as the turkeys wandered aimlessly into the library. I sighed in relief that no one had noticed the turkey expedition, until an hour later, when we all heard a lot of screaming and squawking, and we discovered that the principal and librarian had found the turkeys, who had somehow made their way to the cafeteria. They had also managed to *shit everywhere*. It was actually a little bit impressive, and also horribly revolting. The principal had seen the turkeys follow us to school before (as had most of my classmates, who'd just been too embarrassed for me to point out that they knew I was the turkey-magnet the whole time), so he called my father and demanded that he come to the school to clean up the mess that his turkeys had made. My father explained to the principal that he must be mistaken, because *he* was raising jumbo quail, but the principal wasn't buying it.

A half-hour later, when my class lined up to go to PE, I found my father on his knees, cleaning up poop in the lobby. He was unsuccessfully attempting to shoo the turkeys away, quietly but forcefully yelling, "GO HOME, JENKINS." I froze and tried to blend into the wallpaper, but it was too late. Jenkins recognized me immediately and ran up to me, gobbling with excited recognition like, "OH MY GOD, ISN'T THIS AWESOME? WHO ARE YOUR FRIENDS?" and for the first time I didn't run screaming from him. Instead I sighed and waved weakly, mumbling dejectedly, "Hey, Jenkins," as my classmates stared at me in amazement. But not the *good* kind of amazement, like when your uncles show up at your school in a limo to invite you to live with them, and they're Michael Jackson and John Stamos, but you never mentioned it before because you didn't want to brag, and everyone feels really bad for not inviting you to their slumber parties when they had the chance. It was more of the *bad* kind of amazement. Like when you realize that not having the right kind of leg warmers is really small potatoes compared to being assaulted by an overexcited turkey named Jenkins, who is being scolded by your shit-covered father in front of your entire school. I think this was the point when I realized that I was kind of fucked when it came to ever becoming the most popular kid in the class, and so I just nodded to Jenkins and my father (both equally oblivious to the damage they'd done to my reputation), and I held my head up high as I walked down the hall and tried not to slip in the feces.

All the rest of that day I waited for the taunting to come, but it never did. Probably because no one even knew where to begin. Or possibly because they were intimidated by Jenkins, who I later heard had screamed threateningly at the kindergarteners as he was forcibly evicted from the premises. My sister tried to be blasé and pretended as if this sort of thing was commonplace. She refused to let it affect her social standing, and so it didn't. This same confidence came in handy a few years later, when she was attacked by a pig on the playground. (That story's in the next book. You should start saving up for it now.)

I, on the other hand, gave up completely at ever trying to fit in again.

When other girls had tea parties on the playground, I brought out my secondhand Ouija board and attempted to raise the dead. While my classmates gave book reports on *The Wind in the Willows* or *Charlotte's Web*, I did mine on tattered, paperback copies of Stephen King novels that I'd borrowed from my grandmother. Instead of *Sweet Valley High*, I read books about zombies and vampires. Eventually, my third-grade teacher called my mother in to discuss her growing concerns over my behavior, and my mom nodded blithely, but failed to see what the problem was. When Mrs. Johnson handed her my recent book report on *Pet Sematary*, my mom wrinkled her forehead with concern and disapproval. "Oh, I see," she said disappointedly, as she turned to me. "You spelled 'cemetery' wrong." Then I explained that Stephen King had spelled it that way on purpose, and she nodded, saying, "Ah. Well, *good enough for me*." My teacher seemed a bit flustered, but eventually the principal reminded her that my family had been the ones responsible for the *Great Turkey Shit-off of 1983*, and she seemed to realize that her intervention was futile, and gave up without feeling too guilty, because it was pretty obvious there was no way of turning me into a "normal" third-grader. And I felt relieved for her.

And actually? A little relieved for me too. Because it was the first time in my life that I gave myself permission to be me. I was still shy and self-conscious and terrified of people, but Jenkins had essentially freed me of the bonds of having to try to fit in. It was a lesson I should have been happy to learn at such a young age, if it weren't for the fact that it was a teaching moment centering on a public turkey attack witnessed by all of the same kids that I would graduate from high school with.

Soon afterward, Jenkins and the other turkeys disappeared from our lives, but the lessons I learned from them still remain: Turkeys make terrible pets, you should never trust your father to identify poultry, and you should accept who you are, *flaws and all*, because if you try to be someone you aren't, then eventually some turkey is going to shit all over your well-crafted façade, so you might as well save yourself the effort and enjoy your zombie books. And so I guess, in a way, I owe Jenkins a debt of gratitude, because (even if it was entirely unintentional) he was a brilliant teacher.

And also? *Totally delicious.*

If You Need an Arm Condom, It Might Be Time to Reevaluate Some of Your Life Choices

(Alternative Title: High School Is Life's Way of Giving You a Record Low to Judge the Rest of Your Life By)

I was the only Goth chick in a tiny agrarian high school. Students occasionally drove to school on their tractors. Most of my classes took place inside an ag barn. It was like if Jethro from *The Beverly Hillbillies* showed up in a Cure video, except just the opposite.

I purposely chose the Goth look to make people avoid me—since I was painfully shy—and I spent every free period and lunch hiding in the bathroom with a book until I finally graduated. It was totally shitty.

The end.

UPDATED: My editor says that this is a terrible chapter, and that she doesn't "even know what the hell an ag barn is." Which is kind of weird. For *her*, I mean. "Ag barn" is short for "agriculture barn." It's the barn where they teach all the boll weevil eradication classes. I wish I were joking about that, but I'm totally not. You could also take classes in welding, animal husbandry, cotton judging and cultivation, and another class that I don't remember the name of, but we learned how to build stools and fences in it. I'm fairly sure it was called "Stools and Fences 101." None of this is made up.

UPDATED AGAIN: My editor says this is still a terrible chapter and that I need to flesh it out more. I assume by "flesh it out" she means recover a bunch of awkward memories that I've invested a lot of time in repressing. *Fine.* My ag teacher told us that once, years ago, a student was hanging a cotton-judging banner on the ag barn wall when he fell off of the ladder and landed on a broomstick, which went *right up his rectum*. The idea must have really stuck with my teacher, because he was forever warning us to be constantly vigilant of any stray brooms in the area before getting on a ladder, and to this day I cannot see a ladder without checking to make sure there aren't any brooms nearby. This is pretty much the only useful thing I ever learned in high school. Oh, and I also learned firsthand how to artificially inseminate a cow using a turkey baster (but that was less "useful" and more "traumatic," both for me and the cow). This is what we had instead of geography. It's also why I can never get the blue pie when I play Trivial Pursuit.

UPDATED AGAIN: My editor hates me and is apparently working in collusion with my therapist, because they both insist that I delve deeper into my high school years. *Fine.* I blame them for this whole chapter. Please be aware that you'll probably have horrible flashbacks of high school when you read this. You can forward your therapy bills to my editor.

Let's start again. . . .

Pretty much everyone hates high school. It's a measure of your humanity, I suspect. If you enjoyed high school, you were probably a psychopath or a cheerleader. Or possibly both. Those things aren't mutually exclusive, you know. I've tried to block out the memory of my high school years, but no matter how hard you try to ignore it, it's always with you, like an unwanted hitchhiker. Or herpes. *I assume.*

Since I went to high school with all of the same kids who'd witnessed my peculiar childhood, I had already given up on the idea of becoming popular and perky, so instead I tried to reinvent myself with a Goth wardrobe, black lipstick, and a look that I hoped said, "You don't want to get too close to me. *I've got dark, terrible secrets.*"

Unfortunately, the mysterious persona I tried to adopt was met with a kind of confused (and mildly pitying) skepticism, since the kids in my class were all *acutely* aware of all my dark, terrible secrets. Which is really not how secrets work at all. These were the same kids who'd witnessed the

1980:
It was a look that screamed,
"Ask me about becoming
a sister wife."

Great Turkey Shit-off of 1983, and who all vividly remembered the time my father sent me to our fourth-grade Thanksgiving play wearing war paint and bloody buffalo hides instead of the customary construction-paper pilgrim hats the rest of my class had made in art class. These were the same classmates who owned yearbooks documenting my mother's decade-long infatuation with handmade prairie dresses and sunbonnets, an obsession that led to my sister and me spending much of the early eighties looking like the lesbian love children of Laura Ingalls and Holly Hobbie. I suspect that Marilyn Manson would have had similar problems being taken seriously as "dark and foreboding" if everyone in the world had seen him dressed as Little Miss *Hee Haw* in second grade.

My classmates refused to take me seriously, so I decided to pierce my own nose using a fishhook, but it hurt too much to get it all the way through, so I gave up and then it got infected. So instead I wore a clip-on earring. In my nose. To school. It was larger than my nostril and I almost suffocated. Still, it was the first nose ring ever worn at my high school, and I wore it with a rebellious pride past the principal, who I'd expected would lock himself in his office immediately to stop the Twisted Sisteresque riots that would surely ensue at any moment from all the anarchy unleashed by my nose ring. The principal noticed, but seemed more bemused than concerned, and seemed to be trying to suppress laughter as he pointed it out to the lunch lady, who was bewildered.

1990:
Just as ridiculous, except this time I was dressing myself. (Pro tip: Your faux-Victorian, emo self-portraits in graveyards will look slightly less stilted if you take off your Swatch watch first.)

And who was also my mother.

And it was her clip-on.

My mom sighed inwardly, shook her head, and went back to slicing Jell-O. Neither of us ever mentioned the incident (or wore that earring) again.

Having my mom as the cafeteria lady was a mixed blessing, because she'd let me hide in the school pantry if I was having a bad day, but whenever I'd pass the cafeteria I'd hear her stage-whisper, "Sweetie, stop slouching. *You look so depressed,*" and all the other kids would be all, *"Nice hairnet, Elvira's mom."*

So, yeah, high school was *pretty fucking awesome.* And a lot of people tell me that *everyone* has terrible high school experiences, and that's when I say, *"Really?* So the high point of your senior year was when you had your arm up a cow's vagina?" Then they stop talking to me. Usually forever.

My sister, Lisa, never seemed to have any problems fitting in, and distanced herself from me as best she could while still trying to convince me to join some school activities like everyone else. Lisa was in track, basketball, one-act plays, and had most recently been elected to be the high school mascot, a giant male bird named Wally. We were all quite proud of her, as the competition had been stiff, and she took her new role very seriously, practicing bird attack maneuvers in full costume in the living room. While we waited for our parents to get home from work I'd watch and give her pointers about her technique. "Try to shake your butt wing more," I offered helpfully.

"Tail feathers," she clarified (with a surprising amount of condescension for someone wearing bird feet), her voice slightly muffled by the giant bird head on her shoulders. "They're called *tail feathers*. And if we're giving each other advice, maybe you could stop wearing black *all the time*? People think you're *weird*."

"People think *I'm* weird because I wear a lot of black?" I asked. *"You're dressed as poultry."*

Lisa shrugged indifferently. "That may be true, but I was *elected* to dress as poultry, and when I walk down the hall in my costume tomorrow, people will smile and high-five me. When *you* walk down the hall tomorrow, people will spit and avoid eye contact to keep you from putting voodoo curses on them."

"Okay, first of all, you can't even *get* real high fives, because *you don't have hands*. And secondly, I'd need to have someone's hair or nail clippings to put a voodoo curse on them."

"THIS IS EXACTLY WHAT I'M TALKING ABOUT," Lisa yelled, pausing her bird routine to cross her wings in frustration. "You shouldn't even know *how* to do voodoo curses. *It's bizarre.* WOULD IT KILL YOU TO JUST TRY TO BE NORMAL?"

"Oh, I'm sorry. . . . Could you repeat that last part?" I asked. "I can't hear you through YOUR GIANT FUCKING BIRD HEAD."

Lisa huffily pulled the bird head off and seemed to be working up a lecture, but I really couldn't stomach the thought of someone in a bird costume telling me I needed to be more focused on fitting in, so I locked myself in the bathroom. After a few minutes Lisa halfheartedly apologized through the bathroom door, probably because she realized that her hands were still covered in thick bird wings, and that I was the only person in the house who could help her unzip her costume if she needed to pee. *Yes*, it seemed cruel, but these are the risks you take when you choose popularity over opposable thumbs. It's probably also why Big Bird is always so fucking nice to everyone. You kind of *have* to be nice if you know that you're trapped in a costume, and that your bathroom breaks are at the mercy of people in the vicinity who own thumbs. Honestly, if we ever run out of straitjackets, we could just put crazy people in old mascot costumes. Plus, if they escape from their mental institutions they'll be just as hindered as anyone in a straitjacket, but way less scary. And instead of shouting at terrified children at the bus stop, they'll just look like charmingly bedraggled Muppets who are lost and need a bath. *Everyone wins.* Plus, I think I may have just solved the homeless problem. (*Editor's note: Nope. Not even remotely.*)

Even so, the words of my sister were still ringing in my ears the next day at school, and I decided to make an effort to fit in. And that's how the peer pressure of a sibling in a bird costume led to me getting my arm stuck in a cow's vagina. *This is exactly why peer pressure is such a terrible thing.* Frankly, this entire chapter could be an after-school special.

The weirdest thing about my getting a cow pregnant when I was in high school is that I wasn't even enrolled in that class.[1] I'd taken most of my required classes in my first two years of high school, so I filled my last two years with easy electives. I enjoyed art, but I'd already taken the only three art classes my school offered, so my art teacher allowed me to make up a new one. I chose "Medieval Costume Design," but I got bored after the first six weeks and switched it to "Sequins! The glitteriest buttons!" Then my art teacher pointed out that the school didn't actually have a budget for

--- --- --- --- --- --- --- --- ---

1. *Editor's note: No. That's not even* close *to the weirdest thing about getting a cow pregnant in high school.*

sequins, and that I probably wasn't ready for an advanced sequin class if I was under the impression that they were buttons, so I just stopped going. Instead I was assigned to be an office aide, and I spent the noon hour manning the front desk of Mrs. Williamson, the temporary receptionist of the junior high next door, who spent her lunch hour drinking in her car. She was a nervous, divorced woman who always left incredibly raunchy novels in her top desk drawer, and who once told me that house cats will eat their owner within an hour of their owner's death. She disappeared less than a month after I started (I suspected she'd been fired, but I admitted that it was possible she'd been eaten by her own cats) and had been replaced with an answering machine, so no one really seemed to care anymore whether I showed up or not. I'd taken to spending that hour crouched under Mrs. Williamson's abandoned desk, reading whatever lascivious books she'd left behind, but I'd just finished her last book the day before (a V. C. Andrews novel with the really graphic parts underlined), so I was in no hurry to get to the junior high office. Instead I dallied in the ag barn, slowly packing away the power tools and arc welder.

The ag teacher noticed that I seemed a bit shiftless, and offered to let me tag along and help with the animal husbandry class on their trip to the local stockyard. It was a small class of boys, all wearing tight Wranglers and cowboy boots, and (against my better judgment) I took a deep breath and said, "Why not?" as I nervously climbed onto the small bus. I looked like a Metallica roadie who had been won by Willie Nelson's tour bus, but the guys did their best to make me feel at home, and seemed quietly impressed that I'd volunteer to come along for the trip. It wasn't until we actually arrived at the stockyard that I realized we were there to learn about artificial cow insemination. The teacher suggested that I help him, since my arms were smaller and so "it would be less uncomfortable for the cow." I wasn't entirely sure what constituted "helping," but it became clearer as he rolled a shoulder-length rubber glove up my arm. He slapped an open thermos of semen in my hand, and sucked it up into the turkey baster.

This is probably the point when I should have just run, but there was something about the way he was staring at me that made me stop. It was the look of a man waiting for a girl to run screaming so he could have a good laugh at her expense. Or possibly it was the look of a man who wondered how he was going to explain to the lunch lady that he *had* to give her daughter all that semen, because she was the only one around who could fit in the arm condom. Hard to tell. But either way, it seemed as if he expected me to bolt, and I'll be damned if I was going to be judged by a man who carried semen around in a thermos.

And that's how I ended up shoulder-deep in a cow's vagina, squishing out the semen baster as a bunch of teenage boys looked on. It was the closest I'd ever come to doing porn. Suddenly the cow's vagina tensed unexpectedly and I realized that my arm was stuck. I screamed involuntarily. The teacher panicked, thinking that the sudden contraction was an indication that the cow was going to sit down quickly, and told me to pull out my arm gently, because if the cow sat down it could break my arm. This was disconcerting, both because it sounded painful, and also because "I broke my arm in a cow's vagina" is not something you ever want to have to explain to anyone. I yanked my arm out, and the cow looked back at me in disgust. And that's when I realized that I no longer had the turkey baster.

This is the point when I'd like to say that I gritted my teeth and said, *"I'm going back in,"* with the focused determination of Bruce Willis from that movie I can't remember the name of. The one about Armageddon. (*Editor's note: Really? It's called* Armageddon.) But instead I took a deep breath, held my head up with what little dignity I could muster, slowly peeled off my glove, and walked away. No one called me back, probably because none of them could find an elegant way to say, *"You left your turkey baster in that cow's vagina."* Or possibly because they realized that the first one to speak up would probably be elected to take my place. I'm assuming someone went back in to retrieve the turkey baster (for the cow's sake, at least), but I don't know, because I didn't stick around to see. Instead, I walked off and waited until the rest of the class finally showed up. I was braced for the teasing to begin, but it never did. The guys looked a bit pale and shaky, but laughed at one another as they made bovina jokes, and my ag teacher patted my back reassuringly as we got back on the bus.

We returned to the school just as my sister was walking out of the gym from pep-rally practice. She was still dressed as Wally and was waving her tail feathers with panache. She saw me and slowed down to walk beside me toward the school, and as we walked in silence I realized that we could not have been a more awkward-looking couple. "What's up?" she asked carefully. "You look weird."

"I took your advice about trying to fit in," I said in a voice calmer than I would have suspected.

"And?" she asked.

"*And* I got my arm stuck in a cow's vagina," I replied, staring off into the distance.

Lisa paused momentarily, and glanced at me with what I assumed was a look of disappointment. Or possibly shock. It was hard to tell when she had that bird head on. Then she walked on beside me, staring stoically into the surrounding cotton fields, as if a response to my statement could be found there. "Well," she said, pausing to find the right words. *"That'll happen."* She said it with a quiet sense of dignity, as if a small, wise Morgan Freeman were inside the bird costume with her, feeding her lines.

"I almost lost an arm," I added conversationally, a slight hint of hysteria creeping into my voice. "I almost lost an arm *inside a cow's vagina.*" It was a slight exaggeration, but at this point I was almost daring her to call me out, as I had begun to regard a fair amount of this as her fault.

She nodded carefully, her beak bobbing up and down, seeming determined to keep up a normal conversational tone. *"Inside* the cow's vagina, you say? Well, that's just . . . that's fascinating," she said, in the same way someone might remark that the weather was about to turn cold, or that horses lack the ability to vomit. "So"—she paused—"it's *possible* you might have misunderstood my advice." I glared at her. "But still? *These* are the moments high school memories are made of, right?" She held up her wings and did what I'm assuming was her best version of jazz hands. *"Yay for memories?"* she said weakly, and somewhat apologetically.

And then I punched her.

But just in my head, because frankly, starting my day with my arm stuck in a cow's vagina and ending it decking someone in a bird outfit was too much even for me.

But in a way she was right . . . you *should* enjoy and appreciate your days in high school, because you *will* remember them the rest of your life. Like when you're in prison, or you're getting mugged at gunpoint, you can say to yourself, "Well, at least I'm not in high school." High school is life's way of giving you a record low to judge the rest of your life by. I know this because no matter how shitty it got, I could always look back and say, "At least I don't have my arm stuck up a cow's vagina." In fact, that's kind of become my life's motto. It's also what I say when I'm at a loss for words when talking to people who are grieving the loss of their grandparents. "Well, at least you don't have your arm stuck up a cow's vagina," I murmur helpfully, while patting their arm consolingly. And it's useful because it's true, and also because it's such a jarring sort of image that they immediately stop crying. Probably because they recognize it as one of the great truisms of life. Or maybe because most people don't talk about getting arms stuck up cows' vaginas during funerals. I don't really know. I don't get invited to many funerals.

There are no known pictures of me with my arm stuck up a cow's vagina, but my parents own tons of pictures of my sister dressed as poultry. I don't think I need to tell you who the favorite in my family was.

ADDENDUM: When I first wrote this chapter I realized that people would have a hard time believing it, so I looked up my former high school principal and sent him this (abridged) e-mail, which really only proves that I shouldn't be allowed to use e-mail after I've been drinking:

> . . . I've been thinking of writing about artificial cow insemination, but the problem is that my memory sucks and I can't remember all the details. Probably because I blocked it out. Or because of all the drugs I did in college.
>
> This is how I remember it: Shoulder-length glove and a turkey baster up the cow's vagina. I would have sworn this is how we did it, but I know the preferred method nowadays is to do it rectovaginally. Am I misremembering? Because I'm fairly sure I'd remember if I had my arm up a cow's rectum. Then again, I'm having to ask my high school principal the details of getting a cow pregnant, so obviously my memory is not entirely reliable.
>
> Do any pictures of this still exist? I realize this is probably the weirdest request you've ever received from a former student, and I apologize for that.
>
> I also apologize for sending you an e-mail with the word "rectovaginal" in it. I can assure you I never saw that coming either.
>
> Hugs,
> Jenny

Immediately after sending the e-mail I realized how inappropriate it was, and so I called Lisa and said, "So, I may have just sent our high school principal an e-mail with the word 'rectovaginal' in it," and she was all, "Who is this?" and I was like, "No. Seriously. That. Just. Happened." And after she stopped banging her head on her desk she pointed out that I had learned nothing from her advice, and she agreed that I should probably call his secretary to ask her to delete the e-mail from his account before he opened it. It was too late, though, because he'd immediately opened it and replied to it, and seemed entirely unfazed. Also, he assured me that practically *no one* was doing it rectovaginally back in the early nineties, which is totally true on so many levels. He also looked for photographs, but never found any, probably because no one ever takes pictures of underage girls with their arms up cow vaginas. Most likely because those pictures are more likely to end up in evidence lockers than in books about golden childhood memories.

Draw Me
a Fucking Dog

DISCLAIMER: *My agent and editor don't love this chapter, because it's about me doing drugs (poorly) and it doesn't really fit with the rest of the book, but I pointed out that druggies will totally relate to it, and nondruggies will feel smugly self-satisfied with their life choices when they read it, so I'm basically hitting all the demographics. But then they said that it's just too rambling and confusing to be a real chapter. They may have a point. This is why this chapter isn't a real chapter at all. It's a bonus story that you can skip so you can feel like you accomplished more today. Or you can underline parts and write notes to yourself in all the margins so people in the subway think you're either really smart for reading a textbook on the subway, or just rich enough to use hardback books as Post-its. You aren't allowed to judge this chapter, though, because it's not a real chapter. As a Post-it note, however, it is pretty fucking impressive.*

Special note to any teenage children I may one day have: Anyone who does drugs is a moron. Don't do drugs. They will kill you and make your boobies fall off. It happened to your aunt Rebecca, and that's why you've never heard of her. But we keep her boobies in a box to remember her terrible lesson, and if I ever even smell pot on you I will put them on you while you are sleeping, and you will wake up with a dead woman's boobies on your forehead. Now, skip to the next chapter, because I'm about to start writing about having sex with your father.

PREFACE: *There isn't really a preface. I just wanted to see how many paragraphs I could fit in before actually starting a chapter.*

PREFACE ADDENDUM: *Four. The answer is four.*

I was eighteen the first time I did acid. And it was awesome. And horrible. And also I was kind of an idiot, because I'd managed to unintentionally wait until one week after I could legally be charged as an adult for drug possession.

My friend Jim had been doing acid since he was fifteen, and I was captivated with his stories of LSD experimentation, including his recent drug-induced epiphany that the one thing that brought all of mankind together was our common possession of nipples. "I mean . . . we *all* have them, right?" he asked me feverishly. "And what *possible* reason is there for men to possess these useless body parts unless it's an undeniable sign that men and woman are all *one* in this giant, cosmic soup that we call the universe?! Men and women . . . *we're all the same!* It's all relative!" He'd called his epiphany "The Theory of Relativity," until someone pointed out that that already existed, and so he grudgingly changed it to "*Jim's* Theory of Relativity." At the time I thought it was brilliant, but at the time I was also drunk.

I was both terrified and fascinated by the idea that there was a whole world known only to acid users, and I was completely intrigued by the accompanying drug lingo that Jim so naturally bandied about. I longed to "have a connection" in the drug trade, and I felt that the only way I'd be able to use this phrase in good faith would be to sleep with a pharmacist or to meet someone who occasionally sold speed. The latter seemed easier and less likely to end with VD. And also I didn't know any pharmacists.

Jim once told me about the time he was waiting at his house for some friends to pick him up so they could drop acid together. He decided to get a head start and took three hits while his mom was watching TV in the other room. Unfortunately, his friends had *also* decided to take acid a little early and found themselves completely high and driving to Jim's house, which would have been extremely stupid and dangerous except that they were actually sitting at the dining room table just *thinking* that they were in the car, so it was less dangerous and more just really stupid. And they stayed at that table for the next four hours, because none of them were willing to get out of the car, since no one knew where the brakes were. It was basically the longest car ride in the world that didn't actually involve a car. Meanwhile, Jim began doodling on a phone book in his bedroom, and he'd just finished drawing a little stick figure when the little stick figure dude came to life and said, "Dude. Draw me a fucking dog."

This is when Jim realized the drugs had kicked in, and when Jim's mom walked in a bit later and an enormous eagle flew past her and landed on his bed. Jim told me that the stick figure started screaming, but Jim ignored him, because he *was* high, but not so high that he didn't realize that talking to a drawing on a phone book would probably look suspicious.

Jim noticed that his mom was staring at him warily, but at this point he was so high that he couldn't remember whether he'd asked *her* a question that she hadn't answered, or if she'd asked *him* a question that he hadn't answered, but he thought it would be weirder to follow up whatever question he might have asked her with another question, especially since he couldn't remember the question he hadn't actually asked her in the first place. So basically they just sat there having this really awkward staring contest. Then the stick figure pointed out that if the eagle was not a hallucination his mom would know he was on drugs, because what kind of guy would be all, *"Oh, it's perfectly normal to have this eagle here"*? Jim laughed nervously and tried to give his mom a look that he hoped said something like "Wow. The world is a weird place when eagles may or may not land on your bed, right?"

But in reality it must have said something closer to *"Holy shit, I'm fucking high,"* because the next day Jim's mom sent him to the local psychiatric/ rehab center, which helped him find God and introduced him to narcotics far more addictive than any drugs he could have found on the street. When he came back he was all about lithium and Jesus, and when I mentioned that I really just wanted to try LSD, he rolled his eyes at me as if he were some sort of wine connoisseur and I'd just asked the best way to unscrew a bottle of Strawberry Hill. Druggies can be surprisingly judgmental. It's pretty much the only social circle where the same people you just witnessed shooting horse tranquilizers up one another's butts will actually look down at you for not being as cool as them. Unless maybe there's some sort of horse-enema-fetish social circle, which I'm not sure exists. Hold on, let me check the Internet.

Ohholyshit. Do *not* look that up, y'all.

Luckily, though, when you run with drug crowds you eventually run into the perfect dealer, and for me it was Travis. He was a long-haired blond guy in his late twenties who lived at home with his parents. He always seemed to know someone with drugs but seldom ever actually had any himself, which makes him not really a dealer at all, but whenever my friends and I needed pot we called him, because he was the closest thing we had. He was more like the middleman who protected us from the "real dealers," who we imagined were large, angry black men with pierced ears and pagers, who would probably make fun of us. *To death.* Also, in my mind the angry black men were all badasses and they all carried switchblades that had names like "Charlie Firecracker." (I didn't actually know any black people at the time, which I probably don't even need to clarify here based on this paragraph alone.)

A guy I knew had a house on the outskirts of town and offered to host a small LSD party for me and several other people in our group who'd never done acid before either. So we called Travis and asked him to bring over enough acid for six of us that night. Travis arrived and told us the drugs were on their way, and about fifteen minutes later a pizza delivery car pulled up. The delivery guy came to the door with a mushroom pizza and an uncut sheet of acid. The delivery guy was in his late teens, about two feet shorter than me, and very, very white, but he *did* have a piercing and a pager (which was very impressive, because this was still back in the early nineties, although probably the pager was just used for pizza orders). His name was Jacob. Travis told me later that anyone could buy acid from Jacob if they knew the "secret code" to use when you called the pizza place. At the time I thought it was probably something all cloak-and-dagger, like "One pepperoni pizza, hold the crust," or "A large cheesy bread *and the bird flies at midnight*," but in reality it was probably just "And tell Jacob to bring some acid," because honestly neither of them was very imaginative.

Jacob sold Travis the acid for four dollars a hit, and then Travis turned around and sold it to us for five dollars a hit, which was awkward and also a poor profit margin. We each took a hit and Travis said that for another ten bucks he'd stay and babysit us to make sure we didn't cut our own hands off. This wasn't something I was actually worried about at all until he mentioned it, but now that the thought was implanted in our heads I became convinced that we would all cut our hands off as soon as he left, so I handed him a ten. Travis cautioned us that if we thought the house cats next door were sending us threatening messages, they probably weren't. And he warned us not to stare at the sun because we'd go blind (which might have been great advice if it hadn't been ten o'clock at night). "Ride the beast . . . don't let the beast ride you," our wise sage advised us.

Secretly, I was worried that the acid wouldn't affect me at all. I'd smoked pot before, but I'd never actually felt the full, dizzying pleasure that *High Times* magazine promised. I developed all of the side effects with few of the benefits. While my friends sprawled out on papasan chairs, overwhelmed by the fact that nothing rhymes with "orange," I ate an entire box of Nilla Wafers and became paranoid that the neighbors were calling the cops. *"Schmorange!"* I'd yell, while compulsively spraying air freshener to dampen the smell. "Schmorange rhymes with orange! *Now will someone please fucking help me push this refrigerator in front of the door?!"*

No one ever helped.

My inability to get stoned was probably related to the fact that I was never able to hold the smoke in my lungs. A lot of people say that coughing when you're smoking pot gets you higher, because it makes you suck in more smoke, but those people are liars. I'd take a drag and the acrid smoke would hit the back of my throat like a red-hot poker, and I'd start hacking like an emphysemic coal miner. Who also had tuberculosis. And . . . I dunno . . . bird flu. What's worse than tuberculosis? Whatever that is, I sounded like I had that. Also I was constantly inhaling stray seeds into my windpipe, and none of my friends were sober enough to even *pronounce* "Heimlich," so every hit was like playing Russian roulette. Each inhalation brought on several minutes of spastic coughing where I'd spray everyone with what I'm sure were lacerated chunks of my lungs. I was pretty much the most unsexy drug user ever.

"All right there, Doc Holliday?" someone would ask.

"Coughing like that makes you higher," I lied, my voice sounding like I'd swallowed a gravel slushee. "You're supposed to cough as hard as you can until you feel like you're going to throw up. I think I read that in *Rolling Stone*." And by then everyone else was so high that it sounded plausible, and so *they'd* intentionally cough, and the whole car would be filled with flying spittle, and then eventually someone would almost make himself throw up. And then we'd laugh. Because almost throwing up is kind of funny when you're vaguely high and covered with other people's spit.

Even though I seemed mostly immune to pot, I still never turned down a joint, since it gave my hands something to do in social situations. I was still painfully shy, and would have rather costarred in a Tijuana donkey show than to have to make small talk with semi-strangers. The beauty of marijuana is that it instantly brings people together. Two minutes earlier you're standing with strangers in awkward silence because you brought up dildos, and then someone whispers that the hostess's brother died in a dildo accident, and you feel terrible about bringing up such a sensitive issue, but also really curious, because *how does someone die from a dildo accident?* Unless maybe a box of them fell on his head? But you're afraid to ask, because you already feel bad enough for bringing up the subject of dildos, which may have somehow killed a man, and you inwardly tell yourself that you shouldn't even be bringing up dildos at parties at all, but you know you won't listen, because next time there's a lull in the conversation you already know you're going to blurt out something about the girl you know whose brother died from a dildo accident. And then you'll remember that *that* girl is the girl you're actually talking to at the time. And then, just when it gets so terribly uncomfortable that you consider stabbing someone in the knee just to distract everyone so you can run away, someone pulls out a baggie of pot—and suddenly it's all cool. You're standing shoulder to shoulder, watching the ceremonial rolling of the joint while people give rolling tips and reminisce about flavored rolling papers and proffer treasured Zippos. (Note: *proffer.* It's not "offer" or "prefer." It's a combination of them, and it's a real word that you can use in Scrabble. And now you can tell people that you're reading a totally redeeming educational book and not just one about dildos killing innocent men. *You're welcome.*) Individuals who only minutes before might have disdainfully placed a protective layer of toilet paper over the hostess's toilet seat were now cheerily sucking on a joint moist with the saliva of a dozen strangers, and detailing their botched circumcision as if we are all old war buddies.

In the interest of truthiness I should point out that there was *one* time when I'd actually felt *truly* high. I'd smoked some Mexican weed with my friend Hannah, whom I'd been drawn to because we both had a penchant for wearing baby doll dresses, purposely torn stockings, and combat boots. We both had complete contempt for everyone else in the town who followed the herd mentality and was afraid to be unique and individualistic like us, the two Goth chicks *who were dressed exactly alike.*

When Hannah was a kid she'd had this Betsy Wetsy doll that she carried around everywhere. You were supposed to feed her with a bottle and then she'd pee, but Hannah would always just pry off Betsy's head and fill her up to her neck with the garden hose. She also decided to skip the whole diaper thing and would simply squeeze Betsy's distended midsection, and a half-gallon of faux pee would squirt out of Betsy's rudimentary plastic urinary tract onto the neighbor's bushes. "She takes after her father," Hannah would explain. "Runs right through her." Eventually Betsy's neck hole became stretched out from her head being pulled off so much, and the body was lost, but Hannah held on to Betsy's head, possibly as a reminder that she probably shouldn't have children. Then Hannah got older, and we went through this stage where we made everything possible into a bong: Coke cans, lightbulbs, melons. Then one night we used the baby's head as a bong. (I'm pretty sure that's the only time that sentence has ever been used in a memoir. One would hope. I'd check it out on the Internet, but to be honest; that whole horse-enema-fetish stuff scared the shit out of me, so I'm not even going to look.) We poked some holes into the top of Betsy's head, covered it with a wire screen, lit the pot, and sucked the smoke through Betsy's pink rosebud lips. After a few hits I realized I was giggly and dizzy and nauseous . . . and *totally* high. Hannah cockily claimed it was her exceptional Mexican marijuana, but I suspect it was the toxic fumes from the burned plastic of Betsy's soft spot. Regardless, it seemed worth the accompanying cancer risk, because it was the first time that I actually felt high, and I didn't want to take anything away from Hannah, because honestly this was kind of the pinnacle of bong crafts, and I thought it would be like the first guy Leonardo da Vinci showed the Mona Lisa to asking, *"Why's it so small?"* And this was pretty much exactly what was going through my mind the night I took acid from the pizza boy.

Wow. This is a really convoluted story. I blame the drugs.

Anyway, I waited two hours for the acid to kick in and felt only mildly dizzy, and I began to resign myself to the fact that the only thing that might ever get me high was Betsy's burning scalp. Then suddenly things felt different. My body started to ache and get tight, and I figured I was either about to start tripping or I had the flu. I asked Travis and he assured me that this was normal and was caused by the strychnine. And I was all, "Uh . . . strychnine? Like . . . *the stuff in rat poison?*" and Travis nonchalantly said, "Yeah. They add a little strychnine to get the acid to bond with the paper, and it gives you mini-convulsions, but it's not enough to kill you, so chill out." Then I was like, "I'M PRETTY SURE YOU'RE NOT SUP-POSED TO TELL SOMEONE ON LSD THAT THEY'RE HAVING CONVUL-SIONS FROM RAT POISON, *TRAVIS*," but I didn't say it out loud, because I was suddenly afraid my shouting would go *into* my tongue instead of *over* it and then it would swell up and I'd choke to death, and that's when I realized I was probably high.

Then I got distracted because I could hear this ringing sound, and I kept telling the other people to shut up so I could figure out what it was, but they were too busy licking the walls because they said the texture was exactly like licking a jawbreaker. I considered pointing out that it was exactly like licking a jawbreaker made of lead-based paint, but then I remembered that we had all just ingested rat poison, so I figured the damage was done at this point, and that if we survived it would only make us stronger.

Then I heard the ringing again and I started creeping around the house on my knees, because I thought maybe I could get *under* the sound waves of my drugged-out friends, who were now freaked out at the revelation that no one could ever see their faces in real life because "mirrors couldn't be trusted." I wondered whether Travis thought to hide the kitchen knives before we began, and I was going to find him and ask when the ringing started again. Travis was struggling to pry a can opener out of a girl's hands, and he yelled, *"Could somebody answer the goddamn phone?!"* And that's when I realized what the ringing was.

That's also when I realized the amazing beauty of the ringing phone, a sound I now knew the sober world would never truly appreciate. Even the *idea* of the phone seemed somehow more significant. *"It could be anybody on the other end of the line,"* I thought to myself. *"It could be Mr. T. Or one of the Thundercats."* The possibilities were overwhelming. I picked up the receiver and listened to the sound of the staticky emptiness across long-distance lines.

"Uh . . . *Hello?* Travis?" asked the man on the other end.

Me: "No, this is not Travis. Is this a Thundercat?"

"Who?" asked the man, who seemed really very annoyed.

"I think we both have the wrong number," I said, and I started to hang up, but then the not-Thundercat started getting all shouty, but I couldn't really understand him, and I thought that he was probably just angry at the sudden disappointing realization that he would never be a Thundercat. Then I suddenly realized that it was entirely possible that I wasn't even talking to anyone at all, and that perhaps this was all a hallucination. Maybe I wasn't even on the phone. Maybe I was standing here talking to an apple. Or a gerbil. Then I realized that if it *was* a gerbil it would probably soon burrow into my ear and eat my cochlea, so I dropped it on the ground and walked away, and Travis was all, "Who was on the phone," and I was like, "It was *not* a Thundercat. It *might* have been a gerbil. Does my ear look okay?"

This is when Travis probably should have just turned on the answering machine, but I think he'd actually taken a hit of acid himself, because he seemed to be melting, and it's been my experience that most sober people don't do that. And then I started throwing up. I said, "Wow. I think I'm going to throw up," and Travis said, "No, you just *think* you're going to throw up," and then I was like, "God, *that's* a relief." And then I threw up. On Travis's feet. Then Travis gave me a mostly empty bag of SunChips to throw up into, and I sat in a dark room and threw up—a lot. Like, so much that I suspected I was throwing up things I'd never even eaten. Travis put on a single of the Doors singing "L.A. Woman," because he said it would help, and it actually *did* help, in spite of the fact that the whole house seemed to be dissolving, haunted, and filled with hairy goblins. Also, I was pretty sure all the closets had small fires growing in them, and every time the Doors tape would reach the end, I would start throwing up again and Travis would hear me and have to rewind it and start it again.

This basically happened every five minutes for the next four hours.

But somewhere in between the time when I was stomping out imaginary closet fires and the time when I finally fell asleep, I did apparently have a few moments of clarity and inspiration. I know this because when I woke up later, next to a bag of sullied SunChips, I saw that someone had written a bizarre diatribe about Smurfs on the wall, and it was in my handwriting. And also I'd written my name several times on the wall pointing to it, because apparently I didn't want anyone else to take credit for my discovery that the Smurfs were actually peaceful bisexual communists. And that's when I realized that drugs were bad and I never took them again.[1] Then I left and decided to get all new friends, but first I scratched out my name on the wall and replaced it with "Travis." I suspected that he might try to pin it back on me, so I dotted his name with a heart, since everyone knew that I was not the kind of person to dot *i*'s with hearts. Then again, technically neither was Travis. I was probably still a little high at the time.

Anyway, my point is that drugs are a bad idea, unless you use them only to distract people from embarrassing dildo stories. And also that aside

---

1. Except for pot a few more times. And one time I accidentally did cocaine. And also I did acid a couple more times, but I never did it again at night, so I'm pretty sure that doesn't count. You know what? Never mind.

from all the vomiting and paranoia and embarrassing myself, it was actually kind of cool in retrospect, although really *not at all at the time*. Much like life. Also, you wish Lion-O the Thundercat would call you, but instead you spend a lot of time unnecessarily worrying about gerbils getting stuck inside of you. Which is also kind of a metaphor for life. A really, really bad one.

And That's Why
Neil Patrick Harris
Would Be the
Most Successful
Mass Murderer Ever

The week after I turned twenty-one I had made a series of good decisions. I hadn't gotten drunk yet (because as soon as it was legal it suddenly lost its charm), and I'd been really focused on my anorexia, which is one of the best mental illnesses to have, because at least you look hot while you're starving yourself to death. Except your hair looks like shit because it's falling out in clumps, and you find yourself lying awake at night obsessing about how your hip bones stick out too far and wondering how much it would hurt to file them down with a cheese grater. Wait, did I say *"good decisions"*? Let's start again.

The week after I turned twenty-one I was bored, sober, and dangerously underweight in that way that makes people think you're on heroin or dying of cancer. It was nine o'clock at night when I decided I needed to get out of the house, so I threw on a coat and drove to the only bookstore still open that late in the nearby town. My childhood love of horror novels had side-railed into a brief fling with witchcraft. (Which lasted just long enough for me to realize that none of the spells and charms I made ever worked. When it called for "a white candle waved over newly broken seeds," I would shrug and wave my dad's flashlight over a jar of peanut butter. I would eventually denounce witchcraft as completely useless, but to be fair, it's possible that it was less about the potency of the spells, and more that I was just a really bad cook. Plus, it was the kind of peanut butter that already had the jelly mixed in it, which was a real time-saver, but probably not exactly what the druids had in mind.)

I walked back to the New Age section of the bookstore and for once I was not alone, as there was a guy there about my age who would not stop staring at me. Also, he looked almost exactly like Doogie Howser, M.D. (*Special notes for people reading this book who were born after 1990: (1) I kind of hate you. Please stop looking so good in shorts. (2)* Doogie Howser, M.D., *was one of the first shows Neil Patrick Harris did. It was before he got all hot. No one ever had a crush on him at that point. Then he came out of the closet and suddenly he was totally hot, and every girl in the world wanted to sleep with him. This is just how girls work. We can't explain it either.*) The (probably unintentional) Doogie Howser impersonator was wearing a denim vest, so I was fairly sure he was gay, but this was the nineties, so all bets were off. He wouldn't stop staring at me, and every time I'd pull out a book he'd casually remark, "Oh, I have that book." It was extremely annoying, and I found myself wishing there was a book in this section about tampons just to throw him off, but this was a small-town bookstore, so even if a tampon-witchcraft book existed, they probably wouldn't have had it in stock. Then Doogie smiled, picked up an astrology book, and *asked me what my sign was.* He swears that this never happened, *but it totally did.* And the entire time I was thinking, *"This guy's probably a stalker."* He was thinking, *"I'm going to marry this girl."* Mostly because he'd had a dream that he was going to marry a girl wearing a certain coat, and when I walked into the bookstore I was wearing the same coat as the girl in his dream. (I should mention that this was the same coat I'd had since I was fifteen, when my mom was in the hospital having a hernia operation and she was so high she was all, "Jenny needs a new coat," which my father should have recognized as drug-induced delirium, *because we never got new coats*, but he totally took me out and bought me the coat and I was all, "Oh, and I need a new hat too." And when we got back to the hospital room, my mom was still on morphine and she was all, "Hey, nice hat!" Then two days later she sobered up and was all, *"The hell?* I'm unconscious for one day and suddenly everyone goes crazy with hats?!")

Doogie Howser noticed my coat from the moment I walked in the bookstore and became obsessed with finding out who I was. I refused to tell him my last name or give him my number, and I told him very clearly, *"I have a boyfriend,"* because I didn't want him to stalk me. Doogie introduced himself as Victor and suggested that I was wasting my money by buying any of these books, since he had them all and would lend them to me. I pointed out that I didn't actually have any money and was planning on stealing them. The last part was a lie, but it was one that he genuinely chuckled at, which was a refreshing change from the uncomfortable laughter that I got from most men. He took the book I held in my hand and put it back on the shelf. "You're far too adorable to go to jail. Come to my dorm room and you can steal them from me."

And so I did. Because apparently I've never seen any of those movies where the dumb-ass coed gets mutilated by a serial killer. *And* because no one suspects that Neil Patrick Harris is going to murder you. *And* because he made me laugh in spite of myself. *And* because I'd always wanted to have a gay male best friend who could teach me about false eyelashes and blow jobs. More of the last one, really.

Surprisingly, Victor hardly tried to mutilate me at all, and he actually *did* have all the books he'd claimed to have at the bookstore. He also had the largest selection of vests I'd ever seen a man possess (three). He was only a few months older than I was, but he acted much older and more sophisticated than anyone my age, and we quickly became friends. He was one of the most ardent Republicans I'd ever met, but he consistently surprised me by not sticking to any of the stereotypes I tried to fit him into. He was a strange combination of *Star Wars*–quoting geek, tattooed kung fu teacher, and preppy computer hacker.

He was also the first person I ever met who had the Internet in his room (*Special note to those same people born after 1990: I know. Shut up*), and I immediately used it to look at pictures of dead people, because I thought it would be weird to download porn in front of him. He seemed oddly fascinated with me, in the same way that watching car accident victims is fascinating. I assumed he'd eventually realize I was not the kind of girl his conservative parents would want him around, but he was stubborn and refused to be thrown by anything I lobbed at him.

We both attended the same small college in the nearby town of San Angelo, and I spent long lunches in his dorm room where we talked about life and dreams and childhood, and nothing happened at all *because I'm not that kind of girl*. Until he kissed me. And then he convinced me that he wasn't gay at all, and was very concerned to learn that I equated gay people with vests. *"Not in a bad way,"* I pointed out. "I just assumed that only gay men would be okay with wearing acid-washed vests." (Years later, gay friends would point out that that sentence alone proves just how *little* I knew about gay men at the time, and that I had obviously confused "acid-washed vests" with "assless chaps." Then I point out that I've never confused the two, because one is much more drafty than the other. Then we all laugh and order another round and toast to how great it is to have fun, gay male friends. *Hint: It's awesome.* Go find some right now. Gay people are just like you and me, except better. Except for the ones who are boring, or are assholes. Avoid them.)

A few weeks after meeting Victor he told me, "I've decided I'm going to be a deejay," and I replied, "Well, *of course you are.* And *I've* decided to be a cowgirl-ballerina," but then the next day he was hired as a deejay at the biggest rock station in four counties. *It was unsettling.* Mainly because it was the same confident tone he'd used when he casually said, "I'm going to marry you one day." I snorted and rolled my eyes, because there was no way that was going to happen.

Victor was wealthy, and ambitious, and a member of the Young Republicans, and the exact opposite of the type of guy I went for. And also he was still wearing a vest. So I laughed at his little joke, but he didn't laugh back, and in the back of my head I was a little worried that he was right. In spite of the fact that we had almost *nothing* in common, I found myself completely in love with him, and he casually asked me to marry him almost every day. And I laughingly said no to him every day, because he was very dangerous. Not *physically* dangerous, of course. Although one time he did punch me in the nose. I mean, *technically* it wasn't his fault, because he was just doing his kung fu forms and I was standing in his dorm room, thinking about how boring kung fu is, and then I saw something on the floor and I'm all, "Potato chip!" and I bent down at the exact same moment Victor swung around into a form, and he punched me right in the fucking nose. Then I felt bad, because he was so visibly upset at accidentally almost knocking me out, and also because in the chaos one of us had stepped on the potato chip.

Oh, and another time he gave me a sex concussion. I can't really go into the details, because my mother will probably read this, but basically he had a bunk bed in his dorm room (because he's an only child and only children are *obsessed* with bunk beds for some reason), so we were on the bottom bunk and I tossed back my hair in what I envisioned would be a total porn-star move, except the wooden beam of the bunk bed above us was too low, and so I violently head-butted the wood plank and totally knocked myself out, which is pretty much the least sexy thing you could ever possibly do. Like, if I also lost control of my bowels that would be worse, but not by much. Then when I'd recovered, Victor was all, *"Sex concussion, motherfucker!"* like it was something to be proud of. Basically it was like autoerotic asphyxiation, except instead of being choked you get whacked in the head with a two-by-four. And instead of having an orgasm you lose all muscle control and pee on yourself. *Which I totally did not do because that would be disgusting.* I hardly ever pee on myself.

But none of those things were what I meant when I say he was dangerous. I meant that he was dangerous *mentally*. For one thing, he was rich. I mean, *other people* might not have said he was rich, but he was the first guy I ever met who owned his own tuxedo. He'd spent long summers with his grandparents in the rural countryside, so he felt as if we weren't so different, but when I told him that my parents didn't believe in air-conditioning he gave me this look like I was some sort of starving leper who needed a fund-raiser. The division between us was evident even when we'd go out for lunch. He would order a giant steak, and I'd get some sort of weak peasant broth, because I refused to allow him to buy me anything (and also because of the whole anorexia thing, which actually comes in quite handy when you're too poor to buy solid food).

He was dangerous because he was different, and smarter than me, and he wanted me to be a grown-up. My mother decided that I needed to marry Victor before I slipped back into my pattern of dating poor, mentally unstable artists. About six months after Victor and I had been dating I came home to find that she'd packed up my stuff and told us both that I should just move in with Victor, since I was *"obviously already sleeping with him."* This was when Victor and I both got very quiet, and I wondered when my mother had turned into the crazy parent, because I wasn't really prepared for *both* of them to be unstable. Then I realized that this whole scenario was less about my mom's instability than it was about her saving me from my own. I was pretty sure my mom's infatuation with Victor as my potential husband stemmed from how impressed she was with the whole *"owns-his-own-tuxedo"* thing, and I considered just telling her that he'd rented it and then changed addresses without returning it, but before

I could open my mouth to protest, Victor slipped his arm around my waist and beamed down at me, saying, "*Totally.* You *totally* need to move in with me." I suspected he and my mother had plotted this, because I didn't really *want* to move in with him, but he later admitted that he wasn't expecting it at all, and that although he did want me to move in, he was afraid to do anything other than agree with her, because he assumed my father would shoot him, in some sort of milk-without-the-cow scenario. One where I was the cow, *apparently.* I told Victor that he was being ridiculous, because although my father *did* own several full gun cabinets, the only weapon he actually used was a bow and arrow, because it was "more sportsmanlike." But then I remembered that Daddy *had* mentioned looking at a new crossbow just last week, and decided it was best to just not mention that at all. Victor frowned and pointed out that most people don't own entire pieces of furniture dedicated to weapons, and I began to suspect Victor was not actually *from* Texas. Then we both sort of stared at each other like we couldn't understand what the hell was wrong with each other. This probably should have been my first warning of what my future held.

Victor and I were still poor college students at the time, so we rented a tiny one-bedroom apartment in the worst part of town, and it was surprisingly wonderful. Except that the guy next door to us was some sort of mentally ill hermit who never left his apartment, but would wave to me from his window occasionally wearing pants. I'm not sure where the comma goes in that last sentence, since "occasionally" modifies both "waving" *and* "pants." As in, he waved to me occasionally, and (on those occasions when he waved) he was occasionally wearing pants. But he seemed to do it with less of a lurid *"Look-at-my-penis"* motivation, and more of a sad *"I'm-simply-too-unstable-to-know-how-pants-work-today"* sort of way.

A friendly but bleary-eyed couple on the other side of us seemed to be doing a booming business cooking and selling cupcakes. Except replace "cupcakes" with "meth." "Cupcakes" sounds nicer, though. Unless you're really into meth. Then I think you kind of lose a taste for cupcakes. Unless they're meth cupcakes. Which honestly sounds awful, but would probably sell like *hotcakes*. Which would actually be a great name for meth cupcakes if they existed. *Oh my God, this business plan writes itself.* Someone find me a venture capitalist.

The first time my mother visited us in our new apartment, she seemed worried that she'd made a huge mistake in pushing me to move out, but I reassured her that we were happy, and that (in a way) it was kind of an unorthodox neighborhood-watch program, because technically the meth cookers and shut-ins were always at home to sign for our packages and to keep an eye out for neighborhood burglars (who we all suspected lived in the apartment directly underneath us). It was an uncomfortable, involuntary community, but we were young and didn't know how much it hurt to be shot yet, so we shrugged off the danger, and we began the process of learning how incredibly difficult it is to live with someone who is totally anal and slightly OCD (*ahem . . . Victor*). And someone who is perpetually accidentally hot-gluing herself to the carpet, and who is sort of mentally unstable, but in an *"At-least-I-still-remember-how-pants-work"* kind of way (*cough . . . that'd be me*). Victor remarked that comparing myself with the sometimes naked hermit next door wasn't exactly a strong mental-wellness benchmark, especially since I often ended up pantsless myself. I raised my eyebrow at his seemingly seductive remark until I realized he was referring to the time he found me half naked because I'd just hot-glued my jeans to the carpet.

Still, in spite of everything, Victor seemed to love me in a strange and bizarre way that was never more evident than the day that he proposed to me. But that's the next chapter.

(Aren't you glad you're not paying for this book by the chapter? Because then you'd feel totally ripped off that you paid for this chapter and then it leaves you hanging like *Pirates of the Caribbean II*. I would never do that to you guys. Also, did you know there are some places in Russia where you have to *pay* to use the toilet? It's not really on the same subject, but honestly, *what the fuck?* I would *never* pay to use the toilet. That's like paying someone to let you throw away your own litter in the mall trash can. If I ever go to Russia I'm going to pee on the floor all the time.)

No One Ever
Taught Me
Couch Etiquette

B efore Victor could tell his parents that we were moving in together, he insisted that I go meet them personally in Midland, Texas, which was a few hours' drive away. Midland is a big oil town, and in my mind, everyone who lived there was some sort of millionaire. Victor assured me that his family was not *really* wealthy, but he kept drilling me on how to tell the fish fork from the dessert fork, and then when I walked into his parents' house I noticed that they had a giant, fancy floral centerpiece on the table *and* a skylight, and that's when I started to hyperventilate a little. Victor's stepdad was out of town, but his mother was very polite, in a way that made me feel like I should have worn tiny white gloves to meet her.

Bonnie, his mom, invited me to sit on the couch. And so I did. But when my back grazed one of the little couch pillows, Victor's eyes widened at me in horror as if I'd just stabbed the family dog through the ear. He cleared his throat at me, and I sat up quickly as he surreptitiously re-straightened the pillow and whispered, *"Those pillows are only for decora-tion."* And that's when I learned my first rule about rich people. They never use their cushions. Which is sort of fucked up, *because that's kind of what cushions are for.*

Bonnie excused herself to mix us some drinks and, I imagined, to telephone her husband about the low-class drifter that her son had brought into her home. "You'll love this one," I could hear her saying in my mind. "She can't even use a couch properly. I suspect she might be some sort of a hobo."

I pulled anxiously at Victor's arm and whispered that we should sneak out now before I did any more damage, and he looked at me as if I'd gone insane. "We'll leave a note," I explained. "We'll leave a nice note saying that we saw a monkey outside, and that we need to catch it."

"Are you high?" He looked suspiciously at my pupils. "Seriously, calm the hell down. She's gonna love you. *Just don't sit on the couch cushions.*"

I looked at him in confusion, and he patted my hand and gave me a strained smile as he told me to relax. Then I sighed in resignation and slid down onto the floor, sitting cross-legged, which was fine, because I was wearing jeans and honestly I felt more comfortable there anyway, and Victor whispered, *"What the hell are you doing?"* and I'm all, "Dude. I can't do this. I'm intimidated by your fucking *couch. Clearly this relationship is not going to work out.*"

He anxiously tried to pull me back up before his mother got in the room, but I wasn't worried, because it always takes a long time to make Kool-Aid. "You can't sit on the damn floor. *What're you, seven?*"

"Dude. You *just* said not to sit on the cushions."

"The *decorative* cushions," he attempted to explain, as he yanked me back up on the couch next to him. "*Obviously* you can sit on the *couch* cushions. *That's how couches work.*"

"WHY DIDN'T YOU TEACH ME COUCH ETIQUETTE?"

I guess I may have said that a bit loudly, because when Victor's mom walked back in with the drinks she gave me a strange look, and I was so flustered I couldn't even think straight, so I quickly took a drink of what was the worst Kool-Aid in the world, and (after a small coughing fit) I realized that "mixed drink" actually referred to some kind of wine spritzer, and not a drink that you make from a mix. After it was clear that I wasn't going to die, she tried to fill the awkward silence by showing me pictures of

Victor in his tux with lots of different girls, who all had good hair and formal dresses, and probably never even *heard* of bread-sack shoes. Victor kind of rolled his eyes when his mom went on about all the debutante balls Victor had gone to with these girls, and I nodded, trying to look politely interested. Then she asked me when *I* came out and I said, "Oh, I'm not gay. I'm dating your son," which I thought was pretty clear to begin with. Then Victor started coughing loudly and Bonnie looked confused, but then she got distracted, because Victor sounded like he'd swallowed his own tongue, and then right after that Victor said that we should probably leave.

On the way home, Victor explained that "coming out" is what debutantes do when they reach womanhood. I told him that he sounded like a tampon commercial, and he rolled his eyes. Then I yelled at him for spending so much time teaching me the proper fork to use when we didn't even stay for dinner, and he was all, *"You couldn't even use the fucking couch correctly!"* He had a point, so I sighed and sat in silence, because it's hard to argue with confidence when you've just found out that you've been using couches wrong your whole life.

We stopped at Dairy Queen on the way back, which was comforting, because they give you only *one* set of silverware, unless you order the Peanut Buster Parfait, in which case they give you that extra-long red plastic spoon so you can reach the fudge at the bottom of the cup. And even then there's a picture of an ice cream cone on the end of that spoon, just in case you get confused about what it's for. This is when I started venting about why Dairy Queen is better than fancy restaurants, and Victor stared at me, fascinated, as if he were totally surprised that no one had ever thought of that before, or like he wondered what the hell was wrong with me. It was a look he'd perfected in our last year together.

I took a deep breath and I leaned forward to look at him, grimly. "Look. This is us. *I'm* the Dairy Queen ice cream spoon. *You* are the escargot spoon. That's why this is never going to work."

Victor paused, then leaned into me across the table and whispered, "Fork," and I was all, "I don't get it. . . . Is that how fancy rich people pronounce the F-word?" And he smiled crookedly, like he was trying not to laugh, and said, "No. You eat escargot with a *fork*. Not a spoon." And I yelled, "*Exactly!* This is *exactly* what I'm talking about," and Victor laughed and said, "I don't *care* that you don't know what an escargot fork is. I think it's adorable that you don't. And you will learn all of this. Or you won't. But it doesn't really matter, because *I* happen to like Dairy Queen spoons." And I smiled hesitantly, because he said it so confidently that it was hard not to believe him, although I did suspect that he was just being nice because he didn't want to get dumped by a girl in a Dairy Queen who couldn't even use a couch properly. That's pretty much the worst way to get dumped, ever.

Actual picture of Victor and me on his parents' couch.
Please note how uncomfortable Victor is to even be near the
couch cushions. It's like he's poised to run from them.
And at this point I still think I'm the crazy one.

Just Your Average
Engagement Story

When I was in junior high I read a lot of Danielle Steele. So I always assumed that the day I got engaged I'd be naked, covered in rose petals, and sleeping with the brother of the man who'd kidnapped me.

And also he'd be a duke.

And possibly my stepbrother.

Then one of us would get stabbed with a broken whiskey bottle and/or raped.

Turns out the only part I was right about was that one of us was going to get stabbed.

IT WAS 1996, and Victor and I were still in college. At night he worked as a deejay, and I worked ~~as a phone prostitute~~ in telemarketing. We'd been living together for about a year when Victor decided it was time to get married, and (just to make it all rock-star romantic) he decided to propose on air. The only problem was that if he was on air he wouldn't be there to physically make me say yes, and so instead he took the night off and set up a recording that would make it sound like he was calling in to the radio show to talk to the guy filling in for him. He planned on my hearing the proposal on air, and then getting down on one knee and handing me the ring, but he had no idea how to get me in front of the radio, so he suggested we go for a drive so he could listen to his substitute on the radio. And so we did. *For six. Fucking. Hours.*

6:00 P.M.—We've already been in the car for a half-hour. I'm getting hungry.

6:30 P.M.—I'm hungry, but Victor refuses to pull over to eat.

7:00 P.M.—Victor is acting very strange and jumpy. I start to suspect he's going to kill me. I know this seems like an illogical jump to make, since this was the same man who cried when he punched me in the nose over a potato chip, but I'd always suspected that Victor was a little too good to be true, and it seemed easier to believe that he wanted to murder me than it was to believe he'd want to marry me.

7:30 P.M.—I pretend I'm going to pass out if he doesn't take me to get something to eat. Victor is convinced that the moment I leave the car, his sub will play the recording, so he insists we just go through the drive-thru of Taco Bell.

8:00 P.M.—Victor refuses to turn down the radio while we're ordering our burritos. I assume he wants to drown out my voice in case I ask the cashier to call 911.

8:30–10:30 P.M.—Victor drives in circles. I have to pee. Victor will not let me out of the car. He's sweating a lot. I dimly wonder where he'll dump my body.

10:30–11:30 P.M.—The urge to go to the bathroom has now grown more pressing than the urge to escape. I begin to suspect that Victor is trying to kill me by making my bladder explode. He smiles nervously and I wonder whether I could make myself pee on myself.

11:40 P.M. — No, but not for lack of trying.

11:45 P.M. — Fifteen minutes to the end of the sub's shift. Victor is a wreck. I'm at that point of having to pee where you think you're going to throw up, but then you realize as soon as you throw up you're going to pee on yourself anyway, and I start considering leaping out of the moving car, because even if I peed on myself, the coroner wouldn't judge me, because who *wouldn't* pee on themselves when they were tossing themselves out of a moving car? *Nobody*, that's who.

MIDNIGHT — Victor sighed and turned into the parking lot of our apartment building, and he just stared numbly at the dumpster in front of us, looking defeated and despondent, and that's when I felt really, really bad for him. I put my hand on his arm and he sighed miserably, like he was a total failure. I wanted to cheer him up, but it felt weird wanting to cheer up someone who was possibly depressed because they didn't murder you correctly, and that's when I thought, "*This must be what love is.* When you want to make it less difficult for someone to murder you." And that's when I realized that I was *far* too in love with him for my own good, and also that I probably needed therapy.

It was also when I noticed that he'd suddenly tensed up, and that his own voice was on the radio. And then I thought that I was *definitely* going to get murdered, because this was the perfect alibi, since it would sound like he was in the radio studio when they found my body. But then I noticed he was looking at me and grinning crookedly, and I listened to the Victor on the radio talk to the other deejay about a girl he'd met and fallen in love with, and how at the end of every shift he'd played Sting's "When We Dance" as his signoff, and as a silent "I love you" to that girl. And then he said that he'd grown so in love with her that he was going to propose to her right then. *On the fucking radio.*

And then I turned around and Victor had silently opened my car door and was kneeling and holding a diamond ring so small that I knew he had actually bought it himself. And so I said yes, partly because I loved him, partly out of relief that I was not going to be murdered, and partly because I knew he'd never let me out of the car to pee until I agreed to marry him. And then I kissed him and still he stayed knelt down, blocking my exit. And then I asked him if I could go to the bathroom, and he gave me this pained expression, and I wondered whether I'd fucked up his romantic moment, but then he straightened up and I noticed that he'd accidentally knelt right in a pile of broken glass, which was awesome, because there's nothing more romantic than a proposal that ends with you needing a tetanus shot.

I remember thinking at the time that if I didn't have to pee so badly I probably would have told him that we should wait, because truthfully, I knew I was a little too broken to be married to anyone. But by the time I'd gotten out of the bathroom he'd called everyone we knew and told them I said yes.

I tried to convince Victor several times that he'd made a terrible mistake in proposing, but whenever I insisted that he would be better off with one of his old debutantes, he dismissed it as low self-esteem. Even when I assured him I was kind of insane, he brushed it off as an exaggeration on my part, because he'd witnessed my minor panic attacks and occasional breakdowns and he wrongly assumed that was as bad as it got.

Then one morning, shortly after we got engaged, I woke up as Victor reached over for me, and he stopped suddenly and slowly sat up. In a carefully measured voice he said, "Honey . . . ? Did you . . . did you pee in the bed?"

And I was all, "WHAT?! Of course I didn't pee in the bed!" And then I thought, *"Ew, DID* I pee in the bed?" and I felt around and I didn't feel anything, but then I saw this large puddle seeping slowly though the top of the comforter into the valley between Victor and me. Then I screamed,

"*OHMYGOD*, CAT PEE!" and I threw the comforter off me and the cat pee splashed everywhere.

Victor jumped out of bed, gagging and shouting profanities at both me and the cat, and then I realized that—in spite of his *total disgust* in thinking that I had peed on him—he had still struggled to maintain a calm and understanding demeanor. Because apparently he thought I was just crazy enough to *randomly urinate on him*. And that's when I thought that *just maybe* we had a chance together.

Still, I felt sorry for Victor, because he did know that I was *kind of* mentally ill, but he also thought I was naturally thin, so he was kind of expecting "crazy," but I think he was expecting hot, sexy crazy. Then Victor insisted I start seeing the college shrink, who coaxed me away from the anorexia, and I immediately gained thirty pounds, which was very healthy, but which seemed *not hot at all*. Also, I suddenly started eating solid food, so I cost a lot more than Victor had originally expected. Basically he got a really shitty deal.

And I was even crazier than I'd let on.

It Wasn't Stew

I t's always seemed unfair to me that I'd had so little time to ingratiate myself with my soon-to-be in-laws, whereas Victor had a year to worm his way into my parents' hearts before we got married.

Granted, it hadn't been easy for any of us. One of the first times he'd come to my house for dinner, we were sitting in the living room visiting with my mom. My mom and I were on the couch, and from our vantage point, we could see my father tiptoeing into the room. He gestured with a finger to his lips not to let Victor know that he was behind him and a live bobcat was tucked under his right arm. This probably would have been my exact worst nightmare of bringing a boy home to meet my parents, if I'd ever had enough creativity to imagine my father throwing a live bobcat on the boy I was trying to impress. I assumed that Daddy had accidentally left a bobcat in the house, fallen asleep, realized his terrible mistake when he woke up and heard Victor's voice, and was now surreptitiously sneaking it out the back door so that Victor would never suspect that we were the type of family to keep live bobcats in the house. Unfortunately, that was not my father's intent at all, and my eyes widened in horror as my father leaned over and yelled in his booming, cheerful voice, *"HELLOOOO, VICTOR,"* while tossing a live bobcat on him.

Most people reading this will assume that this was my father's way of making would-be suitors terrified of him so they would always treat his daughters right, but this wasn't even vaguely a concern of his. He would just as happily have tossed the live bobcat on my mother or me, if it weren't for the fact that we'd all become superhumanly aware of the terrifying sounds of my father trying to be quiet. In my father's defense, it was a smallish sort of bobcat that my dad was nursing back to health so he could release it back into the wild, rather than one of the full-grown ones from the backyard. At the time, my dad had several large bobcats he was keeping, but they were seldom indoors, and if my mom found one in the house she'd shoo it into the bobcat cages outside with a broom. I once asked my mom exactly *why* Daddy kept bobcats, and she said it was because "he collects their urine." Because, *yeah*. Whose father *doesn't* have some sort of a collection? (Also, for those of you not from bobcat territory, bobcats are like small, easily underestimated tigers. They'll avoid confrontation if they can, but push them too far and they'll cheerfully eat your face off. They're like tiny, undermedicated badgers and should be avoided.)

Even if I *had* ever wondered how Victor would respond to a giant bearded man throwing a live bobcat on him, I don't think I ever could have foreseen his actual reaction. Victor's jaw clenched and he stiffened, staring with wide-eyed shock at the bobcat and remaining perfectly still. Then (impressively avoiding any sudden movements) he looked up at my father in bewilderment. Perhaps Victor was expecting to see a look of embarrassment from my father, who must've *accidentally* spilled a bobcat on him, or perhaps he thought my father would be just as horrified and shocked to see a bobcat on Victor's lap, and would tell him to remain still while he got the tranquilizer gun. Instead, my dad smiled broadly and held out his hand to shake Victor's, as if an unexpected bobcat weren't sitting on Victor's chair. (A bobcat, I might add, who was looking just as horrified and pissed off himself at being placed in this awkward social situation.) Victor kept a wary eye on the bobcat (who was now making the frightening sort of noises bobcats make when they want to make it perfectly clear that they are *not* house cats and don't want you to snuggle them), and then Victor glanced at me, as if deciding whether or not I was worth this. He took a deep breath, and then turned in slow motion in his seat to shake my dad's hand. "Henry," he said tersely, nodding his head in greeting, the fear in his voice showing only slightly. Then he turned back to my mom and kept talking as if nothing could be more natural. It was awesome, and I think it earned the respect of all of us right that moment. Even the bobcat seemed to realize he was probably safer with Victor than with the large man who was always throwing him on people, and snuggled down beside Victor to glare resentfully at the rest of us.

(*Disclaimer: These aren't great pictures of Victor or of the bobcats.*)

Later Victor told me he'd been totally freaked out by the situation, but that his dad had once owned a cougar named Sonny when Victor was a kid, so he assured me that he understood that some people liked exotic pets. And it was nice that we had this thing in common to bring us together, but the difference was that *his* father owned helicopters, Porsches, and pet cougars because he was wealthy and ostentatious, and *my* father kept wild bobcats for their urine. I didn't point out those differences, though, because we were bonding. And because I still couldn't completely explain the urine thing myself, although I was later told it's simply an organic way some people use to frighten pests out of their yards. Unless those pests are bobcats, I guess. Then you're fucked.

For some reason, Victor was very concerned about what my parents thought about him, and he focused on winning their approval. He'd won over my mom almost instantly by helping her rebuild an old muscle car, but my father always treated him as if I'd inexplicably invited our CPA over for dinner. If we'd ever had a CPA, that is. Victor attempted to woo my father's approval as a *manly man* by asking my dad to teach him about his taxidermy business. It was an endeavor that neither of them seemed entirely excited about, but they both pretended to be happy to do it for my sake, in spite of the fact that I told them both I thought it was a terrible idea. At the end of what would be Victor's first (and only) day of taxidermy, he looked physically ill, and my father looked bewildered.

"What happened?" I whispered to Victor as my father went to go lie down. "Did you throw up? Because *almost everyone* throws up the first time they mount something," I reassured him. "I'm pretty sure that's normal."

"No," Victor answered, his arm slung over his eyes as if attempting to block out the images. "No, your dad had already mounted it. It just needed some touchups. It was a black boar, and he told me I could paint the inside of the mouth, because that's good, quick beginner's work." It *was*, actually, and I gave my dad points for giving him something easy and nongross.

"And?" I asked.

"I spent six hours painting it. *Six hours*. With an airbrush."

"*Wow.* That's . . . that's a *really* long time to paint a boar mouth. How did it turn out?"

"It looked like . . ." He paused for a moment, staring grimly at the ceiling. "You know when Fred Flintstone dresses up like a girl?"

"*Oh.*" I bit my bottom lip to remain stoic, because I knew that laughing would just add insult to ~~injury~~ more insult, and I patted his arm reassuringly. "So, what did Daddy say?" I asked cautiously.

"He didn't say anything. He just looked at the boar in silence and then led me away from it. I've never heard him so quiet. Then he asked me to string his hunting bow for him, and I almost got a hernia doing it. He took me out back to try to shoot it, and I almost shot myself in the leg. For real.

I almost shot myself. In the leg. I think your dad was expecting me to kill myself accidentally so that he could tell you there had been a tragic accident, and then you could just move on with your life and find someone else who doesn't make wild boars look like cheap male prostitutes."

I tried to convince Victor that my dad actually adored him, but then I remembered that two weeks earlier my dad had tried to teach Victor flint napping (the art of making arrowheads out of rocks the Native American way), and Victor had been doing surprisingly well, until he cut himself and had bled so much we started to suspect he'd hit an artery. *"You sure you want to marry a hemophiliac?"* my dad had whispered to me while looking for something to use as a tourniquet. "That's a hereditary trait, you know." It was possible my father *was* trying to kill him.

In a final desperate attempt, Victor decided to make a present for my father of an authentic Native American medicine bag he'd made himself with a found coyote face, a dead turtle, and some braided leather for the strap. When he'd finished his macabre handicraft project he held it up to me triumphantly, and I stared at the eyeless coyote face for a moment, and then went back to reading my book. *"Isn't this awesome?"* he insisted (somewhat manically), and I shrugged halfheartedly, allowing that it *did* seem like the sort of the thing that my father would enjoy. This wasn't saying much, though, since my father also inexplicably enjoyed picking up interesting roadkill, and creating mythical taxidermied creatures out of spare parts. Victor was pissed that I didn't share his enthusiasm, and he gruffly and dismissively waved me off, pointing out that I was "a girl," and thus couldn't understand such masculine endeavors as winning over your future bride's father with such a manly gift.

"You're probably right," I admitted. "It *is* hard for me to appreciate the sheer machismo involved in a man making a purse for another man." Then he clarified (quite loudly) that it was *a medicine bag*, and I replied, "Oh, I wouldn't know about such things. I've never even owned any coyote-face purses, because I can never figure out which shoes to wear them with." Then Victor glared at me and told me I wouldn't understand, and I agreed and blamed it all on my vagina, since it seemed like that was what we were both doing at the moment. Then Victor sighed defeatedly, kissed me on the forehead, and told me he was sorry in a rather unconvincing manner. I suspect he said it less because he realized he was being sexist, and more because I think he was just afraid to argue with my vagina. Which is a pretty smart move on his part, because my vagina is *wily*.

Turns out, though, that Daddy loved his animal-face purse and hung it in a place of honor from the mantel, where it remains to this day. Victor had won my father's respect, and all it had taken was a dead-animal back-pack. I wondered whether there was some sort of secret combination that I could try that would make Victor's parents accept me so willingly. It wasn't really that they *disliked* me. They just seemed uncomfortable around me. They were polite and kind but baffled. It was as if their son had unexpectedly shown up with a neck tattoo that read "MAKE ME SOME BASKETTI." They seemed dumbfounded, and confused, and possibly even hurt, but they also seemed to realize it was too late to do anything about it, and so they hesitantly complimented the unaccountable neck tattoo that he'd asked to be his wife.

This was never more apparent than the day before our wedding, when Victor brought his mom and stepdad to my parents' home so that they could meet and visit before the wedding. My mother and I had convinced my father to stay outside in his taxidermy shop until I'd had a chance to soothe them with a little booze and with reassurances that we were all actually quite normal, before bringing in my father. Unfortunately, as soon as Victor drove up with his parents, my father heard them and waved them all back toward the clearing behind the taxidermy shop, where he had started a very large fire. An enormous metal oil drum was in the middle of the fire, and was filled with a boiling liquid, the steam billowing my fa-ther's gray hair as he stirred the barrel with a broom handle. This was the point when Victor should have waved, pretended that they couldn't hear my father, and then quickly ushered his parents into our house, but instead he smiled nervously and helped his mother, whose elegant heels sank into the dirt as she weaved in and out of stray chickens. My father towered intimidatingly over Victor and his parents, but he welcomed them heartily with his booming voice, even as he continued to stir the boiling cauldron. My soon-to-be mother-in-law attempted small talk as she raised an eyebrow at the strange, bubbling liquid and asked shakily, "So, what are you cooking?" She leaned forward hesitantly, trying to smile. "Is it . . . stew?"

My father chuckled good-naturedly and smiled kindly and condescendingly, as one would to a small child, as he said, "*Nope.* Just boiling skulls." Then he speared a still-meaty cow's head with the broomstick to show it to her. Then the eyeball fell out of the cow's head. It rolled toward them and stopped at my mother-in-law's designer shoe as if it were attempting to look up her skirt. Then my future in-laws stumbled back to the car and left quickly. I would not see them again until the wedding.

Still, they did grit their teeth and gamely try to accept me into the family, as they hesitantly welcomed me into their lives with extreme trepidation and slow movements. They treated me with respect, but also with an equal amount of uneasiness, as if I'd brought with me a dangerous instability that threatened their very lives. It was only later, as I walked down the aisle on my wedding day, that I finally placed and recognized the look in Victor's parents' eyes and numbly realized that I'd seen that exact same look on Victor's face once, long ago. It was then that I realized that *I* had become the unexpected bobcat in the room. And I knew exactly how terrified that damn bobcat had felt.

Married on
the Fourth of July

Victor and I were married on the Fourth of July. It was a lot like the movie *Born on the Fourth of July*, except with fewer wheelchairs and Tom Cruise wasn't there. Also, I've never actually seen *Born on the Fourth of July*, because it looks kind of depressing. But to be fair, I remember very little of my own wedding, so it's entirely possible Tom Cruise was there and I've just forgotten. This will probably be very awkward the next (or first) time I meet Tom Cruise.

On the day of our wedding, Victor and I *both* had misgivings.

I had misgivings because I was barely twenty-two, and immature, and had no clue how to be someone's wife, and, more important, because of what I was wearing (*see "twenty-two, and immature"*). In a strange twist of fate, Victor had bought my wedding dress when he saw it in the window of a rental shop that was going out of business. It was inappropriately virginal white, beaded, bowed, and looked like the sort of wedding dress that both Princess Diana and Scarlett O'Hara would have deemed "completely over-the-top." Each of the billowing puffed sleeves was larger than my head and seemed to be stuffed with newspaper (I suspect it was the *New York Times* Sunday edition), and the hoop skirt, pushing out the yards and yards of white ruffles, dictated that I keep an empty five-foot radius around me at all times, because if anything pressed against the bottom of the hoop, the opposite side of the dress would suddenly lift up and hit me in the head. It was fancy and high-maintenance and pure as the driven snow, *and I would not have chosen that dress for myself in a million years*, but Victor insisted it was "so me," which I think was less of an insult and more of a vision he had of the woman I might one day become. He was wrong on so many levels that I started to lose count.

I wasn't alone in my doubts, though. Victor had misgivings because two weeks earlier we'd had what I referred to as *"a very bad date."* Victor was still referring to it as *"that time you almost killed me."* (Side note: He now refers to it as "the *first* time you almost killed me.") But Victor isn't writing this book, mostly because he's a terrible overreactor. The truth was that we'd been driving down some deserted country roads after sundown, as Victor was looking for snakes. On purpose. He'd developed a fascination for them in the last year, and was making money on the side by finding snakes basking on the hot, empty roads after dark, capturing them, taming them, and then selling them to fellow snake lovers. He was great at recognizing the harmless and easily tamable snakes, and listened to my warnings to never mess with the poisonous, aggressive ones, until the night when we drove up on a very large rattlesnake, which seemed to have been run over by a car. Victor stopped his truck and I told him not to get out, but he said he could tell the snake was squashed and told me to hold the spotlight up so he could make sure the snake was dead and not still suffering. I suggested just running over it again a few times, but Victor looked at me as if I were being ridiculous, and he slowly got out of the car. I opened my own door hesitantly, but refused to get out, standing instead on the edge of the truck's floorboard and leaning over the hood of the truck, certain that other rattlesnakes were probably lying in wait and planning a group attack. Victor looked back at me with frustration. "Come over here and bring the spotlight. *You're too far away.*"

"Oh, I'm just fine, thanks. *Please get the hell back in the truck.*"

He glared at me and shook his head. "Have a little faith, will ya?" He knelt down beside the rattler. "It's dead. Looks like its head was crushed."

"*Awesome*. Now get the hell back in the truck."

Victor ignored me as he put on a glove and stooped to pick up the tail of the five-foot rattler. "We should bring this home to your dad. He could probably— *OHJESUSCHRIST!*"

It was at this exact moment that the "dead" rattlesnake suddenly started angrily striking at Victor's leg. Uncoincidentally, it was also the exact same moment that I ducked back into the truck, taking the spotlight with me and leaving Victor in the pitch-dark blackness on an abandoned road, as the angry rattlesnake he was holding tried to murder him.

"BRING BACK THE LIGHT," he screamed.

"I TOLD YOU NOT TO GO OUT THERE!" I yelled angrily, as I quickly locked the doors (for some reason) and rolled up all the windows. I *was* worried about him and wanted to help him, but I couldn't help but think that he *had* brought this on himself.

"BRING BACK THE LIGHT OR I WILL THROW THIS DAMN SNAKE IN THE CAR WITH YOU," he screamed, which was surprising, both because he sounded very vital for someone dying of snakebite, and also because he'd wrongly assumed that I *hadn't* automatically locked all the doors. *He knows so little about me*, I thought to myself.

I took a deep breath and reminded myself that although he was a macho idiot, he was *my* macho idiot, and I rolled down the window just far enough to put my hand and spotlight through it, and saw Victor still looking very much alive and more than slightly pissed off. Turns out that the snake was still alive and striking, but its mangled jaw was crushed and so it never broke Victor's skin. Victor glared at me with terrified eyes, and put the snake out of its misery with a shovel before walking back to the truck.

After a minute to slow his breathing, Victor's voice was only vaguely controlled. "You left me alone. In the dark. *With a live rattlesnake*."

"No. *You* left *me* alone. In the car. *For* a live rattlesnake," I countered. "So I guess that makes us even." There was a long pause as he stared at me. "But I forgive you?" I said.

"YOU ALMOST KILLED ME," he shouted.

"No," I pointed out. "*A rattlesnake* almost killed you. *I* was just an involuntary witness. *I* wanted to turn the car back on and try to run over the snake to save you, but *you* took the keys with you. Plus, I can't drive a stick. So basically I would have died eventually too, except *way* more painfully and slowly from starvation and exposure. If anything, *I* should be mad at *you*." I hadn't actually been mad until I started defending myself, but then I realized that I had a point. If anything, I had almost killed *both of us*, but Victor was too shortsighted to see that far ahead.

"You left me alone. In the dark. *With a live rattlesnake*," Victor repeated in a whisper.

"Well, I had faith in you," I said sweetly. This is one of my favorite phrases to use in an argument, because it's hard for someone to contradict you without blatantly admitting that your faith in them is utterly unjustified. I use that one a lot. In fact, it sounded so good I said it again. "I *knew* you could handle that snake. Sometimes you just have to have faith."

And *faith* was exactly what I was trying to have in the week before our wedding. Personally, I was terrified of being the center of attention in front of other people, and I'd wanted to just elope and get married in tennis shoes in Las Vegas by an Elvis impersonator, but Victor was an only child and his family desperately wanted a real wedding, so I'd given up and gone through the motions. I was never much of a big-wedding girl, so I gave no thought to unity candles and rehearsal dinners. My mom and I made a veil out of hot glue, mesh, and a flowered headband, and we picked out a cake at the local grocery store.

Neither Victor nor I was religious, so my grandparents bribed their church to let us use their small side chapel. The wedding lasted an entire twelve minutes, as we'd asked the preacher to cut almost all of the Jesus references out. ("Jesus is *totally* invited," we explained to the preacher. "We just don't want him giving any long speeches.") Then we had a twenty-minute reception in the basement, which looked just like a basement except somehow drearier.

But at the chapel of the church where we'd said "I do," none of that seemed to matter. All that mattered was that we loved each other. And while our families made their way to the church doorsteps to prepare to throw birdseed at us, we hid in the empty church sanctuary and I made Victor promise to love me forever. "Have a little faith in me," he said with a proud smile. In retrospect, I probably should have asked for something more substantial, like "Promise me you'll always clean up the cat vomit in the hall," or "Promise me you'll never ask me if it's 'that time of the month' in the middle of a totally rational argument when what you *really* need to do is just apologize and stop being such an asshole."

But no, I was young, and naive, and wished for love, and I tried to have faith that that would be enough.

Sometimes you just have to take it on faith.

*Our official wedding portrait. If you didn't know us you could
almost imagine that we're whirling around a candlelit ballroom
instead of standing in front of the Sears Portrait Studio backdrop
at the mall. Still, there was a Lionel Richie song playing
over the intercom. It was "Dancing on the Ceiling."
It was like even the mall was mocking us.*

There's No Place Like Home

After we were married, I started working in HR. Victor worked in computers. We bought a small seventies house in San Angelo, the same town outside Wall where we'd gone to college. The house quickly grew full of memories. It was the house we were in when I became convinced that Y2K was basically the end of the world, and so on New Year's Eve of 1999 I filled up the bathtub with water, so we'd have something to drink when the water from the tap turned into blood, but my cat didn't realize it was full and fell in it, contaminating the whole thing. Then Victor laughed at my distress, which really pissed me off, because, *Hello? I'm doing this for both of us.* And then he abandoned me at a quarter to midnight to go check on the computers at work, and he wouldn't even load the riot gun for me before he drove off. When he came back a few hours later, I'd barred the doors with couches to keep out the looters. I was too tired to move all the furniture, so I just told him that doors didn't work anymore because of Y2K, and that he should just go sleep under his car. Eventually he convinced me that there were no looters, and so I opened a window for him to climb through.

These were the happy memories I was holding on to a month later when Victor took a job offer in Houston, and left me behind to sell our house. He found us a new place to live, and he expected me to come to Houston within a week or two, but as soon as I had an opportunity to leave the small country area I'd always wanted to escape, I suddenly realized how much I didn't want to leave. I was terrified of even thinking of living in a big city, and did everything possible to keep from selling the house. I parked directly on top of the "For Sale by Owner" sign Victor had left up, and I told multiple people who stopped by (after seeing the ads that Victor had put in the paper) that we were selling the house because "I just can't bear to live in a house where such a gruesome murder occurred."

After six months of waiting, Victor started to suspect I was stalling and came to bring me to Houston, saying that we'd just leave our house vacant until it sold. On the very day he came, he huffily pried the "For Sale" sign out of the grille of my car (I blamed the nonexistent gangs of hoodlums who, I'd convinced prospective buyers, roamed the streets at night looking for stray pets to eat) and stuck it back in front of the house. Two hours later the doorbell rang, and Victor sold the house to a man who'd just been passing by. He planned to give it to his daughter and son-in-law, and started measuring the front lawn for the wooden wishing well he was going to install to "increase the curb appeal." I felt almost as sorry for our house as I did for myself.

After a few months in Houston I came to realize that there wasn't much difference between the two places, except for the change in traffic and the lowered incidences of my parents showing up unannounced with dead animals in the back of the car. But surprisingly, I found myself homesick for both of these things. Victor tried to convince me that it was a whole new adventure filled with sushi and museums and culture and intimidating coffeehouses, and (much as I had done with Wall) I gritted my teeth and bore it, certain that soon we'd leave Houston and go back home to West Texas. And, *as before*, that was how life went on for the next ten years.

Every time we'd go back to visit West Texas it would change a bit. The cotton fields slowly gave way to subdivisions. The tractors were upgraded and new. I'd drive around our old town to find that the snow-cone shack

I'd worked at was replaced by a parking lot. The skating rink was shuttered and abandoned, the sign filled with empty birds' nests. The bookstore where I'd met Victor was gone now, and my grandparents' home was sold soon after they died. Each year, my father's small taxidermy shop grew until it became a true business, with an always-busy parking lot beside my parents' home. One day I came home to visit and was shocked to see that the elementary school I'd walked to each day had become an alternative school for pregnant teens, and the school playground I'd lived in each summer had been ripped out and demolished. My sister and I walked through the aftermath of the playground together and I took a small piece of the rubble to remember it by. Now when I pass by the school I look away and remember it the way it was, with the dangerous metal seesaws and merry-go-rounds that eventually disappeared all over America. All that remains of it today is the memory, still echoing in my head, of the sound of my favorite swing, squeaking rustily and comfortingly, over and over, back and forth.

One day, several years after Victor and I had left for Houston, we came back home to stay with my parents for the weekend and my mother proudly announced that San Angelo now had "some new coffee place" everyone was talking about. We drove up to see what I expected to be some rural cowboy coffee shop, but instead a Starbucks stood largely on the corner, looking wrong and out of place next to the shops that hadn't changed since I was a kid.

"Oh, thank Christ," Victor said. *"Civilization comes to West Texas at last!"* he proclaimed.

It bothered me. Not that Victor equated caramel macchiatos with civilization, but that there had been a turning point, a final tip over the edge when I realized that the small town I'd always expected to come back to no longer remained, at least not in the same way as before.

Later that night I sat out on the porch, looking at the same stars I'd stared at when I was ten and had longed to travel to places that existed only in my mind. They were places like Egypt or France, but they were the Egypt and France of a child's mind, filled with blurry visions of perfect pyramids, and warm sands, and Eiffel Towers, and something that people called "wine." They were visions of places that weren't quite real, but that was long before I discovered that the romanticized places on the map were more than just pretty pictures, and that included things I couldn't have even imagined when I was young. Things like political unrest, and dysentery, and hangovers.

That night I looked up at those same stars, but I didn't want any of those things. I didn't want Egypt, or France, or far-flung destinations. I just wanted to go back to my life from my childhood, just to visit it, and to touch it, and to convince myself that *yes*, it had been real. Victor could tell I was upset, but I couldn't find a way to describe it without sounding ridiculous. "It's nothing," I said. "It's just that . . . Have you ever been homesick for someplace that doesn't actually exist anymore? Someplace that exists only in your mind?"

He rocked with me on the front porch in silence, not knowing how to answer, and eventually he put his arm around me and told me everything would be all right, and then he went inside to get some sleep. He found me the next morning, still outside in the same rocking chair, and stared at me worriedly. He asked me gently, "Are you gonna be ready to go home this morning?"

I rocked in silence, and realized for the first time that "home" wasn't this place anymore. It was wherever Victor was. It was both a terrifying and an enlightening realization, and I took a deep breath and thought carefully before I answered.

"Yes. I'm ready to go home."

It was like saying hello and good-bye at the same time, and Victor stared out at the baseball field that had once been a cotton field. He quietly said (as if to himself) that the memories of the places we'd been before were always more golden-tinted in retrospect than they had ever been at the time, and I nodded, surprised that he'd known more than he'd let on. He was right, but I didn't know if that made it better or worse. Was it worse to be homesick for a time that was once home, but now lived only in your own mind . . . or to be homesick for a place that never really existed at all? I couldn't answer, so instead I went back inside the house to pack. *For home.*

A Series of Helpful Post-it Notes I Left Around the House for My Husband This Week

Dear Victor: This bath towel was wet and you left it on the floor and it was the last clean one in the house. I'm pretty sure this is how tuberculosis is spread. I'm writing all this in my blog in case I end up dead because of your carelessness.

Dear Victor: There is a pile of business suits for the dry cleaner's that have been in the closet for five months. You work from home. *The fuck, Victor?*

Dear Victor: Why is cleaning up cat vomit always *my* job? Was I not here when we picked from the job jar? Is there a job jar at all? Because I'd like to redraw. Also, I'm aware that you always have to clean out the litter box, but that's because at any moment my IUD could fail and I could accidentally get pregnant and then get that cat-poop pregnancy disease, and our baby would be born with no arms or legs. Is *that* what you want, Victor? For our baby not to have arms? *You are so selfish.*

Dear Victor: You make me sick. Why in God's name wouldn't you just throw away the empty pizza box when you were done with it? Are your arms broken? Do you have some sort of disease I don't know about that makes you blind to empty pizza boxes?

Dear Victor: Okay, I just remembered I was the last one to make pizza, so I guess I left this box out. Still, I'm leaving out the note anyway so you can learn from it. *Bad, bad Victor.*

Dear Victor: I do not appreciate your leaving passive-aggressive addendums to my helpful Post-it notes. In fact, *they are the opposite of helpful.* They are just bitter.

Dear Victor: If you leave wet towels on the ground again I will stab you.

Dear Victor: You can't take clothes out of the dryer without telling me and just dump them on the bed in a heap. When I find them they've usually cooled off, and then I have to put them all back in the dryer with a cup of water, and then rerun the dryer so all the wrinkles come out, and then sneak each article of clothing out one at a time and hang it up. *It's called "a method," Victor.* Stop judging me.

Dear Victor: No, actually, I *don't* know how to use an iron. *Because we don't own one.* How have you never noticed this before?! The dryer is our iron, Victor. Also, I would appreciate it if you would talk to me directly instead of yelling at me on a Post-it. These Post-its are for educational purposes. Not to draw lewd caricatures of hands pointing menacingly at me. Also, you're supposed to point with your index finger. This is basic pointing etiquette.

Dear Victor: I've poisoned something in the fridge. Good luck with that.

Dear Victor: I'm sorry. I think I might have PMS. I don't know what's wrong with me.

Dear Victor: That was an apology, you asshole! Now there are two things poisoned in the fridge. *Because you don't know how to accept an apology.*

Dear Victor: I am so sorry you are sick. I swear I was just kidding about poisoning shit in the fridge. I mean, I *did* leave the yogurt out for, like, a half a day, but that was really more by accident because I was so distracted by the wet towel on the floor. If anything, you brought this on yourself. Once again, I apologize.

Dear Victor: I love you but I'm getting kind of weak from hunger, and I know you said you didn't poison anything, but every time I take a bite of something you leer and laugh suspiciously and I have to spit it out. I can only assume this is probably how Gandhi felt when he wasn't allowed to eat. (Here's a hint: He felt *stabby.*)

Dear Victor: Okay, first of all, you don't know that Gandhi went on a hunger strike on purpose. For all we know he was avoiding poisoning too. The people who *survive* are the ones who write the history, Victor. *Not the people who die of hunger because their husbands may or may not have poisoned all the food in the house.* Except guess what? This is all going on my blog, so I can document this in case people find my emaciated body later and demand justice. There will be a reckoning and it will be brutal and swift.

Dear Victor: Great. Now we're out of Post-its. I'm writing this on the towel you left on the ground this morning, since we obviously have no respect for towels anymore. I'm going to the grocery store for more Post-its, and I'm going to eat unpoisoned Triscuits straight out of the box while I'm there, so I will return fresh and renewed. Also, the cat vomited in the hall and I am not cleaning it up. I have had *enough*, Victor. And so has the cat. Whom I'm assuming you poisoned.

Dear Victor: The cat and I are leaving you. You can have the dog. Also, I've decided not to go get Post-it notes after all, because I'm no longer speaking with you, so I'm just writing this on your hand towel. You will never hear from me again.

Dear Victor: The dog started whining when I told him he had to stay with you, so I'm taking him too.

Dear Victor: Yes, actually I *was* holding a bag of dog treats when I told him he had to stay with you, but I don't think that had anything to do with his reaction. Also, we're running out of dish towels, so this will be my last message to you.

Dear Victor: Okay. Fine. You can have the dog. I tried to put him in the car and he peed on me. *You two deserve each other.* I am writing this on the dog because it seemed fitting. Also I couldn't find packing peanuts for the booze, so I just drank it all. YOU WILL MISS ME SO MUCH ONCE I'M SOBER ENOUGH TO WAKE UP AND DRIVE AWAY.

Dear Victor: Wow. That . . . *really* got out of hand. I'm sending this cat in as a peace offering. I forgive you for all the stuff you wrote on the walls about my sister, and I'm going to just ignore all the stuff you wrote about my "giant ass" (turn cat over for rest) because I love you and you need me. Who else loves you enough to send you notes written on cats? Nobody, that's who. Also, I stapled a picture of us from our wedding day to the cat's left leg. Don't we look happy? We can be that way again. Just stop leaving wet towels on the floor. That's all I ask. I'm low-maintenance that way. Also, this cat needs to go on a diet. I shouldn't be able to write this much on a cat and still have room left over.

Epilogue: Victor forgave me and we all lived happily ever after, except for the cat, who had to have his leg amputated, but that was less from the infection and more from his poor circulation because he was so fat. He kind of brought it on himself too. But now he's less fat. By, like, a whole leg.

(Disclaimer: Most of this chapter was exaggerated, except for the part where Victor left a wet towel on the floor. That shit totally happened. I'm still working through it.)

The Dark and Disturbing Secrets HR Doesn't Want You to Know

I worked in human resources for almost fifteen years at a number of different companies, including a religious-based organization where one of my duties was to teach people how to be appropriate and professional. Yes, I do see the irony in this.

Human resources is the place where people come to complain and/or shoot people when they just can't take it anymore. Choosing to work in HR is like choosing to work in the complaint department of hell, except way more frustrating, because at least in hell you'd be able to agree that that Satan is a real dick-wagon without having to toe the company line. The HR department is the place where people stop by to say, "THIS IS TOTALLY FUCKED UP," and the HR employees will nod thoughtfully and professionally as they think to themselves, *"Wow. That is totally fucked up. I wish that this person would leave so I could tell everyone else in the office about it."*

When I was in HR, if someone came to me about a really fucked-up problem, I'd excuse myself and bring in a coworker to take notes, and the employee would relax a bit, thinking, *"Finally, people are taking me seriously around here,"* but usually we do that only so that when you leave we can have a second opinion about how insane that whole conversation was.

"Was that shit as crazy as I thought it was?" I would ask afterward. It always was. Sadly, HR has very little power in an organization, unless the real executives are on vacation, and then watch out, because a lot of assholes are going to get fired.

There are three types of people who choose a career in HR: sadistic assholes who were probably all tattletales in school, empathetic (and soon-to-be-disillusioned) idealists who think they can make a difference in the lives of others, and those who of us who stick around because it gives you the best view of all the most entertaining train wrecks happening in the rest of the company.

People who aren't in HR always assume that people who are in HR are the biggest prudes and assholes, since HR is ostensibly[1] there to make sure everyone follows the rules, but people fail to realize that HR is the only department actively paid to look at porn. Sure, it's under the guise of "reviewing all Internet history to make sure *other* people aren't looking at porn," but people are always looking at porn, and so we have to look at it too so that we can print it out for the investigation. This is also the reason why HR always has color printers, and why no one else is allowed to use them. Because we can't remember to pick up all the porn we just copied. This is just one of many secrets the HR department doesn't want you to know, and after sharing these secrets I will probably be blackballed from the Human Resources Alliance, which is much like the Magicians' Alliance (in that I don't belong to either, since I never get invited to join clubs, and that I'm not actually sure that either of them exist). Regardless, almost immediately after starting work in HR, I started keeping a journal about all the fantastically fucked-up stuff that people who aren't in HR would never believe. These are a few of those stories:

---

1. Did you know that "ostensively" isn't a word? Because I didn't, and apparently I've been using the wrong word for my entire life. Apparently the "correct" word is "ostensibly." *Ostensively.*

— — — — — —

Last month we decided to start keeping a file of the most horrific job applications handed in so that we'd have something to laugh at when the work got to us. We now officially have twice as many applications in the "Never-hire-these-people-unless-we-find-out-that-we're-all-getting-fired-next-week" file than we have in the "These-people-are-qualified-for-a-job" file. What's the word for when something that started out being funny ends up depressing the hell out of you? Insert that word here.

— — — — — —

Today a woman came in to reapply for a job. She wrote that she'd quit last month but now wanted her job back. On "reason for leaving" she wrote: "That job sucked. Plus, my supervisor was a douche-nugget." She was reapplying for the exact same job. I rehired her and reassigned her to her old supervisor, because I totally agreed with her. That guy was totally a douche-nugget.

— — — — — —

In the last two months, six separate men filled in the "sex" blank on their job application with some variation of "Depends on who's offering." Two answered, "Yes, please," and one wrote, "No, thank you." I hired the last one because he seemed polite.

— — — — — —

This afternoon an applicant wrote that she'd been fired from her job at a gas station for sleeping on a cat. Everyone in the office read the application, but none of us could agree on what the hell she was talking about, so we brought her in for an interview. When I asked her about falling asleep on her cat she looked at me and indignantly replied, "What? I never wrote that." Then when I showed her the application she said, "Car. My boss found out I was sleeping on a car. Duh. Why would my boss care if I slept on a cat?"

"Um . . . why would your boss care if you slept on a car?" I asked.

"Because I was the only person working that shift. But I totally would've heard if anyone had driven up. I'm a very light sleeper. It's not like I didn't have a plan."

The lesson here is that sometimes you get brought in for an interview just to settle a bet.

―― ―― ――

Today I interviewed someone who handed me a résumé saying that he'd worked at Helping Hand-Jobs. I choked on my own spit and couldn't stop coughing. Later I showed it to the interviewer in the next office. She told me that her brother had worked there once but had quit because all the manual labor had given him heatstroke. After I started coughing again she realized my confusion and explained that it was actually named Helping-Hand Jobs and was a handyman service. Never underestimate the power of punctuation, people.

―― ―― ――

Today I had to talk to an employee who e-mailed a photograph of his penis to a woman in his department. I knew it was his penis because it said, "This is my penis," in the subject line. Also, his name badge was clipped to his belt and was clearly visible. I practiced saying, "Is this your penis?" over and over in my office until I could say it without giggling, and then I called him and his supervisor in.

"Is this your penis?" I asked, as I pushed the printout of the e-mail over to him.

I think I was expecting him to break into a sweat or try to jump through the window out of embarrassment, because apparently I'd forgotten about the fact that this was the same man who thought it would be perfectly fine to take a picture of his penis in the office bathroom to send it to a shocked coworker. Instead he grinned cockily (no pun intended), saying, "I think the better question is, Exactly how did you get a picture of my penis?"

"It was caught in the e-mail filter. The picture, I mean. Not your penis. If, in fact, that is your penis, I mean." I was flustered, but tried to gain control of the situation again with a deep, calming breath. "Did you mail a picture of your penis?"

He raised an eyebrow. "Would it make it better if I said I was mailing pictures of someone else's penis?"

I've thought about that question for fifteen years and I still don't have a good answer. Instead I said, "Not really. Giving a coworker a picture of a penis is sort of universally frowned on. It's in the employee handbook. Sort of. It's between the lines."

"Is there anything in the handbook about someone in HR handing you a penis picture and asking you whether it's yours?"

I couldn't think of anything to say to that, so I just told him he was fired and made a note that we need to update the employee handbook with more penis-related directives.

———————

As of today I've had to ask five separate men, "Is this your penis?" after their pictures got caught in the e-mail filter. (Side note: When I read this to people who don't work in HR, they stop me here and say, "Really? People actually mail pictures of their penises at work?" And I explain that yes, it happens at least once a quarter. If it's an HR person I'm read-ing this to, they always say, "Really? You worked in HR for fifteen years and you only had to ask five men about their penises?" And I explain that no, I wrote this in my first few years in HR, and there's another one in the very next paragraph. After that they just got so commonplace I stopped writing about them in my journal. I eventually got to where I could say, "Is this your penis?" without blushing or giggling. That's how much practice I had at handing random men photos of their junk and asking them to identify their penis. I never once had to do it with a vagina. Probably because women are better at not getting their e-mails caught in the firewall, because they don't use the subject line "Look at my penis." Also, vaginas seem to have less personality than penises, so "Is this your vagina?" would probably be difficult to answer. If someone asked me to pick out my own vagina's mug shot out of a lineup of vagi-nas, I'd be helpless. And probably concerned about what exactly my va-gina had been doing that constituted a need for its own mug shot.

— — — — — — —

"Are these your penises?"

This is a question I never thought I'd have to ask, because I've never met anyone with more than one penis, but in this case it was two men taking pictures of their penises, together, at work. They hadn't been caught in the filter, but had instead printed out the picture using the of-fice printer and had accidentally forgotten to pick it up. One of the guys just nodded quietly, but the other leaned over to look clinically at the photo before he pointed to the penis on the left. "Just this one," he said. I thanked him for the clarification, because I didn't know what else to say. His friend looked at him, stunned, but I think it was probably a good lesson for him in picking the quality of people his penis takes pictures with. Standards are important, you guys.

— — — — — —

Last week I turned down an applicant who had misspelled or left blank almost all of her application. She came in again yesterday with almost the exact same application, but with a different name. I turned her down again. Today she came in again and turned in another application with another new name. I asked her whether she was the girl with the first name. She said that was her sister. I told her that I couldn't hire her unless her name matched the name on her Social Security card, and she asked for the application she'd just given me, and changed her name back to the original one. I turned her down again and pointed out that everyone lies on their application but not usually about their names. When she left she said, "Okay. See you tomorrow." I'm pretty sure she's not being sarcastic.

— — — — — —

This morning the HR director told us we were going to start hiring transportation workers to bus people to our different locations, and asked for a committee to come up with some standard interview questions for our office to use. I asked whether we should screen them to see whether they believe that they'll be saved during the rapture, because if they do then they're knowingly putting the lives of the passengers at risk when the bus suddenly becomes driverless and spirals out of control. I got some weird looks, so I pointed out that we technically work at a religious organization, so it should totally be okay to ask that.

I was not allowed to join that committee, so my guess is that they totally hired a lot of bus drivers who plan on leaving their buses driverless. I bet those drivers totally know they're putting their passengers' lives in jeopardy but just don't care. Which (based on what I've learned on religion through TV) would probably be considered a sin. So I guess either way, our passengers will still have a driver when the rapture comes. It's gonna be a pretty nasty surprise for those bus drivers, though.

- - - - - - -

Every HR department I've ever worked in has secret codes that no one else knows about, and we use them to talk about you while you're still in the office. Here are the codes from my last job: Tucking your hair behind your ear means, "This bitch is crazy." Tucking your hair back behind both ears means, "Totally fucking crazy." Absentmindedly wiping your brow means, "I'm sorry. Does it look like I have 'dumb-ass' written across my forehead?" Picking your nose means, "Someone needs to call security." Scratching your crotch means, "Steal second." It worked really well until we hired a new girl who had a lot of nervous tics, and then it just became too confusing.

- - - - - - -

Last year they installed panic buttons under our desks so we could alert security if there was someone violent threatening us. We're supposed to test it out once a month, but security is always very slow to show up to turn off the alarm. Yesterday our boss was out, so we decided to push all the panic buttons. After fifteen minutes with no response, we decided to lie down on the floor and put signs on our chests that said things like "I've been shot in the head" and "We're all dead now. Thanks." Mine said, "I'm still alive. I just came in, and I slipped on all the blood and now I'm unconscious and have a concussion. I really shouldn't be allowed to sleep." In true dedication to a role I actually was asleep when security showed up fifteen minutes later. They were not amused, and pointed out that it would be a smart move to be a little less bitchy to the only people in our building who were actually required to bring loaded guns to work. The next day we all got yelled at by our boss because "po-

tential job applicants could have been scared off if they'd looked through the glass window of our office door and had seen you all lying on the floor." I pointed out that finding bodies on the floor and not helping was sort of an interview that they had failed anyway, so technically we were kind of saving time. He was not amused.

At one of my jobs we'd have drills to see how easy it was to smuggle babies out of the building. One employee (usually a new hire, so that he or she wasn't recognizable) was given a baby and everyone else in the building had to stop the person from sneaking out. It was a public building and none of our customers could know that we were doing a supersecret smuggled-baby drill, because it might seem unprofessional, so that made it harder. It was usually a fake baby, but you never knew whether it would be a real one brought from home. Today we had a drill and I stopped someone in the hall and wouldn't let them go for fifteen minutes until security came, because I was sure it was the fake baby. It totally wasn't the fake baby.

This morning we were all praying with the bishop at work (which is legal, because it's a faith-based organization, but also weird because I still don't understand how I got hired here, except that we need to do better background checks). There were about a hundred of us in the hallway when the bishop said—in this really loud and dramatic way—"Oh, heavenly Father: Hear our prayer!" Immediately some guy from engineering's walkie-talkie blasts out, "COME IN, CHUCK!" and I had to walk out in the middle of the prayer because I totally snorted and was drawing attention to myself, because all I could think of was how I bet God was only half listening and then was all, "WTF? Did the bishop just call me

Chuck?" This is when I realized I was probably not getting into heaven, unless God has one hell of a sense of humor, which He probably does because, hello? He's making me work at a faith-based organization. I mean, He's not forcing me work there, but I hear He kind of controls everything, so technically this is probably His fault. If anything, they should blame God for making me snort in the middle of the prayer. When I get fired I'll have to remember to tell the bishop that.

Last week my boss told me to rewrite a twenty-page proposal on engagement benchmarking. I turned it in and he wrote a note on the cover that just said, "No, no. Not this." I had no idea what he wanted, so I just put it off, and then when he came in this morning and told me he needed the final draft in a half-hour I printed out the exact same one as before, but this time on prettier paper. This afternoon he brought the whole team together to tell everyone I was the perfect example of being able to listen to constructive criticism.

There's a very mean girl down the hall who's trying to get me fired. I'm no good with confrontation, so whenever I say, "Have a wonderful day," to her out loud, I'm really saying, "Be nice to me or I will stab you in the face with a fork," in my head. I wish her a wonderful day at least once an hour. She's starting to get paranoid and jumpy about it, but there's really nothing she can do, because she can't complain about me wishing her a wonderful day without sounding totally insane. This is why you should never mess with nonconfrontational people. Because they're too unstable to second-guess. And because they're totally the kind of people who could suddenly snap, and stab you in the face with a fork.

\- \- \- \- \- \- \-

Last month the general manager came in with his usual complaint that the employment office wasn't pulling its weight, because his area was still chronically understaffed. We told him we were running behind and gave him the "Never-hire-these-people-unless-we-find-out-that-we're-all-getting-fired-next-week" folder and told him to let us know which ones he wanted us to call in for interviews. He returned the file the next day and has not complained since then.

\- \- \- \- \- \- \-

Today at lunch my coworker (Jason) was telling me about a documentary he'd seen about this woman who had a tiny upper body, but everything from her waist down was enormous, and I was all, "My God. I bet her labia is huge," and that's when Jason put down his fork and said he wouldn't eat lunch with me anymore. But then I pointed out that scientifically it makes sense that her labia would be enormous. If I were her, I'd roll it up with binder clips. Or foam curlers. And then on special occasions she lets it out of the curlers and bingo: spiral perm. Totally ready for prom.

"Hi," Jason said, waving his hands in front of my face sarcastically. "I'm eating tuna salad over here."

"But just imagine what you could do with it. If you got attacked you could throw it on someone to swat them back, or you could catch children jumping out of burning buildings. I bet it's flat as a pancake too, since it's being squished by her legs. You could put a lantern behind it and make shadow puppets. It's like a gift no one can ever use. Except I would totally use my giant labia. I'd entertain the whole world with it. Because that's the kind of person I am. Saintlike. If I had an enormous labia I would change the world with it."

Jason threw his tuna salad in the trash. "So the only thing holding you back is . . . how small your labia is?"

"Well, it's not like a handicap,*" I retorted. "I mean, I get by."*

Jason was silent.

"I'd say it's roomy, but compact. Like a balloon valance. Or a Honda Accord."

Then Jason got all weird and yelled, "You aren't supposed to tell me your vagina is like a Honda Accord! WE WORK TOGETHER," and I'm all, "You brought it up!" Then there was this awkward silence while I tried to look penitent and Jason tried to look stern, but technically I was just thinking about how a giant labia would be a great lap blanket on cold nights, and Jason was probably wondering what a balloon valance was. So then I was all, "It's like a tiny curtain," and Jason was like, "What!?" and I just said, "Oh, never mind."

Today an applicant who couldn't pass the typing test blamed it on me for giving her "a trick keyboard because the keys weren't in alphabetical order." I tried to explain that all keyboards are laid out the same way and she called me a liar. I apologized and told her that if she wanted to bring in an alphabetized keyboard, I'd be happy to hook it up for her so she could retest, and she yelled, "I'M NOT GOING TO PAY TO REPLACE YOUR SHODDY EQUIPMENT." So I told her to go across the street to the computer store, find an alphabetical keyboard, and have them put it on our account. An hour later the computer store called to ask that we stop sending crazy people over there.

This afternoon my coworker, a sweet but sheltered girl named Collette, called me into her office. "Did you know that amputee porn is a thing?

Because it is. Amputee porn." *She looked like she might be going into shock, and I considered finding a blanket to wrap her in. "This guy's supervisor found porn in a printer, so she asked me to check his hard drive, and it's* filled *with amputee porn."*

I apparently didn't look shocked enough, because she looked at me and slammed her tiny fist on the desk, screaming: "AMPUTEE PORN." Clearly she needed an intervention, as she was stuck in a porn loop.

I pulled up one of the pictures, a legless naked woman. "Okay, see? This isn't even amputee porn. It's just . . . bad Photoshop. *You can tell because there are shadows where her legs were before they were airbrushed out.* I mean, it's still totally porn. *It's just not real amputee porn."*

Collette looked at me with sad, dead eyes, her innocence scarred forever. "So what about this?" *she asked as she enlarged a photo of a onelegged girl in a bikini. "Is* this *porn? Or is it not?* Because I can't even tell anymore. *I mean, it must be porn, because it's in his porn folder, but I just don't know. It's a girl with one leg, who's waterskiing. Is it supposed to be empowering? Is it pornographic? I DON'T EVEN KNOW."*

I didn't have an answer for her. When you can't tell whether something's porn or not anymore, that's when you know it's time to go home. Or to quit. Possibly both.

IT WOULD BE PARTICULARLY fitting (and easy) to finish this chapter with a paragraph about how I personally ended my career in HR because I lost my ability to tell porn from real life, but that would be a lie, as I actually quit because I wanted to give myself a year to find out whether I could be a writer. I told my boss that I had a book inside of me, and that I needed to get it out even if I had to squeeze it through my vagina. Because that's exactly what the world needs. A book squeezed from my vagina.

But it must have been a worthwhile bet, since you're now holding that very book in your hands. Unless this is the year 2057, and you're a police detective holding this stained, unfinished manuscript as you stand over the body of the lonely elderly woman who was found partially eaten by her own house cats, and this chapter ends with a handwritten note that says, "Note to self: Find a more upbeat way to end this chapter, because being eaten by cats is depressing, and also a terrible running theme to have in a book. Also, buy cat food and pay the insurance on the hovercar." If this is the case then I apologize to you for the state of my apartment. Please know that I was *not* expecting company, and that I usually never have dirty dishes in the sink *or* partially eaten bodies on the floor. I can assure you this whole day is a total anomaly for me.

If You See My Liver, You've Gone Too Far

Spoiler alert: Bambi's mom doesn't make it.

Okay, get prepared, because this chapter is kind of depressing and is about dead babies. I know. *Ew.* But they don't *all* die, and in the end everything is fine. Mostly. If you just forget about all those dead babies. Or if you call them fetuses. Calling them fetuses makes it feel more clinical and less sad, but I'm pretty sure I get to call them whatever I want, because they're *my* dead babies. And no, I'm not calling them "babies" instead of "fetuses" for any political reason, because I'm actually totally prochoice and you can do whatever you want with your body, but stop hijacking this chapter, asshole, because this is about me. God, *you have a problem.* Also, my editor is all, "WTF are you doing? How are you going to build up suspense if you just gave away the entire chapter in the first paragraph? Don't you know about the six elements of drama?" and I'm all, "No, but I know that when I go see a sad movie I always want someone to run in right before the sad scene and be like, 'Okay, Bambi's mom's about to bite it, but it's *totally* going to be okay in the end. Don't freak.'" And that's what I just did for you. *You're welcome.* My editor just pointed out that I just ruined *Bambi* for everyone who hasn't seen it, but IT'S FUCKING *BAMBI*, y'all. It's totally not my fault if you haven't seen *Bambi* yet. It's been out for *years.* Hey, have you heard about this new thing called "a sandwich" yet?

It's awesome. My editor says I'm being purposely fatuous. I don't know what that means, but it sounds bad, so I'm going to go back up to the top and add a spoiler alert. I'm like a goddamn saint.

So, how do you write something funny about dead babies? Answer: *You can't.* So get prepared.

I ALWAYS IMAGINED that when I got pregnant it would be awesome, and everything would go perfectly, and I'd pose for all those artfully naked, pregnant Demi Mooresque pictures and put them all over my house, and suddenly I'd have *less* cellulite, and then I'd go into labor while I was standing in line at the bank, but it would be okay because the baby would get stuck in my pants leg, so it totally wouldn't slam into the floor. Thank God for skinny jeans with maternity panels; *am I right?* And that was basically exactly what I expected *would* happen the first time I got pregnant. In real life, though, I found out I was pregnant, promptly got so sick I could hardly move, and threw up into my office garbage can all day long. At the time I was still working in human resources, teaching people how to act appropriately at a nonprofit Christian organization in Houston. That sounds like it's a joke, but I assure you it's not. I was actually really good at pretending to be appropriate (when I wasn't throwing up in front of large groups of people), but it started to become obvious to everyone that I was either pregnant or dying, so Victor and I decided to go ahead and tell everyone. And everyone was thrilled, except for the cleaning lady at my office who had to empty my trash can.

I had always wanted to be a mother. I didn't really like other people's babies, but I never considered that a job requirement, as I assumed that my baby would be kick-ass, or would at least quickly turn into a kid. When I was little I always wanted to have a slumber party, but my parents were too smart to ever agree to have one, and so I told myself that one day when I was old enough I'd have a kid and have a slumber party with her every night. That seems like a ridiculous reason for having a child, but there are worse ones. At my core, though, was a need that I couldn't quite verbalize. I wanted to be part of my family legacy. I wanted to give a child the kind of magical childhood I wanted. I wanted to see a small reflection of myself and the generations before me in a new face, and be reborn again too. I wanted to have someone I could beat at Scrabble.

Victor and I picked out names, bought baby sweaters, and wondered what our lives would be like as parents. I was nervous, but too sick to really worry. A few weeks before the second trimester, Victor and I went into the doctor's office for an ultrasound. I hadn't slept much that night, because I'd had a panic attack and ended up calling my sister at midnight, hysterically yelling, "OHMYGOD, *WHAT IF THE BABY'S A REPUBLICAN?*" Then she hung up on me because she enjoys being unsupportive. Or maybe she was mad that I call her only at midnight when I'm having panic attacks. I don't really know. What I do know, though, was that I was braced to hear almost anything in that exam room.

"It's twins."

"It's triplets."

"It's a Republican."

"It's a small bear."

Granted, that last one seemed unlikely, but I was mentally prepared for almost anything—anything except for what the doctor actually told us: That there was no heartbeat. That the baby was dead. That *"these things happen for the best."* And this is when I broke. It wasn't obvious from the outside. I didn't cry. I didn't scream. I went numb, and then I realized that this was all my fault. If I'd gone to church, or believed in the right God, this wouldn't have happened. The exam room door was the unlucky number that falls after twelve, and I'd wanted to ask for another room but had been too embarrassed to say why. If I'd demanded another room, the baby would still be alive. There were a million reasons why this was happening, and all of them were because of me.

I numbly followed Victor down the halls, and for the first time in my life I seriously considered suicide. I wondered if I would be fast enough to slip away from Victor before he noticed that I was gone. I wondered if the building was tall enough to kill me if I jumped, or if I'd just wake up, broken physically as well as mentally, in a hospital bed. I wondered what I could do to not have to ever deal with this, because I knew I wasn't strong enough to come out whole on the other side. Victor seemed to sense that I was planning on running, or maybe he was just on autopilot himself, because he held on to my arm almost painfully, leaving me no room for escape. We went home, and while I waited to miscarry, I had Victor call everyone and tell them to *never, ever* mention this to me again. No flowers, no "I'm sorrys." *Nothing.* Because I knew that the only way I could survive this would be to block it from my mind.

And that might have been easier to do except for the fact that I *didn't* miscarry. I continued to carry the baby for another month and then I had a nervous breakdown. I'm still not sure what triggered it, but my coworkers found me crying hysterically in my office. I didn't even recognize the sounds as human, and I remember wondering what that horrible noise was, until I realized it was me, keening uncontrollably until I finally exhausted myself. Victor took me home, and my doctor eventually realized I needed this to end immediately and performed the surgery. There were complications from the procedure, and I ended up having a painful, hemorrhaging miscarriage that night. A week later I was diagnosed with post-traumatic stress disorder and put on an antidepressant that made me suicidal. *Which is not really how an antidepressant is supposed to work,* turns out. Victor found me trawling online for suicide message boards, pulled my Internet access, and got me on another drug that worked. My psychiatrist worked with me until I was eventually able to leave the house without having a breakdown, and then he mailed me a letter telling me that he was retiring suddenly, which I'm pretty sure is code for, "You're too fucked up even for me. I'm totally breaking up with you." But that was fine, because I was better and stronger and ready to try again.

And then I got pregnant again.

And then I lost it again.

I switched doctors and demanded to be tested for everything in the books. That's when I found out that I had antiphospholipid antibody syndrome, which I could barely even spell. I went home and looked it up on the Internet and it basically said, "YOU'RE GOING TO DIE," but then my doctor told me that it wasn't that big of a deal. It's a rare autoimmune disease that causes blood clots, and worsens during pregnancy. I told her that I was pretty sure that I also had polio and testicular cancer, and she said that I wasn't allowed to read WebMD anymore.

I was put on a regimen of baby aspirin and I was all, "Seriously? Fucking *baby aspirin?*" But my doctor assured me that it would thin my blood enough to stop having miscarriages. And that's when I had another miscarriage. Coincidentally, this is the same time when I screamed, *"FUCK BABY ASPIRIN,"* and my doctor agreed to prescribe a heavy-duty treatment of expensive blood thinners, and I was all, *"Hell, yeah."* Then she said, "Here's your giant duffel bag of syringes so that you can inject the medication directly into your bloodstream," and I thought, "Oh. *I have made a terrible mistake.*" But by then it was too late to back out, because I'd read all the Internet horror stories about women having strokes because of this blood disease, and I thought that perhaps all the blood thinners would help the polio that I'd also diagnosed myself with, and so I took a deep breath and I started giving myself injections. In the stomach. Twice a day. *Awesome.* It's basically like getting the treatment for rabies, except instead of five shots you have to get seven hundred.

And after many, *many* months of shots I found myself pregnant again. This time I was getting further along than ever before. By the second trimester my stomach had become a patchwork quilt of bruises, and when I would pull up my shirt for checkups the ultrasound techs invariably gasped in horror, until I quickly assured them that I was *not* being pummeled repeatedly in the stomach. They still gave Victor the stink-eye, though, which was actually a nice distraction, since every time we had an ultrasound I would wince in terror, certain that the baby would be gone. But it wasn't.

I kept my appointments and adamantly insisted that none of them fall on the unlucky-numbered day. I took to calling that number "twelve-B." As in eleven, twelve, twelve-B, fourteen. People thought I was insane, and I was. (Still am.) But I wasn't taking any chances, and curing my worsening OCD wasn't as important to me as the possibility that asking the cats to wish me luck was keeping the baby alive. Once, as Victor drove me to work in the morning, I realized that I'd forgotten to ask the cats to wish us luck and I demanded that he turn around immediately. He tried to logically explain that the cats didn't actually have the ability to give me good or bad luck, but it didn't matter. I *knew* that the cats weren't in charge of good luck. These were the same cats who would stand inside the litter box and cluelessly poop over the side. *Of course* they weren't controlling my destiny. *I* was controlling my destiny. I was just doing it by following all the little OCD routines that I'd picked up that had made life keep going. They were, of course, all the bizarre little routines that made my life incredibly complicated as well, but it was a mental illness I was willing to live with if it kept my baby (who we'd just been told was a girl) alive.

When I was seven months along, my coworkers decided to throw me a shower. I'd vehemently insisted against it, because I knew it would interfere with all of my secret little rituals, but they were adamant and decided to throw me an involuntary surprise shower. One that just happened to be on the unluckily numbered floor. I got into the elevator, expecting to go to a budget meeting, but I couldn't bring myself to press the unlucky-numbered button, so I did what I always did, which was to ride the elevator until someone else got on and pressed that unlucky button for me. Except that no one was getting in the elevator to go to that floor. Because they were all already in the conference room waiting to surprise me. Twenty minutes later someone came looking for me and found me sitting helplessly in the corner of the elevator. I told them I was just dizzy and resting, but I think it was probably pretty obvious I was more than slightly unhinged.

By the eighth month my stomach was huge and tight, and I didn't have any extra folds of fat to pinch away that I could stick the syringes into. My doctor insisted that although the needles were quite long, they were not long enough to actually reach the baby, but I was terrified that I would end up injecting blood thinners into her head, and so I would yell, "MOVE, BABY. GO TO YOUR LEFT OR YOU'RE GOING TO GET STABBED." Then Victor would point out that most fetuses don't speak English, but I'd been talking to her a lot and I felt sure she'd picked up a few basic phrases. I *did* worry, though, that she didn't know which direction "left" was, and so I'd yell, "*My* left. Not *your* left. Unless you're facing my belly button. Then it's your left too. If you can see

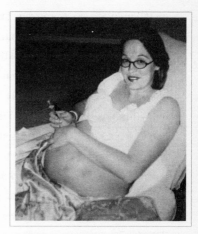

One of hundreds of injections. Ah, the simplicities of motherhood.

my liver you've gone too far." Then Victor looked at me worriedly and I was all, "You know, you *could* help," and he was like, "*What the fuck can I do? You have obviously lost your mind.*" Then I glared at him until he finally sighed resignedly, walked around me, leaned down, and shouted at the left side of my stomach, "THIS WAY, BABY. MOVE TOWARD MY VOICE!" And I smiled at him gratefully, but after I finished the shot Victor muttered, "If this doesn't work out we're just getting a puppy," which was kind of a crazy thing to say, because we already had a puppy. Clearly Victor was losing his mind and it was up to me to keep our family together. Me and the cats, who were granting me luck only when I specifically asked for it, that is. So, yeah . . . there was a lot riding on me.

Time crept by until it was finally time to induce. We went to the hospital maternity ward, and Victor quickly turned the television up to drown out the woman across the hall who was enthusiastically screaming, "JESUS-GODKILLMENOW."

"She's praying," Victor said unconvincingly.

In a twisted sort of serendipity, the TV screen buzzed on to reveal the bloody-stomach scene from *Alien*, which should probably be banned from all labor rooms. Victor attempted to switch it, but I asked him to leave it on because it seemed to fit the theme.

A nurse came in to start my IVs and told us that she was sorry about the woman screaming next door, and that she'd told her that she needed to keep it down. I wondered what the nurse would do if the woman refused to keep quiet. The nurse was a petite black woman, but you got the feeling that she could easily drag a screaming pregnant woman out into the street if she needed to, and she struck me as being someone who should not be tested. "It's because she's black," explained the nurse matter-of-factly.

"Um . . . *what*?" I asked, certain I'd misheard her.

"The lady yelling in the other room. She's black," the nurse continued. "Black women are *always* the loudest when they have babies. Screaming to Jesus, usually. White women are much quieter, right up until the baby starts to crown. Then you can't tell a white woman from a black woman. Asian women make no sound at all. *Quiet as church mice.* We have to keep an extra-careful eye on them, because if we don't keep checking their hootchies they'll give birth without even letting us know."

"Oh," I mumbled, as I found myself near speechless . . . less from the racial profiling and more from hearing a medical professional use the word "hootchies." Mostly because I'm pretty sure that the word she was looking for was "coochies." She must have noticed my look of concern, because she patted my hand and said, "It's okay. I'm black, so I can totally say that out loud. The other nurses on the floor just have to think it. And," she added proudly, "I've just distracted you so much that you didn't even notice that I put all your IVs in." And she was right. I had totally been distracted by Asian hootchies. ~~And not for the first time.~~

Victor knew I was scared, but I wasn't so nervous about the pain. I was terrified because the risk of stillbirth is so much higher with antiphospholipid syndrome. I was so focused on getting my daughter out of my body (which I still viewed as a veritable deathtrap) that I hardly noticed the pain. Victor murmured sweet, supportive things in my ear, but they sounded so unnatural coming from his mouth that I couldn't stop giggling hysterically, and everyone looked at me like I was the crazy one, and so I told Victor he wasn't allowed to speak anymore. Then one more push, and there was silence. And then the beautiful sound of crying. It was me crying. And then it was Hailey crying. My sweet, beautiful daughter. And it was amazing.

It wasn't until that very moment that I actually let myself believe that I really might be able to be someone's mother. As I held her in my arms, Victor cried, and I was filled with so much wonderment and awe that it felt as if my chest would explode. Then the epidural started to wear off and I remember thinking that it would be nice if this baby's mother would come and take her so that I could get some sleep. And then I remembered that *I* was that baby's mother. Then I felt a little scared for both of us.

A few minutes later Hailey was whisked away by the staff, and I prodded Victor out of the room to follow her, because I was certain that the doctor would somehow switch her with another baby who would grow up to be a sociopath, because I'd been watching too much of the Lifetime channel.

And that's how I found myself half naked, completely alone, covered in my own blood, and still strapped into the stirrups of the labor table, in what was possibly the most unflattering position imaginable, as I added a frightened, confused janitor to the long list of people who had seen my vagina that day.

Totally worth it.

Me and Hailey—2004.
We both needed a bottle at that point.

My Vagina Is Fine.
Thanks for Asking

I f you are not a parent you are going to get here and assume this is a potty-training chapter (since almost every mom-penned book follows the labor-and-delivery chapter with the potty-training chapter), and you'll start gagging and you'll want to skip it. But you shouldn't. Because this chapter will make you feel very superior about using birth control and/or infertility.

If you *are* a parent, you're probably going to think that you should skip this chapter, because you've already heard it all. But I guarantee you haven't. And also? The nonparents reading this are totally going to read it and smirk at you later, and you should at least be prepared. This is the same reason I listen to a lot of über-conservative Republican radio. Because I want to know what is on the minds of my enemies. Also because I live in Texas, and there aren't a lot of alternatives. And besides, this chapter isn't even *about* potty training. I don't even know where you got that idea. Potty training is not a fun subject to reminisce about. It's more like a horrible death march through a haunted forest, and the trees are made of angry bears that you're allergic to. And you have to look at pictures of dead people at the same time. Like, it's so awful you want to just make your kid go live outside for the rest of their life, but you can't do that because the dog's out there. And that's why I'm not going to write about potty training, and instead I'm going to write about perspective.

THE FIRST YEAR after having a kid felt sort of foreign to me, and I keep stumbling across it in my head, much like when someone you know dies and an hour later you're laughing at *Hee Haw*, and then you think to yourself, "Oh, fuck, I just remembered that Grampa died," and you get sad again, but then your head goes somewhere else and you're all, "I wonder why you never see elderly biracial couples?" And then a minute later your mind yells, "*Shit*. I forgot Grampa died again." And you keep crying and getting distracted, and you consider that you should probably just turn off *Hee Haw*, because obviously that's not helping, but then you think to yourself, "But Grampa loved *Hee Haw*," and you convince yourself it's an homage to him, even though, really, you just kind of want to watch *Hee Haw*. It's probably also some sort of self-preservation thing to help you deal with grief, *so back off already and stop judging me.*

And this is exactly what being a mom is like. You're just going about your day, thinking about how awesome it would be to make nachos, and suddenly you're all, "Holy shit, *I have a baby*. I should, like, feed it or something." And you do, but then a half-hour later you forget again, and you hear her giggling in the other room and you think, *"WTF? Whose baby is that?"* and then you remember, "Oh, yeah. It's mine. *Weird*." And then you come up with these great ideas to turn the spare room into a bar, so you can charge your friends for all of the alcohol of yours that they're already drinking anyway, and then you draw up the plans and bring over a contractor, and then you're all, "Fuck. *Wait a minute*. This isn't a spare room. This is the room the baby lives in." Right?

Wrong. I was with you up until that last one. If you agreed with the last one then you need to put down this book and go find your baby, because she's probably out drunk on some tree limb somewhere. *You are a terrible parent*.

Special note to people who are childless and are smugly smiling right now: Stop judging. It's entirely possible that you aren't really childless and that you've just forgotten you had a baby. Because that shit totally happens. Check your vagina. Does it look kind of broken? If so, you probably had a baby. Seriously, mine was all Franken-gina for a good year before it was presentable again. But not "presentable" like I'd lay it out at the Thanksgiving dinner table. I wouldn't have done that even *before* it got destroyed. I mean, *not that it wasn't a good trade-off*, because it totally was. And it's fine now. *Great*, actually. *My vagina is great.* Slimming, even. Thanks for asking. It was just fucked up when Hailey was born, but I didn't really care so much at the time, because I was so relieved that she was alive, and so I lay there on the hospital table thinking that is the only time in life when you're too blissfully happy to notice that people are stitching up your vagina.

Also, I just want to say that I think when the doctor is stitching your vagina back up (for real, child-free people: *Stitching. Your. Vagina. Up*), I don't know why they don't throw in some cosmetic surgery while they're down there, to make it look cuter. Like, when my gynecologist told me that she'd probably have to cut my vagina, I was all, "YOU ARE A FUCKING PSYCHOPATH," and she was like, "*Not for fun* [unspoken: *"dumb-ass"*]. To get the baby out." And I said, "Oh. Well, if you're going to have to scar me, could you do it in some kind of kick-ass shape? Like, how about a lightning bolt?" And she just stared at me, so I explained, "You know . . . like Harry Potter's?" Then she just looked at me like I shit on the floor, and I thought maybe it was because the sentence structure kind of implied I was referring to Harry Potter's vagina, and so I clarified: "But not on my forehead like his was." And she still didn't respond, so I pointed down and said, *"On my vagina."* Then she shook her head like she'd known all along that I wasn't referring to Harry Potter's vagina, and said, "Uh, we don't really do that. In fact, we prefer for you to tear naturally, because it heals better," and I'm all, "MOTHER. FUCKER. Are you fucking serious?" And I kind of suspected she was just making that up because she didn't want me to have a nicer vagina than hers, because she'd never had a kid and so hers was probably all perfect and cheerful, and she probably didn't want me rubbing my vagina in her face when it was all lightning-bolt awesome. *Like I would even do that, Dr. Ryder.* I would never rub my vagina in someone's face, even though it would be the most badass vagina in the world. And whenever I have menstrual cramps I could just pretend that Voldemort was close.

Later, during the labor, I did tear *and* get *cut, and it was totally not in a lightning-bolt shape,* and I immediately regretted not doing some sort of perforation in a lighting-bolt shape, but I was so big at that point that I couldn't even *see* my vagina, and when I asked Victor whether he'd draw a dotted line in the shape of a lightning bolt (with little scissors indicating "cut here"), he just walked off. I suspect it's because he didn't want to admit he can't draw scissors, because honestly he is a horrible artist, but when I started badgering him the next day he said confidently, "Oh, I already did it. While you were asleep." Which seemed suspicious, because I'm a pretty light sleeper. But I couldn't even see myself with a hand mirror, and so then I just wondered whether he was fucking with me so that I'd leave him alone. And if he wasn't just fucking with me, then what the hell did he draw? Probably a gun, or a cougar, or something stupid. And also, that doesn't even make sense about tearing being better than cutting, because if that's true then why don't they tear people open when they pull out their gallbladder or remove their appendix? There's really no other sort of surgery where the doctor prefers to just let you get torn apart rather than cut you, and I'm assuming that's because gynecologists are just really lazy.

Holy crap, y'all. Remember back when I was talking about how my Grampa died but I got distracted with *Hee Haw?* That same thing just happened here when I started to talk about perspective and got distracted by my vagina. *I didn't even plan that.* That's how natural this writing shit comes to me. It's like my brain is subconsciously sticking to the theme *in spite* of my distracting vagina. I am so fucking going to win a Pulitzer for this.

Anyway, having a kid is an excellent exercise in perspective. Because it teaches you to embrace the horror and indignity of life. You simply have no other choice.

Take, for example, the first time that you take your child to the community pool. You're self-consciously trying to still appear hip in front of your thin, childless neighbor, who probably got more than two hours of sleep, when you notice that your child's ass seems to be exploding. Then you realize with horror that your husband failed to put a swimming diaper on your toddler, and so now the real diaper is soaking up all of the pool water and expanding like a giant mushroom cloud, and your kid is looking at you like, *"What the fuck is happening to my junk?!"* and you're all, *"DON'T PANIC.* Walk slowly toward the bathroom," but the kid is all, "Pick me up! I AM BEING EATEN BY MY OWN DIAPER," and so you do, but then the pressure makes the diaper seams burst, and now you're covered with this gel stuff from inside the diaper which, *it turns out*, is a bluish, crystal-like jelly. And you're repulsed and fascinated all at the same time, and you run to the bathroom, but the crystal-jelly stuff is leaking out behind you like a trail of bread crumbs, and the lifeguard is giving you the stink-eye, and you finally get to the bathroom, but the gel inside the diaper is continuing to expand. And so as soon as you yank your kid's suit off, the diaper rips open from the sheer internal pressure and lands with a splat and the diaper jelly sprays *all. Over. Everything.* And right at that exact moment, your thin, childless neighbor walks breezily in, and then backs up against the wall in shock as she sees you bending over in the middle of the bathroom, splattered with blue diaper filling and trying desperately to use wads of ineffective brown paper towels to clean the (probably cancerous) diaper jelly off a naked toddler. And you try to smile at her reassuringly, as if this is the sort of thing that happens all the time, and you consider standing up to explain casually *that this is really all your hus-*

band's fault, but before you can straighten up your child sees your giant boob perched precariously at the edge of your bathing suit and she punches it and it falls out of the top of your bathing suit. And then your neighbor backs silently out of the bathroom, like she's stumbling away from a murder scene, and you scream after her, "YOU CANNOT RUN FROM ME. BEHOLD! THIS. IS. YOUR. FUTURE!"

Get ready.

That sort of thing happens *all the damn time.*

I can assure you,
it was traumatizing for all of us.

Phone Conversation I Had with My Husband After I Got Lost for the Eighty Thousandth Time

ME: Hello?

VICTOR: Where are you?! You've been gone an hour.

ME: I'm lost. Don't yell at me.

VICTOR: You went to get milk, dude. You've been to that store a hundred times.

ME: Yes, but not at night. Everything looks all strange and I couldn't see the signs. And I guess I must've taken a wrong street and I've been driving aimlessly, hoping for something to look familiar.

VICTOR: How can you get lost every damn time you leave the house?

ME: I don't even think I'm in Texas anymore.

VICTOR: Motherfu—

ME: DON'T YELL AT ME.

VICTOR: I'm not yelling at you. Just turn on the GPS and put in our address.

ME: I left it at home.

VICTOR: What the hell is wrong with you?!

ME: You said you wouldn't yell at me!

VICTOR: That was before you left the GPS at home. I BOUGHT IT EXPRESSLY BECAUSE OF YOU.

ME: Can't you just tell me how to get home?

VICTOR: How am I supposed to help you get home, Jenny? I DON'T KNOW WHERE YOU ARE.

ME: Okay . . . there are a lot of trees. And bushes. Or they might be horses. It's too dark to tell.

VICTOR: Oh, yeah, I know *exactly* where you are.

ME: Really?

VICTOR: No. You're someplace where there *may or may not be* bushes. *How is that helpful?*

ME: Hell. I need to find a street sign.

VICTOR: You NEED to remember to put the GPS in your car.

ME: No. I'm not using it anymore.

VICTOR: Why not?!

ME: It's trying to kill me.

VICTOR: [stunned silence]

ME: Remember last week when I had to go into town and I got the driving instructions from MapQuest and you made me take the GPS as a backup, but then halfway there the GPS is all, "Turn left now," and I'm all, "No. MapQuest says to go straight," and it's like, "TURN LEFT NOW," and I'm all, "No way, bitch," and then she's sighing at me like she's frustrated and she keeps saying, "Recalculating," in this really judgy, condescending way, and then she's all, "TURN LEFT NOW!" And then I'm all freaked out, so I turn left *exactly like she says* and then she's all, "Recalculating. Recalculating," and I'm like, "I DID EXACTLY WHAT YOU SAID TO DO. WHAT'S WITH THE TONE, WHORE?"

VICTOR: You're not using the GPS because you don't appreciate the tone of the robot?

ME: No, that's just the start. Because then she told me to turn on West Lion Street, *but there was no West Lion Street*, so I kept making illegal U-turns and finally I realized that she was mispronouncing Wesley-Ann Street. Probably on purpose.

VICTOR: It's "Wesleyan Street." You still haven't seen a street sign?

ME: Oh. Sorry. I kind of forgot I was driving.

VICTOR: You forgot you were driving *while you were driving?*

ME: It's not like I ran into a cow. I just forgot I was looking for signs.

VICTOR: If you ever make it home I'm hiding your car keys.

ME: Anyway, then I'm all, "Okay, one of us is mispronouncing 'Wesley-Ann' and one of us is lost and I think they both might be me," but that's when I came up with what might be the greatest invention in the history of the world.

VICTOR: Street signs. Look for street signs.

ME: Haven't seen any. Feels like I'm on a highway now. Ask me what my great idea is.

VICTOR: No.

ME: GPS for stupid people.

VICTOR: [silence]

ME: I'm totally serious. Because I'm no good with directions, but I'm really good with landmarks, so if you tell me to go north on Main, I'm fucked, but if you say, "Turn at that Burger King that burned down last year," I totally know what to do, so we should build a GPS system that does that.

VICTOR: [sigh]

ME: And here's the genius part: We make it able to learn so it adapts to you personally. So, like, if I say, "Huh. There's a homeless guy masturbating," it'll put that in its data banks, and then when I want to go somewhere later, instead of just naming random streets it's all, "You know where that homeless guy was masturbating? We're going there. Turn left at that Sonic you like. Turn right at the burrito place you took Sarah to that time she was dressed all slutty. Yield at the place you gave that guy a hand job."

VICTOR: *What the fuck?*

ME: *Exactly.* See, that's the downfall of this system, because really I just gave a guy a hand by telling him how to get a job. But robots don't get the subtle intricacies of human languages, so there'd be a learning curve. We'd have to put that in the brochure. Like a disclaimer.

VICTOR: How long do you have to be missing before I can start dating again?

ME: I'm just saying this robot isn't perfected yet, dude. It's close, though. I wouldn't use it with your mom in the car, though, just in case. OHMYGOD, I TOTALLY KNOW WHERE I AM!

VICTOR: You're at the place you gave that guy a hand job?

ME: No. I'm at that abandoned building that looks like it's owned by Branch Davidians.

VICTOR: Huh. The rest of the world calls that "Dallas Street." So can you get home now?

ME: I think so. Left at that spooky bar that looks like it's out of Scooby-Doo, left at the place we saw that wild boar that turned out to be a dog, and right at the corner where I threw up that one time. Right?

VICTOR: You make my head hurt.

ME: DUDE, WE ARE GOING TO BE MILLIONAIRES.

EPILOGUE: I made it home.* Victor duct-taped the GPS to my windshield and refused to build me a robot. It's like he *wants* us to be poor.

*DISCLAIMER: By "made it home," I mean I got lost again and Victor had to come find me so I could follow him home. The point is, I made it home. And that I had no robot. This whole incident is kind of a tragedy. Victor says he agrees but probably not for the same reasons.

And Then
I Got Stabbed
in the Face
by a Serial Killer

People with anxiety disorders are often labeled as "shy" or "quiet" or "that strange girl who probably buries bodies in her basement." I've never actually heard anyone refer to me as the latter, but I always assume that's what people are thinking, because that sort of paranoia is a common side effect of anxiety disorder. Personally, I always labeled myself as "socially awkward" and reassured myself that there are *lots* of perfectly normal people who don't like to talk in public. And that's true. Unfortunately it's also true that my fear pushes slightly past the land of "perfectly normal" and lands well into the desert of "paralyzing pathological handicap."

Even simple conversations with strangers in the grocery store leave me alternately unable to speak or unable to *stop* speaking about something completely inappropriate to talk to strangers in the grocery store about. For a long time I beat myself up because I thought it was something I could control if I were strong enough, but in my twenties I began having full-scale panic attacks and finally saw a doctor, who diagnosed me with generalized anxiety disorder.

It's been my experience that people always assume that *generalized* anxiety disorder is preferable to *social* anxiety disorder, because it sounds more vague and unthreatening, but those people are totally wrong. For me, having generalized anxiety disorder is basically like having all of the other anxiety disorders smooshed into one. Even the ones that aren't recognized by modern science. Things like *birds-will-probably-smother-me-in-my-sleep anxiety disorder* and *I-keep-crackers-in-my-pocket-in-case-I-get-trapped-in-an-elevator anxiety disorder.* Basically I'm just *generally* anxious about fucking *everything.* In fact, I suspect that's how they came up with the name.

My doctor was extremely tactful when she diagnosed me with anxiety disorder. *So* tactful, actually, that it wasn't until several visits later that I finally realized that that was what I had. She was blathering on about a patient who sounded to me like a total nutcase. I wasn't really paying attention to her talking about anxiety disorders because I was too busy wondering whether she'd consider it a step back in my therapy if I hid under the couch while we had our sessions. Then I suddenly realized that the crazy person she was talking about was me. I assume she was hesitant to give my condition a name before then out of fear that I'd be ashamed of having a genuine mental disorder. But in all honesty, I felt relieved. Now instead of being "weird," my inability to carry on an appropriate conversation was suddenly labeled a *"painfully devastating and incurable medical disability that torments both the victim and those around her."* By me, that is. My doctor, on the other hand, refers to it as a *"minor disorder easily treated with medication."* I suspect, however, that if she were ever forced to have a conversation with me at a dinner party she would agree that my definition is far more accurate than hers.

During dinner parties or social events I usually say hello to the hostess and then hide in the bathroom until the party's over. It's usually best for everyone involved. I used to read books about people who were naturally good conversationalists, and I'd wonder why *I* couldn't just be innately confident and charming while relating humorous anecdotes about my time spent with Jacques Cousteau. Frankly, I suspected that even if I *had* ever met Jacques Cousteau, I would still be a bad conversationalist. Most party conversations start with me safely nodding along to whatever dull bit of nonsense someone is talking about, and then a few minutes later I panic because the same person asks me what I think about whatever I wasn't paying attention to, and I hear myself blurting out the story of the time I accidentally swallowed a needle. Then I explain how it probably *wasn't* actually a needle, but that I'd thought it was at the time, and then the silence gets louder and louder and I can't stop talking about how terrible it is to *not* know whether you've swallowed a needle or not. And that's when I notice that the room has gone completely silent except for the now-slightly-hysterical sound of me trying to find an end to a story *that doesn't even fucking have one.* Then I just physically *force* myself to stop talking, and (after several awkwardly painful seconds of silence) someone else will change the subject and I can slink away to hide in the bathroom until it's time to leave. And this is the best-case scenario.

On more than one occasion my panicked ramblings were so horrific that everyone was rendered speechless, and the silence got more and more palpable, and in desperation I just blurted out my credit card number and ran to the bathroom. I did this both because I hoped that yelling random numbers would make the baffled spectators suspect that I must be one of those eccentric mathematical geniuses who is just too brilliant for them to understand, and also because I felt a bit guilty for making them have to listen to the whole "*I may or may not swallow needles*" story, and if they wanted to charge their wasted time to my credit card then they now had that option. Except that I'm not actually good with numbers at all, so I can never remember my real credit card number and instead I just make up a random string of numbers. In short, some random strangers are paying for my shortcomings because I have a bad memory. *And* because I can't carry on a conversation like a normal human being. *And* because identity fraud is so lucrative. So basically, we *all* lose.

I assume this must be quite confusing for people whom I've communicated with only via e-mail and texts, since I *can* actually come across as reasonably witty and coherent in e-mail, because I have time to think about what a normal, filtered, mentally stable adult would write before I press "Send." This is why I prefer to talk to people only electronically. I'll write up an e-mail and then ask myself whether normal people would bring up the fact that Lincoln died from a lot of people sticking unwashed fingers into his bullet hole, and then I'll convince myself that they don't, and I'll also take out the part about how vegetarians are allowed to eat human placenta because no animal died for it, and then I'll be left with a tight little e-mail that just says, "Congratulations on your baby!" which is much more bland, but is also something I've totally heard normal people say before, so it seems safe.

A lot of people assume I'm comically exaggerating this point, but the only people who really think that are the people who don't have an anxiety disorder. The rest of you are nodding your head in agreement because you, too, have been stricken by this rather shitty disorder that makes an e-mail conversation (which should take only minutes) stretch on for hours of rewrites.

For example, here's a reenactment of the work that went into a simple e-mail conversation with my coworker Jon this morning:

> Jon: I just wanted to email all of you to let you know I won't be into work today because we have to put our beloved dog to sleep.

> Me: I have one testicle. In a jar. A dog testicle, I mean. Not like, I *personally* have one testicle. Because that would be weird. For a girl. I guess, probably for a guy too. I'm just saying that when my dog had to have one cancerous testicle removed I thought I should keep it because I never got to keep my tonsils when they removed them and I thought, "*Next best thing, right*?" And thank God I kept it because like two weeks later my dog ran away and now all I have is this testicle to remember him by.

Me: I'm so sorry, Jon! I'm reminded of what my grandmother once said to me. "Losing a pet is like losing a family member." Except that it's way less expensive because you don't have to get it embalmed and instead of buying a casket you can just bury it in the backyard.

Me: Penis.

Me: Jon, my heart is with you today. Attached is a copy of Rainbow Bridge, and a small poem by Maya Angelou.

Jon: This is exactly what I needed. How did you know?

Me: I know how difficult it can be to let go. I still can't bear to throw away my dog's testicle and it's been fucking *years*, Jon. I mean, I don't even know if he's *dead*. He might have just run away because he didn't like me. Or maybe he was afraid I was going to take his other testicle. Or maybe he was just an asshole, Jon. Sometimes dogs can be assholes too.

Me: I know how hard it is to say goodbye.

In short? *It is exhausting being me.* Pretending to be normal is draining and requires amazing amounts of energy and Xanax. In fact, I should probably charge money to all the normal people to simply *not* go to your social functions and ruin them. Especially since I end up spending so much money on sedatives to keep my anxiety at least *slightly* in check, and those expenses are not even tax-deductible. Still, it's worth the personal expense, because being drugged enough to appear semicoherent is preferable to being treated like an unwelcome polar bear at a dinner party.

See that last sentence? A sane, rational person would have written "an unwelcome *guest* at a dinner party," but not me. I *started* to write "unwelcome guest," and then my brain said, "Hang on. What's even *more* unwelcome than an unwelcome guest? *A fucking polar bear.*" Then the normal, slow-to-intercede, good side of my head comes over and says, "*No. No one is going to get that. Just write 'guest' instead.*" Then the bad side is all, "*Really?* Because it makes *total* sense to me. If an unwanted guest shows up at your party the worst thing that'll happen is maybe you'll run out of Tostitos early. If a *polar bear* shows up at a party there's going to be blood everywhere. Polar bears aren't welcome ANYWHERE." And then the good side would smile patronizingly and sigh, saying, "No one understands your logic, asshole. And also polar bears *are* welcome some places. Like zoos. And Coke commercials." But the bad side of my mind isn't having it and he's yelling, "*The cage at the zoo is there to keep them from us. BECAUSE* THEY'RE UNWELCOME," and then the good side is all, "Well, if you hate polar bears so damn much then why did we go to the zoo on Saturday?" and the bad side is all, "Because you promised me a blow job, *you condescending bitch*," and then the good side just gasps like she can't even believe the bad side would even go there, because *that shit's supposed to be private, bad side,* and she gets all sullen and sanctimonious and maybe we should just leave now because this whole thing is uncomfortable, and why does this feel like domestic violence? And also how can the bad side of my mind even *get* a blow job? Is it a dude? This whole thing is confusing, and feels somehow sexist. See, if I were trying to impress you I would have deleted this whole paragraph and just changed "polar bear" to "unwanted guest," but I'm leaving it all out there because I'm too lazy to erase it. And also *to show you the difficult truth about the pain of living with a mental illness.* Mostly that first part, though. And basically this entire paragraph is what it's like in my head all the time. *So, yeah.* It's a goddamn mess in here.

I thank God, though, that I do at least *possess* the good side of my brain, because I once had a neighbor who lost the impulse-control part of his mind in a car accident and would randomly yell strange things at me when I'd go check the mailbox. Things like "Hi, pretty lady! Your butt is getting bigger!" and "I'd still plow that ass!" I'd always just force a smile and wave at him, because, yes, it was kind of insulting, but I'm fairly sure he meant it to be complimentary. I mean, that guy didn't even *have* a good side of the brain to filter his thoughts, so it seems a bit selfish of me to not be thankful for mine, even if it is kind of broken and seems to recognize how fucked up the things that I'm talking about are only after I've already said them. It's like I have a censor in my head, but she works on a seven-second delay . . . well-meaning, but perpetually about seven seconds too late to actually do anything to stop the horrific avalanche of *shit-you-shouldn't-say-out-loud-but-I-just-did.*

In a way it's a gift to be able to recognize your faults, but in real life I find myself saying terrible things to people, and the part of me that recognizes how inappropriate what I just said was screams at me, *"No!* We don't talk about vibrators to clergymen!" Then I get distracted by all the screaming going on in my head, and I panic and here come the credit card numbers again. Or I'll blurt out something else to fill the awkward silence, but for some reason the part of my mind that doesn't have a filter can think only about necrophilia, and the part of my brain that recognizes that necrophilia is *never* an appropriate topic yells, *"NECROPHILIA IS BAD,"* and so then I panic and hear myself start talking about *why* necrophilia is bad, and the part of me that is slightly sane is shaking her head at myself as she watches all the people struggle to think of an appropriate way to respond to a girl at a cocktail party who is against necrophilia. I feel sorry for those people. Not just because they have to be there to witness that train wreck, but also because who is going to disagree with the evils of necrophilia? *Nobody, that's who.* And if you try to change the subject it's just going to look like you're a secret proponent of necrophilia who just doesn't want to admit it in public. That's probably why, when I'm speaking to groups at dinner parties, those people slowly back away to join any other conversation, and I end up standing alone and talking to myself. Which is awesome. Because if there's one thing more awkward than a girl talking to strangers at a cocktail party about sex with dead people, it's a girl at a cocktail party talking to herself about *the exact same thing.*

This is why whenever I see disheveled homeless people on the street, screaming to no one in particular about how bears are evil masterminds trying to take over the city, I immediately assume that years earlier they'd found themselves discussing this subject at a dinner party, horrified themselves into a complete mental breakdown, and then everyone else just wandered away. And now here this homeless woman is, *years later*, still trying to find a way to wrap up this conversation with dignity and failing miserably. This is why I always give homeless people a dollar and some Xanax. Because I know exactly what they're going through. Also, I like to nod and try to add something to the conversation, like "It's an interesting theory, however, I'm not sure whether bears have the cognitive ability to create a complex system of government," but usually the person I'm talking to just stares past me, fixated on a long-gone horrified audience that now exists only in her head. Then my husband will pull me away, lecturing me about the dangers of provoking the homeless. He doesn't see what I see: the desperate face of a person who has been driven mad by a dinner party.

You would think Victor would be more sympathetic, since he's actually witnessed the emotional devastation I leave behind when forced to mingle, but until only recently he had dismissed my ability to completely destroy both our reputations in a single dinner party as an overexaggeration on my part. I can only assume that he placed so little importance on my inability to deal with social situations because (a) my actual anxiety attacks were so severe that in comparison my social awkwardness seemed mild, and (b) he just wasn't paying that much attention.

And to be fair, the anxiety attacks are much more disturbing to watch, and I'm very lucky that the worst of them happen only a few times a year. One moment I'm perfectly fine and the next I feel a wave of nausea, then panic. Then I can't catch my breath and I know I'm about to lose control and all I want to do is escape. Except that the one thing I can't escape from is the very thing I want to run away from . . . *me*. And inevitably it's in a crowded restaurant or during a dinner party or in another state, miles from any kind of sanctuary.

I feel the panic build up, like a lion caught my chest, clawing its way out of my throat. I try to hold it back but my dinner mates can sense something has changed, and they look at me furtively, worried. *I'm obvious.* I want to crawl under the table to hide until it passes, but that's not something you can explain away at a dinner party. I feel dizzy and suspect I'll faint or get hysterical. This is the worst part, because I don't even know what it will be like this time. "I'm sick," I mutter to my dinner mates, unable to say anything else without hyperventilating. I rush out of the restaurant, smiling weakly at the people staring at me. They try to be understanding but they don't understand. I run outside to escape the worried eyes of people who love me, people who are afraid of me, strangers who wonder what's wrong with me. I vainly hope they'll assume I'm just drunk, but I know that they know. Every wild-eyed glance of mine screams, "MENTAL ILLNESS."

Later someone will find me outside the restaurant, huddled in a ball, and lay their cool hand on my feverish back, trying to comfort me. They ask if I'm okay, more gently if they know my history. I nod and try to smile apologetically and roll my eyes at myself in mock derision so I won't have to talk. They assume it's because I'm embarrassed, and I let them assume that because it's easier, and also because I *am* embarrassed. But it's not the reason I don't talk. I keep my mouth closed tightly because I don't know whether I could stop myself from screaming if I opened my mouth. My hands ache from the fists I hadn't realized I'd clenched. My body shouts to run. Every nerve is alive and on fire. If I get to my drugs in time I can cut off the worst parts . . . the shaking involuntarily, the feeling of being shocked with an electrical current, the horrible knowledge that the world is going to end and no one knows it but me. If I don't get to the drugs in time, they do nothing and I'm a limp rag for days afterward.

I know other people who are like me. They take the same drugs as me. They try all the therapies. They are brilliant and amazing and forever broken. I'm lucky that although Victor doesn't understand it, he *tries* to understand, telling me, "Relax. There's absolutely nothing to panic about." I smile gratefully at him and pretend that's all I needed to hear and that this is just a silly phase that will pass one day. I *know* there's nothing to panic about. And that's exactly what makes it so much worse.

Those are the painful days that I think distort Victor's view of just how badly I deal with people. They're the days when I'm certain he thinks that a little anxiety-induced social awkwardness is really nothing in comparison to a full-blown attack. And then I have to prove him wrong.

Case in point: This weekend Victor took me to a Halloween dinner party for his coworkers. I'd reminded him beforehand that he was making a terrible mistake, because he'd seen over the years a few examples of me fucking up parties. But he patted my leg and assured me I'd be fine. It was exactly the same way he'd patted our cat reassuringly right before we'd had it euthanized. It was *not* reassuring.

The drive to the party was long, which worked against me, because already the sedatives I'd taken were wearing off, and it gave me more time to worry about our choice of costumes. We were dressed as Craig and Arianna, the Spartan cheerleaders from *Saturday Night Live*. When I'd bought the costumes I'd thought it was a pretty iconic pop-culture reference, but when Hailey's babysitter arrived she'd had *no damn idea who we were.*

"You know? *The Spartans? From Saturday Night Live?*" I asked, trying

Victor and me as Craig and Arianna. One of us is not even fucking trying.

not to let the hysteria seep into my voice as Victor (who had never wanted to be a male cheerleader in the first place and still hadn't forgiven me for picking out the costume) just glared at me. The babysitter stared at me blankly. *"COME ON, YOU KNOW THIS!"* I may have shrieked a little, and then Victor pulled at my arm to go because we'd lost our first babysitter that way, and so I took a deep, calming breath and said, "It wasn't *that* long ago, Dani. *Remember?* It was in the nineties?" and then she said, "O-o-oh. I was *born* in the nineties." And then I kicked her in the stomach. But only in my head, because that's kind of how we lost our second babysitter.

Still, Dani's saucy ignorance of *shit that was on TV before she was born* was still fresh on my mind as we drove to the party. I tried to clear my head by reminding myself to not accidentally show people my vagina. This is not a usual worry for me; however, the cheerleader skirt was made of a clingy polyester material that kept riding up on my underwear whenever I moved, so rather than continually pulling down my skirt all night long, I'd decided it would be wiser to just go commando instead. I was still a little nervous about this decision when we pulled up to Victor's boss's house, though, and as we walked up the long driveway toward the large home I quickly whispered to Victor, "By the way? *I'm not wearing any underwear.*" He stopped in his tracks and furrowed his brow in undisguised panic.

"I'm not trying to seduce you," I assured him. "I'm just telling you so that you would, ya know, *be aware.*"

Victor stared at me, horrified. "Be aware of *what?*"

"You know," I explained, "in case you decided we needed to do any really physical cheers, you'd be aware of the whole '*careful around the old vagina*' thing."

Victor paused at the doorway and stared at me, his mouth slightly agape. A small sheen of sweat was beginning to form over his forehead. "We are *NOT* going to do any cheers. I didn't even want to *wear* this damn costume, for Christ sake, and *WHY THE HELL ARE YOU NOT WEARING UNDER-WEAR?!*" Then I told him to be quiet or his boss would hear him, and that's when Victor started shaking a little bit. It worried me, because only one of us was allowed to have a panic attack at a time, and I'd already called dibs. I wondered internally whether I should explain *why* I wasn't wearing underwear or just stay quiet, because at this point he seemed so irrational I didn't even think that I could get him to understand the science of panty lines. Then I looked through the beveled-glass door of Victor's boss's house and noticed four people on the couch watching TV.

And exactly none of them were in costume.

This was when I considered running away, because forcing your husband to wear a cheerleader costume for Halloween is grounds for divorce, but dressing him as a male cheerleader at his boss's party where everyone else is in Dockers will totally get you stabbed. Then I realized that if I ran back to our car now, Victor would probably notice that no one inside the house was in costume, and then he'd quietly follow me back out to the car and stab me in private, and the last thing I wanted was to be stabbed anywhere. I quickly decided I was probably safer with witnesses, so I rang the doorbell before Victor could realize the severity of the situation. Then he pulled his (still aghast) face from mine to turn toward the door, and that's when he noticed that no one in the house was wearing costumes.

"What. *The. Fuck?*" was all he managed to get out before a man in his late fifties opened the door. The man looked at us strangely, which I thought was rather rude for a host, and I thought I'd just get it out of the way, so I blurted out, "*You know . . .* the Spartans? From *Saturday Night Live?*" He just kept staring, with his brow furrowed like he was still trying to place us, and I shrugged in defeat and said, "Meh. Don't worry about it. The babysitter didn't get it either."

Victor cleared his throat and gave me the *"Please shut up"* look, while the man at the door said, "I'm sorry. Can I *help* you?" Then Victor explained that we were here for the party and that *apparently* we'd read the invitation wrong (*insert unnecessary glare at me*), because we'd thought it was a costume party, and that's when the guy stopped us and said, *"There's no party here."* I assumed he was just trying to get rid of us, but then Victor pulled out the invitation and the man helpfully pointed out that we were on North Cleveland Street and we wanted South Cleveland Street. He seemed very relieved to clear this up until I suddenly blurted out, "Oh, *thank Christ!*" Then he looked at me oddly again. Probably because he's an atheist who doesn't understand how thankful I was to God that I wasn't going to get stabbed for forcing my husband to wear a cheerleader outfit to a business-casual affair. Atheists never understand that sort of thing.

A few minutes later, Victor and I arrived at the proper address to find a house covered in Halloween decorations and several people milling around outside in costume. I said a quiet prayer, except I guess it wasn't quiet enough, because Victor gave me the stink-eye and asked whether I could please try to be on my best behavior tonight. He gave me a list of things to *not* talk about in front of mixed company. "Divorce, death, politics, heroin, sex, cancer, *swallowing needles*," he droned on. "These are all things *not* to talk about."

"Got it," I assured him.

He looked at me dubiously. "Also, most of these people are conservative Republicans, so *please* don't talk about how much you love Obama. I have to work with these people. And nothing about vaginas or necrophilia"— he'd actually been there for that one—"or ninjas or how your great-great-great-uncle murdered your great-great-great-aunt with a hammer." I tried to nod an assent, but all of those things he'd just mentioned got stuck there in my head, and I struggled vainly to think of anything to talk about besides the prohibited subjects. I had nothing.

Luckily, the party was fairly loud, and, this being Texas, most of the guests were already drunk and talkative, and so I was able to just smile mindlessly and nod in agreement to whatever everyone else was saying. Victor and I settled into the periphery of a large group of his colleagues. Truthfully, it would have been difficult to get a word into the conversation dominated by a man dressed as John McCain (I shit you not), who launched into a tirade about Obama coming to steal all our guns (*"Where would he even keep them?"* I wondered), and I could see the panic in Victor's eyes as he tensed and silently begged me to stay quiet. I bit my tongue and forced a smile. I could see the relief in Victor's face as he sighed deeply, and I smiled and rolled my eyes at his doubt, but costumed McCain must've noticed our exchange, because he chuckled and raised an eyebrow suspiciously as he asked, "What's this? Do we have a bleeding-heart liberal in our midst?" And that's when everything started to get all fuzzy, because I was *explicitly* warned not to talk politics, and so I froze in panic and searched my mind for any appropriate response that would change the subject. Then, after a moment of painful silence that seemed to hush everyone around us, I blurted out what was likely the most improbable sentence ever uttered at a dinner party:

"One time I got stabbed in the face by a serial killer."

And even *more* unsettling was the fact that I'd managed to utter the baffling non sequitur in a completely serious, nonchalant fashion. As if people got stabbed in the face all the time. Also? *I have no fucking idea why I said that.* Then Victor looked at me like he was having a stroke, and he started to change colors, and through a clenched jaw he forced out, "Ha, ha, honey! What the *hell* did *that* have to do with anything?" and I knew he was trying to give me an out, or possibly just trying to distance himself from me. I probably should have just blamed the booze, but instead I thought I could salvage the situation by explaining that not-McCain had mentioned guns, which reminded me of knives, and *that's* when I was reminded of the time that a serial killer stabbed me in the face with a knife, but then it got even weirder when I explained all that, and people began looking uncomfortable and laughing nervously. Then Victor started glaring at me and I got kind of caught up in defending myself, because I'M TRYING TO HELP HERE. If anything, Victor should have been mad at McCain, because this was basically all *his* fault. The guy in costume, I mean, not former presidential nominee John McCain. He wasn't even there. I'm not even sure why I have to clarify this.

Then Victor started clearing his throat and tried to change the subject, but there's honestly no way to put the lid back on an open serial-killer story, and people start pressuring you, and then they notice the faint scar across your face, and that's when you *have* to tell the serial-killer story. In fact, right now you're thinking, "Did she really get stabbed in the face by a serial killer?" And don't bother to deny it, because you just read it, so you *have* to be thinking about it. This is the way books work. Also? *Velociraptors.* Ha! I just made you think about velociraptors. *Awesome.* This is probably why Stephen King writes so many books. I am *totally* controlling your mind right now.

But the answer to your question is, "Yes. *Yes*, I did totally get stabbed in the face by a serial killer. *Sort of.*" Which is exactly what I told all the people at the party. Then Victor almost divorced me. And what's really tragic here is that *technically* this is sort of Victor's fault, because at this point I was prepared to just tell everyone I was drunk and then go hide in the bathroom, but Victor decided to tell everyone I was drunk first and then I got too irritated at him to be worried about talking in front of strangers, because *clearly* he wasn't taking my being stabbed in the face seriously. Victor then pointed out that that was because it wasn't entirely true that I'd been stabbed in the face by a serial killer, and he did have a point, but by then everyone was a little riveted and intrigued. Also, none of them had ever seen the horror ride that my dinner party conversations take, so instead of agreeing with Victor's suggestion that I go lie down, they demanded that I tell the story. Those people were fucked.

I realized almost immediately that this was a mistake, but I figured I could still salvage this situation, so I took a deep breath and explained that I had simply fallen asleep watching a documentary about serial killers, and that it must've stuck with me, because I started having this dream where I was getting chased by the Night Stalker, who was wielding a large knife, and *AND HE STABBED ME IN THE FUCKING FACE.* And the pain in my face got hotter and sharper, and all of a sudden I started screaming, and that's when I woke myself up and realized that it was all just a dream.

This is where people always laugh politely. Coincidentally, it's also where I should stop telling this story. I'll try to remember that for next time.

But, of course, I *didn't* stop there, because my internal censor was still seven seconds behind and she was too busy freaking out about the fact that I'd just said the F-word out loud to tell me to *shut up now.*

So I leaned forward conspiratorially, saying to the relieved crowd, "But then I kept hearing screaming and it turns out it was *me* screaming, because I ACTUALLY *HAD* BEEN STABBED IN THE FACE."

This was when everyone stopped laughing and Victor began looking physically ill. It was also when I started to panic and I began speaking way too quickly so that I could finish and run away.

"So then Victor wakes up and sees my face covered in blood and is all, 'WHAT THE FUCK?!'" I related to the group of awestruck bystanders. "And I'm like, '*I KNOW, RIGHT?* THE NIGHT STALKER STABBED ME!' and right then Victor jumps up and unsheathes his sword and runs down the hall brandishing his sword after the Night Stalker, which was weird, because the documentary had said he was still in jail, but I guess when you wake up and your wife's been stabbed you probably aren't thinking terribly straight, and personally I was just impressed at how quickly he'd unsheathed his sword to run down the hall after a dangerous serial kill—"

Victor interrupted me: "Please, *for the love of God, stop talking.*"

I looked at him curiously and wondered what part of the story he was most appalled by, and then quickly clarified, "*Oh!* When I said he 'unsheathed his sword,' I didn't mean his penis, y'all. I was referring to the samurai sword we keep next to the bed. Victor wasn't running down the hall waving his penis at a serial killer. *I mean, that would be ridiculous.*" I laughed. No one else laughed.

"*Aaaanyway,*" I continued, "Victor searched through the house, but no one was there but us, and all the doors were still locked. Victor tried to convince me that I must have accidentally scratched myself, but I was doubtful. Then the next day at work my coworkers assumed that Victor must be battering me, and so I explained the serial-killer dreams, and of course *none of them believed me,* which is pretty insulting actually, because I can assure you, if my husband *had* actually stabbed me in the face I'd have enough sense to come up with a better story than one about a serial killer attacking me in my dreams."

This is the point where I really, really want to stop talking, but I couldn't because I was so freaked out at how badly this whole thing had gone that I was desperate to find an end and was too panicked to do it correctly. I vaguely wished that Victor would set fire to the house to distract everyone, but he didn't, because Victor is very unhelpful.

I continued. "Of course, then I was terrified that perhaps now everything that happened to me in a dream would actually happen to me in real life, so I could potentially wake up wearing a dress made out of pickles at my high school. Or with arms made out of marshmallows, or with a leg missing. Then, about a week later, Victor and I were lying in bed when suddenly there was a scratching noise coming from the window above the headboard, which sounded like a knife scraping deliberately down the wall. I was paralyzed with fear, but I slowly turned my face up toward the window, and that's when I saw *THE GIGANTIC ASS OF MY CAT*. Turns out that our fat-ass cat, Posey, was trying to perch on the tiny window ledge, but he didn't fit, so he had one of his back legs clawing desperately at the wall as he slowly lost his footing, and that's when I figured out what had happened. My enormous, fat cat had fallen on my face and scratched me with his huge, catty talons while I was dreaming about serial killers. And *that's* why ten years later I still have this scar."

Then everyone looked at me in bafflement, and Victor made me leave, swearing to never take me to another dinner party again. It was hard to argue with him, but I did point out that the party was kind of a win, because no one saw my vagina. Victor says we have different definitions of what a "win" is. Then he told me that stories about serial killers who are really just cats are now at the top of the list of "shit-I'm-not-allowed-to-talk-about," and that's when I really got a little indignant, because technically he kind of *owes me*, because he came out looking like a damn American hero in that serial-killer story for charging through the house to kill a serial killer who was actually a cat. Then he pointed out that cats aren't serial killers, and I retorted that technically cats are *more* dangerous than serial killers because they are too fluffy to be suspects, and that if Posey had landed a few inches lower he could have sliced my jugular. Basically, Posey is the silent killer. Much like cholesterol.

I tried to calm Victor by explaining that when we got home I could patch this all up with a witty e-mail to his coworkers that had nothing to do with getting stabbed in the face by anyone.

"And then what?" Victor asked.

"And *then*," I explained, "it will be fine, because I'll be so charming that they'll forgive me. Besides, most of the people who were there seemed drunk anyway, and there's no way they'll believe I *actually* told that horrible of a story when they wake up tomorrow." But then Victor pointed out that even if I *did* manage to convince them of my normalness through e-mail, I would just end up doing this again, and he was right, which is why next time I'm at a dinner party I'm just going to pretend I have laryngitis and insist that everyone bring their cell phones so I can simply text them. Except, I grudgingly admitted to Victor, I'll probably panic and tell the first person I see that I can't talk because a leopard ate my larynx, and then I'll use my phone to show people how much the magnified human larynx looks like a vagina. Victor looked at me in defeat and I pulled out my phone to find larynx videos to prove my point. And that was when Victor sighed deeply and made me stop talking to him. Which is to be expected, I guess.

Me, hiding in the bathroom.

I'll apologize to him tomorrow.

By e-mail.

Thanks for
the Zombies, Jesus

Car conversation with Victor:

ME: Oh my God, did you see the name of that cemetery we just passed? *"Resurrection Cemetery."* What a horrible name for a cemetery.

VICTOR: It's because they believe in the resurrection of believers, dumb-ass.

ME: *Still.* Some things just shouldn't be resurrected. Just what we need is a bunch of damn zombies wandering the earth.

VICTOR: That's not "resurrection." That's *"reanimation."*

ME: Same difference. Although I guess *"Reanimation Cemetery"* would sound way more creepy.

VICTOR: It's not the same difference. Zombies are reanimated, but they don't have their previous mental capacity, so it's not a resurrection. *Technically* that's a "zombification."

ME: Well, if you want to get all *technical*, then how about vampires?

VICTOR: Um . . . *they're fine?*

ME: What I mean is, vampires have their "previous mental capacity," thus by your logic they are "resurrected." Might as well name it "*Jesus-Is-Bringing-You-Vampires* Cemetery."

VICTOR: No. That's not the same thing, because when you resurrect someone from the grave they aren't undead.

ME: No, they are TOTALLY undead. That's like the very *definition* of the undead.

VICTOR: No. A vampire is undead. The resurrected aren't undead.

ME: I think you don't know what "undead" means.

VICTOR: I THINK *YOU* DON'T KNOW WHAT "UNDEAD" MEANS!

ME: Oh my God, *calm down, Darwin.* Don't get all crazy just 'cause I threw a vampire monkey wrench in your faulty Jesus-zombie logic.

VICTOR: [sigh] Look, there are all sorts of exceptions you aren't considering. You can reanimate someone without making them a real "zombie." For instance, you could bring them back simply to perform a task.

ME: Yeah. And that's called *a zombie.*

VICTOR: *No,* because it wouldn't crave brains. It'd just have a job to do. *Look it up.*

ME: Oh, I *will* look it up. I'll look it up in *The Dictionary of Shit That Doesn't Exist.*

VICTOR: [glower]

***** *Five minutes of angry silence* *****

ME: So, I was talking to the organ donation lady at work the other day and she told me a secret way that you can't *not* give away my organs.

VICTOR: You know what? I fucking *dare* you to make less sense.

ME: Well, I know you're anti–organ donation, and so I told her I was afraid that you wouldn't let the doctor take my organs if I died first, but she said if I list my mom as my next of kin on my donor card then they won't even ask you for your permission.

VICTOR: If you want to throw away all your organs I won't stop you. Just don't come complaining to me when I see you in the afterlife and you're all, *"Oh my God, I just peed all over myself because someone else has my bladder."*

ME: *Fine.* And if you die first I'm totally donating your organs too.

VICTOR: *Like hell you are.* I may need them.

ME: Why would you need them? YOU'RE DEAD.

VICTOR: What if I become a zombie? Huh, smart-ass? I'd be a pretty shitty zombie if they took my eyes out. I'd be biting poles and cats and shit.

ME: So you're making a decision to not save someone's life on the off chance that it *might* be inconvenient *if you turn into a less efficient zombie?*

VICTOR: It sounds stupid when you say it.

ME: Fine. I'll just donate the parts that a zombie doesn't need. Like your skin. Or your brain tissue.

VICTOR: Zombies need brains.

ME: No, zombies *eat* brains. And then those victims become other zombies, even though their brains have been eaten by other zombies, so obviously you could donate your brain and still be a functional zombie.

VICTOR: Yeah, and then I've gotta spend eternity wandering the world as a mindless idiot.

ME: [snort]

VICTOR: Shut up.

ME: I didn't say anything.

VICTOR: If zombie-me finds out I've got parts missing you will be the very first person I eat.

ME: What if you die in a car crash and Hailey is badly injured and the only way she can survive is if she can have your kidneys?

VICTOR: She'd be a pretty fucked-up-looking toddler with my gigantic man-size kidneys in her.

ME: Okay, what if she's sixteen when it happens?

VICTOR: If she's sixteen and I die then she can totally have my stuff. But just the nonessential stuff . . . like an arm or some fingers.

ME: I'm sure she'll be the most popular girl in school with your hairy old man arm.

VICTOR: Ooh, and if a boy started getting fresh with her she could be all, "Don't make me get my dad hand out!"

ME: I wonder if this is the weirdest fight we've ever had.

VICTOR: Not. Even. Close.

Making Friends
with Girls

For the majority of my life I lived with a small, terrible secret: I've never really liked girls. I realize this is stereotypical and hypocritical, since I am one myself, but to be fair, I probably wouldn't choose to hang out with myself if given the option.

It's always been this way. I was too much of an anxious misfit to properly bond with girls when I was young, and I never really got the hang of it. I consoled myself by thinking of how much money I saved on Christmas gifts for friends that I never made, and reassured myself that not having bridesmaids or friends to give me a bachelorette party was perfectly normal. Whenever I hear of women who are still best friends with the girls they went to school with, I always make a mental note to avoid them, because I assume they're compulsive liars.

Even as an adult I had mostly male friends, and I looked at most girls as judgy, cruel, fickle, and likely to borrow your Cabbage Patch doll and never give it back. Victor always pushed me to find girlfriends, but I'd convinced myself that girls are like small bears: cute to look at, but far too dangerous to have lunch with.

This all changed when I discovered blogging and found other people online who were misanthropic misfits like me, and I found myself proudly telling Victor of my new best friends whom I would almost certainly never meet.

"OHMYGOD, Raptor99 is going to have another baby!" I'd say excitedly, as Victor pointed out that he had no idea who that was. "You know," I explained. "Raptor99 is that person who survived cancer last year, and is considering coming out of the closet? Remember all the time I spent on the computer last month, convincing someone that they needed to get help for their bulimia? *That was Raptor99.*"

"Huh. Is Raptor99 a boy or a girl?" Victor asked.

"I don't actually know," I said. "Their avatar is a dolphin."

Then Victor pointed out that it didn't really count as being "great friends with someone" if you didn't know whether they were a boy, a girl, or a dolphin. I had to admit he had a point, so I decided to get out of the house and meet a fellow mom blogger named Laura for lunch, whom I'd bonded with online over the mutual terror of raising a toddler. It was surprisingly awesome, but it was also a slippery slope that led to meeting more and more people. My anxiety-ridden personality clashed with the very idea of making friends, especially girlfriends. Laura tried to convince me that there *were* actually interesting and fairly nonjudgmental women who wouldn't make fun of the fact that I often had to hide under tables when I was overwhelmed. I didn't believe her, but I took a deep breath and decided to trust her, because if nothing else, this would be the perfect experiment to prove my theory that most grown women are just as dangerous as the kids on the playground who wouldn't let you play tetherball with them because you didn't have Wonder Woman Underoos.

Over the next two years, I became tentative friends with the bloggers Laura introduced me to, and I was eventually invited to go to a weekend all-girl retreat in California wine country for a small group of bloggers. It would include wine tasting and group yoga, and I could not have been less enthused, but Laura was one of the hostesses and told me I was being ridiculous. "Besides," she reminded me, "you *did* tell me that one of your goals this year was to make friends with girls." She was right, but at the same time she reminded me why girls make both great and terrible friends: They actually listen to your goals, even when you're too drunk to know what you're saying. I *had* said that I felt I needed to try to find girlfriends, but what I really wanted were down-to-earth chicks who drank Strawberry Hill slushees nonironically, and who would respond to an invitation of "Let's go to a wine tasting and a day spa" with the same sort of horrified reaction as if someone had said, "Let's go join the circus and then burn it to the ground."

Laura stared at me as I tried to come up with an excuse. "It's true, I *did* say I wanted girlfriends," I capitulated hesitantly, "but couldn't we start with something smaller and less terrifying? Like maybe spend a weekend at a crack house? I heard those people are very nonjudgmental, and if you accidentally say something offensive you can just blame it on their hallucinations."

"Tempting . . ." Laura replied, "but let's try this first. We can always check out the crack house later."

The four-day getaway was headed up by a blogger named Maggie, whom I knew in passing, and who had recently gotten a giant corporation to sponsor her life list. She'd been to Greece, had a giant public food fight, and swum in Puerto Rico, all paid for by the sponsor, and possibly by selling her soul. Next on her list was hosting a small girls' retreat, and so she'd decided to host *The Broad Summit,* so named because we were a bunch of broads. I can only assume *The Vagina Venue* was taken.

Women scare me enough, but bloggers can be even more frightening to deal with. Most bloggers are emotionally unstable and are often awkward in social situations, which is why so many of us turned to blogging in the first place. Also, they are always looking for something to write about, so if you fuck something up it will be blogged, Facebooked, and retweeted until your death. It would be lot like Lindsay Lohan spending a weekend with *TMZ* and the *National Enquirer*, and I suspect that one day my gravestone will simply read: JENNY LAWSON: SHE WAS MISQUOTED ON TWITTER.

I assume that to most people wine country sounds wonderful, but it's not my thing. Wine tastings and massages and facials and pajama parties at a small hotel sounded like something that would be fun for rich people who weren't me, and who actually owned pajamas. I was trying to think up excuses to get out of this party when my invitation arrived: It was a small wine box with a bottle of booze and a crazy straw. Victor saw it and encouraged me to go and make new friends, and I RSVPed "yes" because I got drunk on the invitation. Then I spent the next week regretting that decision.

A conversation with my sister three days before the event:

ME: I'm going to Napa Valley for a party and I'm terrified. Everyone at this retreat is probably fashionable and hip, and a lot of them are designers, and I don't have anything designer to wear.

MY SISTER: Just pretend to be bohemian, and they'll think you're avant-garde.

ME: Well, I *do* have a fancy purse, but I've never used it. This sex company sent me a giant metal dildo wrapped in a Kate Spade bag in hopes that I'd blog about it.

MY SISTER: You owning a Kate Spade bag is even weirder than the fact that someone sent you a dildo in it.

ME: I know. That's why it's still in the box, along with the dildo. I'm totally going to bring it with me, though, and use it like a shield, so people will think I belong there. Basically I'll use it the same way you use crucifixes on Draculas.

MY SISTER: The dildo?

ME: The purse.

MY SISTER: Ah. Don't tell that story to anyone there.

ME: It's probably the first thing I'm going to say. The last e-mail I got about the get-together suggested several shoe changes *in one day*. I only have one pair of nice shoes and they're flats.

MY SISTER: Well, you have arthritis, so you have a good excuse.

ME: Yes, but I feel like I need to put that on my shirt: "Please don't judge my flats. I have a disability." I won't have anything to change into when everyone else changes shoes. I have socks, though. I can change into socks.

MY SISTER: Oh, you're totally fucked.

Two days before the event:

ME: Okay, I just saw the invitation list, and I'm *completely freaked about this party*. It's like everyone else there is part of the cheer squad, and I'm that weird girl with the back brace who ate too much glue.

LAURA: You need to stop freaking out about this. It's going to be super laid-back and casual, and you need to relax and have fun. Just bring a few pairs of jeans and some shirts and you're set.

ME: I don't own any jeans.

LAURA: *You're a damn liar.*

ME: How many years have you known me? Have you *ever* seen me wear jeans?

LAURA: *Wow.* No. There might be something wrong with you.

ME: *This is exactly what I've been trying to tell you.*

The day before the event:

Karen (a wonderful and sweet blogger whom Laura had introduced me to) found out that I didn't own jeans, and decided to have a shopping intervention.

KAREN: I can't believe you don't wear jeans. Jeans are fabulous, and crazy comfortable. Jeans are like underwear. It's like just wearing your underwear around.

ME (from inside the fitting room): No. *Dresses* are like wearing underwear, because guess what I'm wearing under my dress? Just underwear. And sometimes? *Not even underwear.*

I stepped out of the dressing room.

KAREN: Ooh. *See?* Those are cute jeans. You should get them.

ME: Mmm. No. My knees look fat in these.

KAREN: Um . . . *what?*

ME: *You* wouldn't understand, because you've always been thin, but when you're fat your kneecaps get tired of supporting all of your weight, and so when you lock your knees they bend backward. That's why I always concentrate really hard on always bending slightly at the knee, so that I don't have fat-girl kneecaps.

KAREN: I love you, but I can't even tell you how insane you sound right now. Like, most of the time you're fine, but right now? *Totally insane.*

ME: You probably just weren't listening those other times.

The first day of the party, on the plane:

You know when the captain comes on over the overhead speaker and says, "We're going to take off in a few minutes, but we're going to be without air-conditioning for a bit because we don't have auxiliary power, and we're having problems with one engine so we're going to have to get out on the runway before we can get it started"? That's when you should probably just get off the plane. But I couldn't, because I was too terrified to move, so instead I just asked the guy next to me whether he thought this was some sort of joke. He didn't, and told me it was nothing to worry about. "Yeah," I said, my voice becoming shrill with fear, "but they just said we don't have both engines working. *I'm pretty sure two engines are preferable.*"

He rubbed my hand patronizingly and told me I'd be fine, and I assumed he was hitting on me, so I said, "I'm married." Then he looked at me strangely and said, "Congratulations?" He probably wasn't hitting on me at all. More likely he just wanted me to shut up. Then the stewardess came on the speaker, and instead of saying, "At this time we ask you to turn off any portable equipment," she said, "If you're on a cell phone, tell them good-bye." And I'm all, *"Why did she say 'Good-bye' with such an air of finality?"* The guy sitting next to me didn't respond. Probably because he knew we weren't going to make it out alive.

Amazingly enough, we landed. I was supposed to meet a fellow blogger at baggage claim so we could share a ride, but I'm terrible with faces, and

I suddenly realized that unless she was wearing the trench coat from her blog picture I was in huge trouble. Instead I called her and told her to come find me. "You'll know me by my black hat," I said.

"*I know what you look like, Jenny.*" She laughed good-naturedly. "You don't need a hat for me to recognize you."

Fuck. Now I'm wondering whether we've met before. Which stories have I told her? Have I offended her in the past? Panic. Plus, she said it in a way like "Duh. *Of course* we'll know each other," and so I began just staring at every single girl in the airport with a smile and a fake look of familiarity until they looked away awkwardly. That's how you know they aren't looking for a stranger in a hat. Turned out, though, that Susan actually *was* wearing the trench coat from her bio picture, but I'd walked right past her because it seemed too obvious. Then she yelled out, "JENNY! *Where are you going?*" I'd failed the first test and it wasn't even a trick question.

The hotel was small, quaint, and simple, and when we first walked in we were greeted by the owner's dog from the hotel ad, who had gotten the hotel Frisbee in his mouth. The logo was perfectly lined up and everyone was all, "OMG, he's so cute!" but all I could think was, "They totally stapled that Frisbee to his tongue so it would stay like that." Because that's where my mind goes. I considered putting one of my blog stickers on the Frisbee when the owners weren't looking, but those things don't come off easily, and the owners would probably be all, "FUCK. Now we have to staple a new Frisbee to the dog's mouth." That's not even worth the publicity. Mostly because it was a tiny hotel and not many people would see it. And also because stapling advertisements to dogs' mouths is wrong.

I was wearing the jeans Karen had persuaded me to buy, and a 1930s-style black hat that I'd hoped screamed, "I'm a bohemian vintage shopper."

Then I realized that there was an orange Target price tag stuck to the back that said "Now $7.48." Awesome. Plus I was very aware how fat my knee-caps looked in these jeans. I needed to lie down.

I spent the next hour meeting girls who seemed very warm and friendly, and I immediately forgot all of their names and personal stories because I was too busy reminding myself to not say something offensive. Then I saw Evany Thomas, and I was fan-girly and gushy because I love her writing, and I heard myself admitting that I have a tiny paper figurine of her that I'd cut out to put on my desk. I suddenly realized that I'd just stepped into "I want to wear your skin for a jacket" territory, but she was totally gracious about it, because she's just as weird as I am. That's the good thing about hanging out with bloggers. Most of them are kind of fucked up in the same way you are.

For dinner we ate out of a taco truck. It was delicious, and I turned to the girl next to me to introduce myself. She said her name, but it didn't sound familiar, because all I had memorized were people's blog names.

ME: Oh! I know you! You have that great design blog!

HER: No, that's the other Asian woman here. I write a fashion blog.

ME: Holy crap. I can't believe I just did that. I am an enormous racist.

HER: No worries. So what do you do?

ME: I write a blog about all the ways I mortify myself in public. This'll go in there.

HER: I imagine so.

ME: I'd probably put this whole episode on Facebook right now, but I can't get reception out here. Also, almost all of my clothes are from Target, and I'm aware my knees look fat in these jeans. I feel like I need to just admit that right now. I'm sorry; I can't tell. Are you judging me?

HER: Well, not on your clothes.

ME: I like you. You're honest. We will be best friends.

She looked doubtful. I considered telling her I have lots of Asian friends, but I was pretty sure that would make it worse. The sad truth is I couldn't tell any of the white women apart either. In fact, at that point I'd had way too much to drink and I wasn't even sure who I was. I dimly hoped I was Evany Thomas. I love that girl.

Pajama-party time. Except it was fucking cold, and I don't own pajamas. Everyone was in adorable matching sets with robes. Our hostess, Maggie, was wearing a red silky robe over what looked to be a wedding dress, and she had fluffy slippers on. She looked like she'd just come from Wardrobe. I was wearing a muumuu with sweatpants on underneath, a giant men's hoodie, and my red confidence wig. I'd started wearing a wig in social situations for several reasons: (1) It makes me feel like someone who isn't terrified of people, and (2) if I really fuck something up I can excuse myself, pull off the wig, and say, "Who was that weird redhead and why was she talking about dildos? They *really* need to be more cautious about who they let in here." The wig is a form of protection, a sort of talisman, allowing me to pretend that I'm anyone else who isn't me. Except that I can't afford an expensive wig, so mostly I just look like I'm pretending to be a cancer patient.

I looked at my outfit unhappily in the mirror, but Laura assured me I just looked like a mysterious spy. I stared at her suspiciously. "Or like a homeless woman who just wandered into a fancy cocktail party?"

She looked at me objectively for a few seconds. "Maybe a little," she admitted. "But *way* more like a spy."

I have good friends.

All twenty of us sat around an open fire pit in our pj's and no one was tweeting, or texting, or on the phone. We were all forced to make conversation out of desperation, because cell coverage was so sporadic there. Surprisingly, it came naturally, and no one looked panicked but me. The booze helped. I whispered to Laura that this was the closest I'd ever been to sleepaway camp, and that this was exactly when the serial killer would be deciding whom to pick off. We decided that the girl on our left would be the first one to be murdered, because she was frail and adorable and the audience would love her. I would miss her. The girl in the cabin next door would be next, because she's a buxom hot blonde, but she'd probably ask her roomie to help her shower up first, because you have to be naked for the second murder, and that one's always the most violent. Probably because you don't have any clothes on to soak up the blood. I felt sorry for her roommate. We decided that everyone else would be murdered during the night, except for the quiet girl on our right who wasn't drinking, and who would eventually avenge us all, and would be the perfect person to strike down the murderer, because she was pregnant and Mormon and full of brunettey wholesomeness. Then we'd find out that the murderer was Maggie, because turns out being a serial killer was on her life list. And it was sponsored. But the audience would probably forgive her because she's adorable, and you have to admire someone who follows their dreams like that.

———

Three a.m. I couldn't sleep. Luckily I was sharing a bed with Laura, who sleeps like the dead, but I still felt bad for tossing, so I bundled up in ten layers of clothes and a hoodie so I could sit by the pool and watch cartoons on my phone without disturbing anyone. Except the woods reminded me of *Twilight* and I found myself worried about vampires.

Four a.m. I decided it was late enough in Texas to call Victor. He was getting Hailey ready for school, but about ten minutes into the call I got attacked by a giant bear. Except not really, but it felt like it. Basically I was on the phone and this big animal walked into the pool area from the forest, and I whispered, *"Holy SHIT. What the fuck is that?!"* and Victor was all, "Where's Hailey's brush? *Why don't you put things back where they belong?"* and I yelled, "THERE IS A FUCKING WILD ANIMAL SLUNKING UP TO ME," and Victor said, "Huh?" but I could still hear him rummaging around for a brush.

Then I yelled, "I'M GOING TO BE EATEN BY A COUGAR. Wait, are there cougars in California?" And Victor was all, "Yeah. I think so. Oh! So I never got to tell you my idea for an iPhone app I'm going to make." Then I considered calling him an asshole, but the animal was edging closer, and although it was dark I could see it didn't have a tail, so I whispered, "Bobcat! I'm going to be attacked by a bobcat. Or a cougar that lost its tail. Probably because it got gnawed off by a vampire. And now it's a vampire cougar. I am totally fucked." But I said all that in my mind, because I was being quiet so that I wouldn't attract its attention. It looked up, saw me, and then slunk off.

Victor was yelling, *"Hello? Dumb-ass by the pool at four a.m.?* Are you still alive?! TALK TO ME!"* and I shakily said, "I'm fine. It ran away," but before I could start talking about my traumatic experience he started talking about iPhone apps again, and I screamed, "WHY ARE YOU TALKING ABOUT COMPUTERS WHEN I COULD HAVE BEEN KILLED?"

VICTOR: *You're fine.* So do you want to hear about my iPhone app idea I had?

ME: No.

VICTOR: Too bad. I made an iPhone app that tells you when cougars are near you. It doesn't work when you're on the phone, though.

ME: I hate you so much right now.

Six a.m.:

ME: *OH MY GOD, LAURA, WAKE UP.* I totally just got attacked by a cougar!

LAURA: [still groggy] *What?*

ME: It might have been a bobcat.

LAURA: YOU SAW A BOBCAT?

ME: It was small, though, so probably a baby bobcat.

LAURA: [silence]

ME: It might have been a house cat. BUT IT WAS ENORMOUS. And it totally looked at me in a threatening way.

LAURA: Did it growl?

ME: No. *But I could totally tell it wanted to.*

LAURA: How big was it?

ME: Big enough that I could put it in a cardboard box and carry it around, but it'd probably be heavy. Like, I could fit it in my suitcase *but just barely.* We could put it in your enormous suitcase, though, and it could probably live comfortably for weeks.

LAURA: I'm going to throw cougars in the room if you don't stop making fun of my suitcase.

ME: [to the ten people eating an early breakfast the next morning] Did Laura tell you I got attacked by a bear last night?

EVERYONE: *WHAT?*

LAURA: She did *not* get attacked by a bear.

ME: Bear . . . cougar. *Same difference.*

LAURA: There was no attack. *She's fine.*

ME: I think someone should ask the owners how many cougars they keep on the property.

LAURA: I already asked the owners what it could have been, and they said there are some feral cats around.

ME: I'm pretty sure "feral cats" is code for "vampire cougars."

ME: [to everyone else who came to breakfast one hour later] So last night I was attacked by Sasquatch. It was like a smaller version of the Loch Ness monster. But on land. So, yeah. It was *pretty* fucking terrifying.

No one really responded, but it didn't surprise me, because it's hard to know what to say in those situations. It's like when someone tells you they got stabbed. There's not an easy response in that situation. Unless it *just* happened. Then I suggest, "Lie down and tell us who the murderer is," because that way it'll save the homicide detectives a lot of time later.

The morning I found out that we were all going to wine education class I felt like I was in some kind of finishing school and I'd missed all the prerequisites. Our teacher was an author who'd apparently been on the *Today* show a lot. There were five full glasses of wine in front of me, but the wine teacher told us that we were not allowed to drink any of them until after we finished the lesson. I imagine this is how dogs feel when you put a biscuit on their nose and tell them not to eat it. Except I totally stole sips of the wine when the teacher wasn't looking, because I'm really shitty at being an obedient dog.

We spent a lot of time learning how to swish the glass of wine. I'd always assumed people did that to seem snotty, but apparently the more oxygen you get in your wine, the better it tastes, so when you swish it, it spreads out all over the glass and gets more air. I felt sorry for the girl sitting on my right, because apparently I'm a bit of an overachiever when it comes to wine swishing, and so she was sloshed by me several times. Luckily she was nonchalant and simply licked the excess wine off her arm, a move that I considered both ecological and classy. Our teacher looked displeased, so to distract her I asked why people don't just serve wine on large dinner plates with straws to suck it up, and she smiled at me stiltedly and told me she'd never been asked that before. I was pretty sure that was code for "I am totally going to steal your brilliant idea." I wrote my number down on a napkin and told her that if she started marketing wine plates I wanted a cut. She agreed but then left quickly. I'll probably never see any of that money.

Five vans of chicks took off to visit wineries for wine tasting. *Only four came back.*[1]

By my tenth glass of wine I started to wonder whether there was something wrong with my palate. Everyone else was marking the wine list with notes like "Pleasant finish. Robust spices." Meanwhile, I was doodling pictures of vampiric cougars. Then I noticed people staring at my doodles, and so I started writing notes next to the wine. Things like "Tastes of NyQuil, but in a good way," and "This one will get you *all* the way fucked up." "I can't feel my feet anymore." "Did I leave the garage door open? I wonder whether the cat is on fire. I should probably stop drinking now." Everyone else there had a sophisticated palate. I had one that needed therapy, and possibly an intervention.

The last winery looked totally haunted, and the ducks outside reminded me to be on the lookout for hungry-looking homeless people, but I was quickly distracted when the servers brought out cheese. I whispered to the girl next to me that I was very excited about having my first cheese tasting because I love cheese. Especially cheddar. I like *all* the flavors of cheddar. Sharp, very sharp, smoky sharp. I'm kind of a connoisseur. But then when the cheese came it was all unrecognizable and THERE WAS NO

---

1. Really, all five came back, but this way sounds more dramatic.

CHEDDAR AT ALL. I was all, "WHAT KIND OF A FUCKING CHEESE PLATE IS THIS?" but I just said it in my mind (or possibly only with my indoor voice, because I was tipsy but still trying to be a professional). The servers explained that they were a bunch of "art cheeses" that had won contests, and truthfully they were pretty delish except for one of my pieces, which had a Band-Aid in it. So I said, "There is a Band-Aid on my cheese," and the Asian girl I'd offended earlier bent forward and was all, "No. That's bandage-wrapped blah-blah-French-something-blah," and I thanked her, but I ate only the end farthest from the Band-Aid just in case she was still trying to get even with me for being unintentionally racist. An hour later, though, we bonded when we got lost in a labyrinth of wine casks in a desperate search for the bathroom, and she assured me that she was not trying to make me eat a Band-Aid. The desperate need to get rid of your urine is the great equalizer.

There was apparently some sort of yellow-jacket infestation at one of the wineries, because they were everywhere. The guy who poured the booze joked that the color of that particular wine came from all of the ground-up yellow jackets that fell into the casks. I peered into my glass suspiciously, and he laughed and explained that he was just kidding, but that yellow jackets really do like the wine, so there might be some in there. I still drank it. "No biggie," I said casually, "but I'm deathly allergic to yellow jackets, so I'm probably going to die here." The rest of the table was all, "Really?" and I was like, "No, not really. *But wouldn't that be a great way to die?*" Everyone at the table was silent, probably because they were busy thinking that yeah, that totally *would* be a great way to die.

Eight p.m. I was supposed to be downstairs eating barbecue, but I was on the verge of an anxiety attack, so I bowed out, and everyone was very sweet and understanding. That's the great thing about hanging out with bloggers. They already know that you're broken, and most of them are, too, so they just nod and make you go take Xanax and go to bed. They're very supportive. Also they probably wanted me to leave so they could talk about me.

Laura dropped off a plate of barbecue and some water, and patted my head reassuringly when I told her how bad I felt that I wasn't down there. "It's fine, I promise. Everyone totally understands." She walked out the door but then turned back quickly to say drily, "But you *are* getting kicked off cheer squad."

I love my friends.

Four a.m. I woke up and found that Laura was missing. I looked outside for her but I couldn't see her. I vaguely wondered whether I might have accidentally murdered her in my drug-induced state. *"Probably not, though,"* I thought to myself. *"Not enough blood around. Unless the blood is in the bathroom."* I decided to look later.

Eight a.m. LAURA WAS NOT DEAD! She had fallen asleep somewhere else, and came back because she was worried that I'd think she'd gotten kidnapped.

ME: No, I thought I'd murdered you and then blocked it out.

LAURA: You thought you'd murdered me?

ME: Just for a second, but there wasn't enough blood. But the shower-head was askew, so I thought maybe I'd just washed off all the blood in the shower. But it didn't seem like me. I'm *terrible* at cleaning up after myself.

LAURA: Well, it's nice to know that I'd be the first person you'd want to kill.

ME: No way. I adore you. You're the *last* person I'd want to kill. That's why I figured I'd blocked it out. I figured I'd recover all those memories later with therapy, and then also I'd suddenly remember being abducted and probed by aliens. Which would suck. I'm glad you're not dead, though, because I'm already fucked up enough without remembering an involuntary probing.

LAURA: And I guess that whole "murdering your best friend" thing would be a downer too, I suppose.

ME: That too. Mostly the probing, though.

Ten a.m.: Yoga in the rain.

We were all doing the downward-dog position and all I could think was, *"For the love of Christ, just don't let me fart."* I'd begun to pray to the baby Jesus to deliver me from accidentally passing gas, and then someone else farted. It wasn't me, but all I could think was that I felt total empathy for her, and also that I really wanted to say, "That was totally not me," but it probably wouldn't be appropriate, since we were all supposed to be meditating.

I worked up enough courage to talk to Maggie and thanked her for inviting me, and then found myself telling her that I'd decided that if anyone there was a mass murderer it was she. She was silent, and I pointed out that I meant that in a good way, because she was the most organized. Then she asked the cook for a cleaver and I got a bit nervous, but turns out it was because she thought it was brilliant and wanted to act out a murder scene. And so we did. . . .

And it was awesome.

The final morning we all sat around by the pool, wrapped in blankets with mussed hair and no makeup, and I listened to the conversations around me the same way I had in high school, but instead of trying to block them out or sneer at them internally, I smiled and nodded. I forced myself to join in and listen to all the conversations going on around me, rather than hide my head in a book to avoid rejection. And I realized just how awesome girl conversations could be. Random snippets of overheard conversations:

> "I've never said this to anyone before, but sometimes I think my baby is a real asshole. Is that normal?"
> "Oh, yeah. My baby is a total dick sometimes."

> "You know when you're in Nepal and there are all these Japanese people around and it's two a.m. and you're in a basement and you're trying to find breakfast and suddenly a magician shows up?"
> "Oh, I know *exactly* what you're talking about."

"My dad had anger problems, so his doctor recommended he go to mime school to learn how to deal quietly with his emotions. It wasn't until I grew up that I realized that everyone doesn't have this memory of taking mime classes with their angry dad."

"I don't like mimes. I don't like the fact that they fake a disability."

"*Right?* Why stop at mimicking the mute? Where are the clowns pretending to have polio?"

"I once slept with this guy who had an ENORMOUS penis. Like, it was a problem. The condoms wouldn't even fit. I was so overwhelmed that I accidentally laughed at it. Then it shrunk. He was not pleased."

"That should be a comic book. *Penis giganticus* is his superpower, and women laughing at it is his kryptonite."

"Do you ever get on the subway and think, '*Who is that guy in the back? He looks familiar. Did I sleep with him?*' That happens to me all the time."

"No. That's never happened to me. *Whore.* But it *has* happened to me on the bus a lot."

The final hour:

As we all dragged our luggage out to the waiting vans, I looked with a surprising amount of affection on these women who only days ago I would have immediately dismissed as being snobby or mean, but who all turned out to have backstories and struggles just as damaged or bizarre as my own. Sure, I was the only person there with just one small carry-on and a single pair of shoes. But I was embarrassed to realize that those things that set me apart from other girls had turned from what I'd considered "self-proclaimed badges of honor" into defensive shields that I had used to keep others out. I'd used those same shields to judge and dismiss people who I suspected had more than me, in the exact same way that *I'd* been judged for having less as a kid.

I tossed my small bag in the van and went back to help my newfound friends with their enormous luggage sets and hanging garment bags, and they smiled in appreciation, shocked that I'd managed to pack for such a long trip using only one small bag. I smiled back in silence and felt a little guilty at their praise. They may have all had suitcases three times as big as mine, but I realized that the emotional baggage I'd brought with me was big enough to put theirs to shame. It was a little lighter, though, now that I was leaving.

I was leaving behind my assumptions that only snobby, rich people liked wine, and that everyone would immediately break into cliques based on who had owned the right kind of underwear. And most important, I was leaving behind the idea I'd been carrying around for years that girls were not to be trusted. Yes, some girls could be complete douche-canoes, but so could some guys (and even some babies, apparently), and I was slowly losing a prejudice that I hadn't even realized was holding me back. Girls were fine and (until proven to be assholes on an individual basis) were worthy of my trust. Women were great and relatively harmless.

It's the four a.m. vampire cougars in the woods you really need to be worried about.

I Am the Wizard of Oz
of Housewives
(In That I Am Both
"Great and Terrible"
and Because
I Sometimes Hide
Behind the Curtains)

Victor and I have very different definitions of what constitutes a clean house.

Victor's definition involves absolutely everything perfectly in its place (except for the eight thousand wires and extension cords sticking out from every electronic device in our house, which are all apparently invisible to him). It also includes all of this happening magically, without his actually ever being involved in the cleaning *at all* (except for the one time when I ran into the living room because I thought I heard him doing whip-its,[1] but turns out he was just spraying furniture polish. It's amazing how alike the sound of canned whipped cream squirted directly into the mouth and lemon-scented Pledge can be. I'd felt guilty for a second that Victor was actually cleaning without me, but then I realized that he was just polishing the gearshift of his car and I went back to watching zombie movies).

My definition of a clean house is much simpler. I'm fine with the clutter of mail and magazines and toys lying around as long as it's clean and sanitary underneath the clutter. As far as I'm concerned, a house should look lived-in, and I consider it clean as long as I don't stick to it and it doesn't give me cholera. I can ignore the piles of clothes on the guest room bed because I know they're all straight from the dryer and just waiting to be folded. Victor, on the other hand, will glare at the growing pile and huff loudly over and over until I finally break down and ask him why he sounds like he's deflating. We look into the same guest bedroom and see two entirely different things. Victor sees a dangerous volcano erupting with clothes that I must be *intentionally* refusing to hang up because I'm lazy and am purposely trying to make him have a nervous breakdown. I see it as a personal achievement . . . a physical manifestation of all the laundry I've done over the last few months. It's like a strange trophy made of clothes that I've forgotten I even owned. Victor says it's like a crazy person lives in our house and is sculpting Mount Vesuvius out of the sweaters that need to be in storage. This is when I remind him exactly why doors were invented, and I close the guest bedroom door. "See?" I say. *"Problem solved."*

––– –– –– –– –– –– ––

1. After I read this chapter to my editor she pointed out that I've been using the phrase "whip-its" incorrectly for my entire life, as it really refers to getting high from nitrous oxide and can totally kill you. Which explains why people look at me so strangely when I tell them that some of my most cherished childhood memories include doing whip-its with my grandmother. My editor consoled me with the fact that maybe people thought I was talking about the dog (whippet), but then admitted that didn't make it much better.

"You can't fix a problem by *just not using rooms in the house*," he argues, and I point out how ridiculous he's being, as I use that room *all the damn time*. I use it as a giant drawer for clothes that need to be hung up. And also to store my elliptical trainer. Victor then points out that I'm no longer even using the trainer "for its intended purposes," and I calmly explain that he's wrong, because I'd bought it years ago *intending* to work out with it until I got bored with it, and then to eventually use it as a frame to air-dry our freshly washed comforters and coverlets. If anything I should be getting points for being so farsighted, and also for not shrinking all of our comforters in the dryer. If it were left up to Victor we'd all be sleeping on comforters the size of hankies. I'm not even sure why I even have to explain this. Victor says he's not sure either, but I suspect we're not talking about the same thing.

This exact conversation was still running through my mind this morning when I was cleaning up the house. I'd loaded and turned on the dishwasher, but a few minutes later I noticed that the laundry detergent container was out on the counter next to the dishwasher, even though I hadn't done laundry in days. I felt a little sick to my stomach as I thought, "Fuck. *Did I just put laundry detergent in the dishwasher?*"

And this is when I kind of panicked, because last year I'd accidentally put hand soap in the dishwasher, and when I came back the entire house had exploded in foam. It looked like one of those foam parties that teens have at raves, except not as awesome, because Victor was pissed and I didn't own any cool techno music or Ecstasy. It had been a nightmare to clean up, and I was terrified that I'd just done it again, so I prayed that Victor would just stay in the bedroom and I logged on to Twitter. (For those of you who don't know what Twitter is, it's like Facebook except easier, and you can use it to tell people what your cat is doing and also to ask for advice. It's like accessing the hivemind and it is both great and horrible.) I logged on to Twitter and wrote, "Hypothetically speaking, if I accidentally put laundry detergent in the dishwasher will that make my dishwasher

A picture of the dishwasher being comforted that I took to show everyone on Twitter. Please note how nice and unshrunken the comforter looks. That's all me, people.

explode? I kind of need to know as soon as possible." Half of the people responding were all, "Oh, you'll be fine, dumb-ass," and the other half were like, "THE CALL IS COMING FROM INSIDE THE HOUSE. GET OUT NOW." One guy wrote, "Actually, it'll help remove the bloodstains," which just made me wonder what he uses his dishwasher for. But I was still worried, so I wrapped a comforter around the dishwasher in case it started to leak, because comforters are a lot like giant maxipads. I felt pretty proud of my ingenuity. This pride lasted for about ten seconds, until Victor walked in and said, *"Why in the hell is there a comforter wrapped around the dishwasher?"* and I didn't want to explain it, because he *still* hasn't stopped talking about the last time I set the oven on fire, *and that was years ago, people.* Like, let's live in the present already, right? But then I remember that in the present I may have just destroyed our dishwasher by dumping a bunch of Tide into it. I wasn't ready to admit that yet, though, because it was still vaguely possible that I'd used the right soap all along, so instead I just told Victor that the dishwasher was cold, and he was all, "What. The. Fuck?"

"Well," I explained, "it has to heat up to wash the dishes properly, right? And I figured it would help save energy if I insulated it so it could get hot faster. And then our dishes would be cleaner. I'm always thinking." Victor stared at me unblinkingly, with his arms crossed, and after about ten seconds I cracked and admitted that I *may* have used laundry detergent in the dishwasher, because I couldn't think of why else the Tide would be out. Then he sighed and shook his head at me. "You'd make a *terrible* secret agent. Honestly, you are the worst liar ever. But no worries, because I put the laundry detergent out on the counter after you started the dishwasher just to remind myself to buy more."

"SO THIS IS ALL *YOUR* FAULT," I shouted, and Victor said, "*What?* How is this *possibly **my*** fault?" But I yelled, "*J'ACCUSE!*" and stormed off before he could say anything else, because it's a refreshing change when Victor fucks something up for once, and I wanted to go and appreciate the moment.

I'd venture that Victor and I fight about the state of the house more than anything else, which is really saying something, because Victor and I have had weeklong arguments about whether Franken Berry is a girl (he's not) and which one of the Chipmunks is most likely to die first (it's Alvin, probably from an overdose). But arguing about the house is the most common one. In fact, here is a typical argument Victor and I had soon after I decided to quit my job in HR and try to be a full-time writer:

VICTOR: This house is a fucking *wreck.*

ME: This house is a "creative haven."

VICTOR: No. It's just a wreck.

ME: Well, I don't know why you're telling *me* about it. It's not *my* job to clean the house.

VICTOR: Yeah, actually, it is. Remember? You were going to quit your job and work on your book? And clean the house. And do the errands. That was the deal, remember?

ME: Not really. That doesn't sound like a deal I'd make.

VICTOR: "I'm going to be the best housewife EVER. I'll just write and clean and cook." Sound familiar?

ME: Fuzzy. I was probably drunk when I said all that.

VICTOR: "FREE BLOW JOBS FOR EVERYBODY!"

ME: Oh. That *does* sound like something I'd say. Are you mad about the blow jobs?

VICTOR: No. *I'm mad about the fact that we both work at home and that this home is a fucking wreck.*

ME: It's not *that* bad. You're overreacting because you're kind of an anal freak.

VICTOR: You are using a Frisbee as a plate.

ME: *What?* I'm not using a— Oh, *hang on*, this *is* a Frisbee. *Weird.*

VICTOR: [glare]

ME: Dude, calm down. I'll wash it afterward. It's probably dishwasher-safe.

VICTOR: It's not about whether the Frisbee is dishwasher-safe. It's about the fact that *you're using a fucking Frisbee to eat on because there are no clean plates.*

ME: There are *totally* clean plates. I just saw this on the counter and grabbed it. Technically it's a kick-ass plate. It even has a lip on it so you don't spill anything.

VICTOR: *How does this not bother you?!*

ME: IT *TOTALLY* BOTHERS ME. I can't believe I ever agreed to clean the house in exchange for quitting my job. I can't believe you'd even think that would work. If anything *you* should have known better when you made that deal. This is all sort of your fault.

VICTOR: I'm going to strangle you.

ME: And I'm going to replace all our plates with Frisbees. *Because I'm a motherfuckin' visionary.*

VICTOR: I'm being totally serious here.

ME: SO AM I. THESE FRISBEE PLATES ARE AWESOME. Besides, I don't have time to clean, because I'm busy doing important social media stuff.

VICTOR: *Really.* So what did you accomplish today?

ME: A lot. Social media maven . . . stuff.

VICTOR: No. What *exactly* did you do today? Quantify it for me.

ME: It's not quantifiable. *There aren't even metrics for the shit I do.*

VICTOR: Try.

ME: Um . . . I drew this cartoon about Hitler?

The truth. We're all a little jealous of Hitler.
Apparently.

VICTOR: That's . . . not even *remotely* funny.

ME: Dude, it's *totally* funny. You know? Because people always say, "They only hate me because they're jealous." But then it's Hitler, and everyone really *does* hate him and isn't jealous at all?

VICTOR: Not funny.

ME: I think I just need drawing lessons. It took me, like, two hours just to work out how to put a scarf on a stick figure. And *that's* why I didn't have time to clean all the soup I spilled in the microwave. By the way, don't look in the microwave.

VICTOR: I'm going to lie down until the urge to kill you passes.

Then he left and never came back. And I had to clean the microwave, because *I'm* the responsible one in this relationship, and also because it started to smell like clam chowder even in the bathrooms. This is why it sucks to be me. Also, I'm pretty sure that my husband is anti-Semitic.

P.S. Victor says that not laughing at a joke making fun of Hitler doesn't make you anti-Semitic, but I'm pretty sure that's exactly what an anti-Semite would say. They have *terrible* senses of humor. He also says this is a conversation about "why I can't act like a grown-up," but I'm pretty sure it's really about why he loves Hitler so damn much.

P.P.S. I just want to point out that I actually *am* a fairly good house-wife and that the only reason that I set the oven on fire in the first place was because we were trying to sell our house and I'd read that you should bake cookies before the open house because it makes your house smell homier. So I threw one of those frozen cookie logs on a plate and put it in the oven, and then ten minutes later there was a terrible smell and I raced to the oven to find out that if you don't cut those cookie logs into cookie shapes they explode all over the plate. And also that when people install an oven they put the paperwork inside of it, because apparently they want you to die painfully when you catch the house on fire from the burning instructions you just tried to bake. Also, they put the instructions in a plastic sheet, which smells terrible when it melts, and it makes it very hard to sell a house when you have to tell prospective buyers that the oven was used only once but that it was used to cook a bunch of plastic and that's why it smells so terrible at the open house. Also, Victor was surprisingly critical of the whole event, considering that I was only trying to help, and he told me that our insurance company was making us install a halon fire extinguisher system in the new house unless I promised to avoid the kitchen from then on. I did not think that was funny at all and was really pissed off, until the next day, when I tried to heat up the oven again in an attempt to scrape off all the melted plastic still in there, and I accidentally shut a tea towel in the oven and caught it all on fire again. I'm really glad we sold that house, because, honestly, *that oven was a goddamn death trap.*

P.P.P.S. In my defense I just want to point out that I *can* actually cook a meal, although possibly not a meal by anyone else's standard definition. For instance, I have never in my life intentionally made a dinner salad for my family and I don't intend to. Using that many ingredients and utensils to prepare a dish that's just served raw anyway seems like a waste, and I've never seen a family look at a salad as anything other than something you have to survive and drench in dressing just to finish so that you can get on to "the real food." I'm not falling for it. Instead I jump straight to the real food. I recently made microwave macaroni and cheese, and when my family didn't seem properly appreciative, I pointed out that it had taken me a half-hour to make it. Victor refused to believe it until he opened the trash can and found ten single-serving just-add-water macaroni cups. He stared at me in disbelief, as I patted myself on the back for taking out the other trash sack from earlier, which had included an *additional* ten single-serving macaroni dishes, which had sort of fused together into a single, melty pile. Apparently if you want to cook ten plastic serving bowls for three minutes each you shouldn't just shove them all in the microwave all together for thirty minutes and then leave to take a shower. This is my advice to you, and is something Julia Child never covered.

P.P.P.P.S. Also, if you try to make a shrimp boil but the bag of spices bursts and so you just toss it all in along with whatever spices you can find in the pantry, you can make homemade pepper spray. Unintentionally. And everyone at your dinner party will run outside for the next hour, coughing and tearing up as if they've been Maced. Because technically they kind of have been. Because mace was one of the spices I found in the pantry. I blame whoever makes spice out of Mace, and I reminded my gasping dinner guests that even if I did Mace them, I did it in an old-fashioned, homemade, Martha Stewart sort of way. *With love.*

The Psychopath
on the Other Side
of the Bathroom Door

A few weeks ago my friend Lotta told me that her doctor told her that her antidepressants weren't working because she had too many toxins in her body, and that she needed to use a "colon cleanse" to flush everything out of her system. It sounded completely insane and I told her that, but then she mentioned that when she took the colon cleanse she lost three pounds that very day—I was immediately in. I convinced myself that I owed it to my family to have my crazy pills work properly, but really I just wanted to lose three pounds without working out. And that whole last sentence kind of proves why I need to be on crazy pills. *Awesome*.

So I went to the grocery store but I couldn't find the colon cleanse. I considered asking the pharmacist, but as I was waiting in line I had a conversation in my head that went like this:

ME: Yes, I'd like some colon cleanse.

PHARMACIST: I've never heard of that. Sounds like something deviants use.

ME: It's something that cleans out your colon so your antidepressants work better.

PHARMACIST: I think you're using your antidepressants wrong. They go in your mouth.

ME: You are surprisingly unhelpful for a health care worker.

PHARMACIST: I'm calling the police, deviant.

I'm not sure why I jumped right to the pharmacist calling the police, but once the thought was in my head it was stuck there, and so I panicked a little when the pharmacist asked what I needed. I paused awkwardly and then asked where the reading glasses were, and then he said they didn't carry reading glasses, which is weird because most pharmacies do, and I always like to try them on and pretend that I'm a naughty librarian. So instead of the colon cleanse I decided I would just take a bunch of ex-lax, because I figured, *next-best thing, right?* I bought the extra-strength stuff because it was the same price as regular strength, and so technically it was like I was *saving* money, and I thought that would help my argument when Victor demanded to know why I bought twenty dollars' worth of "unnecessary" laxatives (although it turns out he didn't really care about cost-effectiveness because he hates being economically feasible, or wants me to be fat or something). I already knew he'd be all judgy about the whole thing, because he was also very unsupportive when I wanted to buy those Chinese foot-pad things that suck all the toxins out of your feet while you sleep. He claimed the whole Chinese foot-pad thing was a scam, but I think it's just because he wants me to suffer, or maybe that he's racist. Then when I called him racist he got all mad and screamy, and I was like, "I DON'T EVEN KNOW WHAT I'M SAYING! THOSE ARE THE TOXINS TALKING," but he still wouldn't let me buy them. And this is exactly why I waited until the week he left for a business trip to New York to actually do the cleanse.

I took two chocolate squares of ex-lax that night, but then I noticed that the directions said it would bring "gentle results," and it seemed like a good colon cleansing shouldn't be "gentle" at all, so I took three more tabs. And they were chocolaty and delicious and I was kind of hungry, so I ate another one. And then *nothing happened at all*. So then next morning I took two more (because at this point I thought maybe there was something wrong with me, and that I had some kind of freakishly high laxative tolerance), and then I went to Starbucks and picked up a giant Frappuccino. This might have been a mistake, because apparently coffee is kind of a laxative too, although sadly I wasn't thinking about that at the time, because I was too busy thinking about the phone conversation I'd had with Victor last week about Frappuccinos when he called me at work:

[Ring]

ME: This is Jenny.

VICTOR: So why don't they make chocolate Slurpees?

ME: Um . . . what?

VICTOR: Chocolate Slurpees. Why don't they exist?

ME: They do. They're called *mocha Frappuccinos.*

VICTOR: Nope. Not the same thing. Frappuccinos don't have that little spoon on the end of the straw like Slurpees do.

ME: Those are Icees. Not Slurpees.

VICTOR: Next time I go into Starbucks I'm going to be all, *"I want a spoon on my straw, a-hole!"* How else are you gonna get that little last bit in the bottom, huh? Spoon straw!

ME: ?

VICTOR: They need to join forces, 7-Eleven and Starbucks.

ME: Mochaslurpeeccino?

VICTOR: Or maybe a slurpeemacchiato. Now, *that* would be an unholy union.

ME: So did you actually *need* something from me or . . . ?

VICTOR: *Doo-doo, wa-wa.*

ME: Huh. What was that?

VICTOR: That's my Antichrist music.

Please note that he doesn't even start the conversation with a "Hello," which is kind of more upsetting to me than the Antichrist stuff, because a greeting is a basic building block of polite society, and is one of the only things that separates us from bears.

So I drove back to my home, drinking my Frappuccino and making a mental note that I should let all of Victor's calls go through to my voice mail, and then *my intestines exploded.* I mean, they didn't *literally* explode, but it totally felt that way. And at first I was all, "Okay, pain is good, feel the burn," but then I realized that this was not like yoga and that I had, in fact, made a *horrible, horrible mistake.* I'm not going to get graphic, but it basically felt like my legs melted and an elephant crawled inside my stomach and was clawing his way out. And the elephant had claws, apparently. And his nose was made of snakes.

Since Victor was in New York, and Hailey was in school, I had the house to myself, which was good, because honestly there would have been no way to maintain the sensual mystery of womanhood if anyone had heard the noises coming from that bathroom. At a certain point I started worrying that I might be OD'ing. I wasn't sure what OD'ing on laxatives looked like, but I was fairly certain it would be messy and that you'd probably shit out your entire colon. I'm not sure if this is actually medically possible, and I thought about calling Lotta to ask her whether she felt like she was shitting out her colon when she was doing her cleanse, but I wasn't sure I could talk without screaming, and also I didn't have her phone number. And so I sat there, thinking that this would be a horrible way to die, because basically no matter what I'd accomplished in my life it would always be overshadowed by "And she died on the toilet from pooping out her own lower intestine." Like, if it had happened to Thomas Edison that would totally be the very first thing it would say in his Wikipedia entry. It'd be all, "Thomas Edison, *who pooped out his own colon*, made a variety of inventions and changed the way we live today. Did we mention *he pooped out his colon*? Because he totally did. *Thomas Edison pooped out his colon.* Honestly, we can't stress this enough."

It was about this time that I decided I needed to take action, so I found some Pepto-Bismol and took a full dose. I considered taking more, but at this point I was concerned that I might have to call 911 for help and I didn't want to have to explain why I'd taken three times the recommended amount of laxatives *and* three times the recommended amount of antidiarrhea medicine, because even to me that sounded like some sort of poorly planned suicide attempt. Taking just *one* dose of the antidiarrheal seemed somewhat rational, comparatively. *"Surely,"* I thought, *"this will make me seem much more credible and less likely to be put on suicide watch."*

Of course, the Pepto-Bismol was no match for the raw power of the exlax, and was much like wearing shin guards in the middle of a tornado, except even less effective, because at least with shin guards, when they found your body later you could still wear a skirt in your coffin (unless your legs got ripped off entirely, which could totally happen). But the Pepto-Bismol didn't do anything at all except turn my tongue black.

It crossed my mind that maybe eating a bunch of cheese might help, because I once went to school with a girl who ate too much cheese and got so constipated that she had to go to the hospital to get the poop removed *by a doctor*. And after I heard that I could never really look at her the same way, and I often wondered whether she got to keep the poop they removed, like when you get to keep your tonsils. And then I remembered that I didn't *have* any cheese in the house, and that even if I did, it wouldn't matter, because I couldn't leave the toilet long enough to get it. And that's when I heard the noise at the bathroom door.

It sounded like someone leaning against the door and tapping it lightly with his knuckles, and I was all, *"Oh, my God, I didn't lock the bathroom door,"* and then I thought, "Wait, why would I even *need* to lock the door, since I'm the only one home?" My initial thought was that it was a murderer or a rapist, which was quickly followed up by the thought that if it *was* a rapist, he was going to be terribly disappointed. And then I thought how it was kind of weird that I'd even shut the bathroom door in the first place, since I was alone, but technically I think you should never leave the door open when you go to the bathroom, because that's how society breaks down. Then I heard the possible rapist again, and so I coughed, because I thought it might be a burglar who didn't realize I was home. I hoped that the coughing would give him a hint that he needed to leave, although technically the other noises coming from the bathroom were probably much more intimidating than coughing, but I was trying to be polite, *because I'm a lady*.

And then someone slid a note under the door.

And I just stared at it, because seriously . . . *what the fuck?* It was so baffling that I couldn't even get scared. I tried to slide my foot over to reach the note (which was a small, white slip of paper), but I couldn't reach it, so I just yelled weakly, *"Hello?* Did . . . *did you just pass me a note?"* but no one answered, and then I started to get freaked out, and I silently thanked God that I'd thought to bring the phone into the bathroom just in case I needed to call to report the laxative overdose. I picked up the phone to call the police, but then I considered how it would sound when I told them that I was calling from inside my bathroom, where I'd OD'ed on laxatives, and that a possible rapist was quietly passing me notes under the bathroom door. And then I thought that it would be really weird if the note said something like "Do you like me? Circle yes or no," and I probably would have laughed if it weren't for the laxative/rapist combo bearing down on me. Then another note came slowly peeking out from under the door, and I realized it wasn't a note at all. It was actually the wrapper from a Band-Aid, and that's when I realized I was probably dealing with a psychopath, because *why would anyone pass me a Band-Aid wrapper unless they were completely insane?*

So I yelled, *"I'M CALLING THE POLICE! AND I HAVE DIARRHEA! From . . . AIDS!"* because I thought that would discourage a rapist. I wasn't really sure whether AIDS caused diarrhea, but I figured it probably did. And then it got really quiet, and suddenly the Band-Aid wrapper was violently pulled back out from under the door and I was all, "What the hell?" Then it shot back into the bathroom again, but this time I could see that it was being pushed under the door *by a fucking cat paw*, and that's when I realized the cat had knocked over my purse and was just shoving receipts and assorted purse flotsam under the door. Then I murdered my cat, but only in my mind.

It occurred to me that I should write all this down, but I didn't have anything to write on, except for the paper the cat had pushed under the door, and so I yelled, "Posey, push the paper farther!" but he didn't, because he's an asshole. And also he's a cat, so he doesn't speak English. So instead I wrote this on toilet paper with lipstick (but just the key words, and not this whole thing, because *that* would be ridiculous). Then I said a little prayer thanking God for saving me from getting assaulted, and also for not making me have to explain to the ambulance drivers that I'd accidentally mistaken my cat for a rapist after purposely overdosing on laxatives in order to make my antidepressants work better. Mainly because that's the kind of story that gets told over and over again to the new ambulance-crew recruits. But then I remembered that girl from high school who had to have the poop bubble removed, so maybe in comparison my story wasn't really so weird after all.

Except when Victor came home I told him about it (because how could you *not* share that story?), and he got all testy about the laxatives and implied that I "couldn't be trusted in the house unsupervised," and I'm all, *"Glass half full, asshole.* I didn't get raped, right?" and he shouted, *"You were never in danger of getting raped,"* but I think he just said that to hurt my feelings, and so I retorted, "Oh, I am *ALWAYS* in danger of being raped, *thankyouverymuch,"* and he was all, "I'm not questioning your rapability. I'M JUST SAYING I CAN'T GO AWAY FOR TWO DAYS WITHOUT YOU OD'ING ON LAXATIVES." And that's when I made a mental note that from now on I would never tell him about OD'ing on *anything.* And also that I should probably make friends with ambulance drivers, because I bet they have some kick-ass stories.

An Open Letter to My Husband, Who Is Asleep in the Next Room

H*i.*

I know. The weird pattern in the butter dish, right? By now you've surely discovered it and are probably freaking out. Well, last night I discovered that if I make Eggos I can skip the butter knife and just drop the waffle directly in the butter tub. It's awesome. Except that the hot waffle melts a weird pattern in the butter, like an all-yellow plaid, and the plastic tub melts a bit. I know you'd prefer I use a knife, because you're kind of neurotic about this stuff, but honestly, *I'm just not that kind of girl.* Mostly because I'm trying to save the environment by not dirtying a knife that would have to be washed. I'm kind of a hero. Also, the knives are, like, all the way on the other side of the kitchen. Poor planning on your part. And by "on your part," I mean "by letting me unpack the kitchen when we moved in." I mean, *I guess* we could just switch the utensil drawer with the take-out menu drawer, but that seems like a lot of work. Unless I just pulled out the drawers completely and switched them!

Okay, now we have two drawers lying on the kitchen floor. I got them both out, but I can't get them back in. I'm sorry. I don't know what's wrong with me. Don't look in the butter dish.

P.S. If anything, you should be *thanking me* for the butter texturizer. Remember that fucking ridiculous Burberry-plaid car we saw, and you were all, "*Wow!* I wish someone would do that to my car and/or butter!" Well, *Merry Christmas, asshole.*

P.P.S. I'm sorry I called you an asshole. That was uncalled-for. Also, by now you've read this letter and will surely claim that you did *not* ask me to Burberry the car or anything else, but really, you've got more important things to focus on. Like fixing the three drawers that are on the kitchen floor.

I know.

But I thought if I took one more out slowly I could see how it worked, and then I could fix the others before you wake up, but that totally didn't work. But I stopped at three. *You're welcome.*

P.P.P.S. *Shit.* Okay, I thought maybe one more would give me the secret putting-the-drawer-back key. Turns out? Not so much. At this point I'm considering setting fire to the kitchen to cover my tracks, but I'm sure you'd just blame that on me too. So I won't, because I know you'd be a jerk about it. And also because that would be wrong. I would never set fire to our house.

P.P.P.P.S. Okay, I just set fire to the house, but it was totally on accident. I was trying to make you a pizza for breakfast, and I accidentally put a bunch of towels in the oven. I know it seems suspicious, since I was just talking about burning down the house, but it's just a horrible, horrible coincidence.

I have to think that this never would have happened had our builders not put the bathroom so close to the oven. It's like they *wanted* me to set fire to the house. *Those guys* are the assholes. Not *you*. I *love* you.

P.P.P.P.P.S. I'm going to stop at the store on the way home and buy you your very own tub of butter so you don't have to see the melty Burberry one. I'm sorry. I don't know why I didn't just think of that in the first place.

P.P.P.P.P.P.S. None of this is actually true except for the butter part. Aren't you relieved? I know you are. And now you're much less likely to freak out about the butter, because, *Jesus, it's not like I tried to burn the house down* (except for that one time when I did, but that really was an accident, and the builder's fault too, because who the hell leaves the oven instructions inside the oven? Someone who wants us all dead, *that's who*). This was all just an exercise in perspective.

P.P.P.P.P.P.P.S. Don't look in the butter dish.

Just to Clarify:
We Don't Sleep
with Goats

I think there's a goat in our house," my sister says, making no attempt to get up as she turns her head slightly to listen to the strange noises coming from down the hall.

She's wrong; I'm certain. Not because there *couldn't* be a goat in the house, but because this isn't *our* house anymore. It's the home we grew up in, and still feels warm and familiar, but I've managed to disassociate myself from being responsible for shooing errant goats out of a home I haven't lived in for more than a decade.

"No," I explain, looking back down at the photo albums we'd spread over our old bedroom floor. "There is a goat *in Mom and Dad's house*."

She pointed a finger at me and winked. "Ah. You have a point. Hey, look at these pictures of you in wigs when you were a baby. What the hell's going on there?" I stare at the album and start to answer, when the clomping from the next room gets louder and then the screaming starts.

"There is *totally* a goat in the house," she repeats. "Or maybe a pony."

It's the kind of thing that would be shocking if it happened in either of our houses, but this week we've both come back to Wall to visit our family, and this sort of thing is practically expected in a small house with eight people, one shower, and too many goats.[1]

I continue to flip through the photo album as if nothing is happening. "I'm just going to stay in this room until it's gone. This is *so* not my responsibility." Something heavy bounces off a wall. *"I swear to God I am having such childhood flashbacks right now."*

Lisa sighs as the screams get louder. "That's the PTSD talking. But"—her voice quavers with a slight doubt—"our kids *are* out there, so maybe we should go check on them."

Lisa is under the impression that we are responsible for protecting our children from whatever my father is getting them into, but I tend to follow my mother's lead in regard to this. *"How will they learn if we continually rescue them?"* I ask. "By the time *we* were their age we'd have learned to duck and cover until the noises die down. Besides, I'm pretty sure those are happy screams, so it's probably all good. Or possibly the next few hours will be very tragic."

"Oh, that reminds me," Lisa says, frowning at a picture of herself as a one-year-old surrounded by empty beer bottles. "The day before you got here, Daddy came in and asked my kids whether they wanted to see his 'new pets,' and when they said yes he dumped a sack of live ducklings on the living

The weird thing about this picture is that my parents don't drink. I can only assume that Lisa had some sort of problem.

---

1. My mom just read this chapter and asked me to clarify that the goats are outside animals. They don't live here in the house with us. I'm not sure why I have to clarify that, but then I reread the chapter with new eyes and I guess that goats sleeping at the foot of our beds wouldn't be that strange, comparatively. So, yeah, the goats don't live in the house with us. That would be weird. And unsanitary. Plus, the goats aren't even ours. They're rented goats, because my dad has too much grass, and his friend has too many goats. This all makes sense if you live in the country. Probably.

room floor for the kids to chase down. Mom was *pissed*. And Daddy never thought to count them first, so who knows whether we even got them all."

"Who carries ducks in a sack?" I asked myself, but I had only one answer. The screams had died down and I heard giggling and running and possible quacking. *"Shit,"* I said, with resignation. I wasn't worried about the kids (who ranged from age two to nine, and who usually watched out for one another), but I *was* concerned for the ducklings. I stared at Lisa and rolled my eyes in defeat. *"Fine.* I'll get the broom. You man the front door so I can shoo them out without letting goats in."

The scene was chaotic but familiar. The ducklings quacked and ran everywhere, hiding under the recliner and attempting to tunnel under the decorative but nonfunctional piano. When cornered by the children, they'd be picked up and would immediately poop, sending the kids screaming with peals of laughter as they dropped the ducklings and started the cycle all over again.

"HENRY. What did you do?" my mom yelled, as my dad laughed at the mayhem he'd created, the twinkle in his eyes still bright after all these years.

"What?" he asked teasingly. "I put down paper first."

It was true. There was a small, empty square of newspaper in the middle of the living room.

"And you thought the ducks would understand to stay on paper?" she asked sarcastically, as she pried a terrified-looking duckling from a toddler's sticky fist.

"Well, I guess not," my dad admitted, but he was gleeful to see the kids laughing, and we all knew this would continue to happen. My mom shooed him outside, since he was only making things worse with his cries of "WHOEVER CATCHES THE SPOTTED ONE WINS A SILVER DOLLAR."

The scene had taken on a dangerous carnival quality, and I was grateful that Victor had stayed home in Houston to work, since he would never let me hear the end of this. Eventually we captured the last flustered duckling and placed them in a bucket in the quiet, dark bedroom, so they could calm down (and so that Daddy wouldn't just throw them back in the house again as soon as they were returned outside), and Lisa and I settled back down on our old bed again and picked up the albums as if nothing had happened. It's a little disconcerting when shit like this becomes old hat, but this is the way things are, and you have to learn to roll with the punches, even if the punches are coming from the clawed feet of angry ducklings who don't understand that you're helping.

Whenever we came to visit my parents, Hailey would play with the moonshine still. She'd ride Jasper, the miniature donkey, in the backyard. She and her cousins would play on the old tractors and the ancient stagecoaches littering the acreage behind the house. They laughed and played and explored my father's taxidermy shop, and wore cow skulls as masks. They looked for buried treasure with antiqued maps my dad

It'd be easier to judge this moonshine still harshly if my daughter hadn't helped build it.

"found," and would dig up wooden boxes filled with coins and costume jewelry and arrowheads that Daddy had buried for them. They'd roam around the property, chasing goats and having fun, and Lisa and I had to admit that their joy made up for the occasional stray duckling that would walk into your bedroom in the middle of the night.

The next day Victor drove to my parents' house so that we could celebrate our anniversary, except I don't celebrate anything with *that certain unlucky number in it*, because I'm still OCD. I made him swear to just tell people that this was simply "our second twelfth anniversary," which would have worked perfectly if Victor took my phobias seriously and didn't have a death wish. Instead he kept saying the unlucky number over and over, and I was all, "This is *exactly* why I didn't want to celebrate at all this year, because if you don't stop saying that number I will divorce you, and that's *totally* the kind of thing that would happen on an unlucky year, so fucking *stop tempting fate.*" Then he raised an eyebrow and said innocently, "*What number? You mean, ___?*" *AND THEN HE SAID THE NUMBER AGAIN.* This is when I decided I would just cut one of his testicles off sometime this year, because that will take care of all of our bad luck in one fell swoop, and then we'll still stay married, because all the unluckiness will have been used up in an intentional ball-removal accident. Victor explained that there was no such thing as an "intentional accident," and was a little baffled that I'd jumped right from divorcing him to removing one of his testicles, but this is our second twelfth anniversary, so he really should be used to that sort of thing from me by now. Plus, you don't even *need* two testicles. Lance Armstrong seems to be doing pretty well with just one.[2] And also, I'M SAVING OUR MARRIAGE, ASSHOLE.

For our anniversary my mom babysat Hailey so that Victor and I could go to *Summer Mummers*, a melodrama-vaudevillian play that's been going on every summer since the forties in Midland, Texas. There's lots of booze, and you're encouraged to scream for the hero and boo at the caped villain, and to buy bags of popcorn to throw at the stage whenever the evil mustachioed bad guy comes out. Unfortunately I have a weak arm, and so I ended up just throwing it at the people directly in front of us. They turned around, and Victor surreptitiously pointed at the people sitting next to us as if to blame them for it, but our neighbors noticed, and then a terrible popcorn battle broke out. Then Victor stood up on his chair and yelled, "I WILL END YOU PEOPLE," and bought three hundred dollars' worth of popcorn. It was one of those moments when I realized how lucky I was to be celebrating a second twelfth anniversary with someone willing to spend all the money we'd planned to use on a fancy hotel room in order to buy pallets of popcorn just so he could bury perfect strangers in a drunken, Napoleonic endeavor. We fucking *destroyed* those people.

---

2. Please ignore this sentence if Lance Armstrong is dead when you read this. I swear, he looked totally healthy when I wrote this, but the guy isn't going to live forever, *because he's not a vampire, y'all.* So I thought I should clarify that as of this moment Lance Armstrong is awesome. Even with only one ball. Hell, *especially* with only one ball. I'm going to stop now.

The evening was perfect, except for the one time when Victor went to reload (buying another pallet of popcorn) and I was attacked by a guy who looked exactly like Sam Elliott, and I got so much popcorn down my dress it looked like I'd developed a series of horrible tumors. Also, you know when you get that annoying piece of popcorn stuck in your teeth but you can't get it out because it would be too embarrassing to dig it out in front of strangers? Imagine that happening, but instead of it being in between your teeth, it's stuck in your ear canal. And by "ear canal" I mean "vagina."

Then the cancan girls came out and everyone sang along to "Deep in the Heart of Texas" and "The Yellow Rose of Texas" with the live orchestra. Then a man onstage quoted Sam Houston, saying, "Texas can make it without the United States, BUT THE UNITED STATES CANNOT MAKE IT WITHOUT TEXAS!" and everyone *in the entire fucking audience* yelled it along with him, and I thought, "*Wow.* It's really no wonder that the rest of America hates us."

Not blood.

After the whole play/melodrama/burlesque thing ended, I looked down and saw these small patches of blood on the floor, and I was a little unsettled, because Victor *had* been threatening to put rocks in his popcorn in order to take out the front row. But it turns out that the carpet was red, and that was the only part of it you could see under the piles and piles of popcorn.

As we walked out, I noticed that a woman I'd seen sitting off in a corner was walking in front of us. She'd obviously been expecting something else when told she was going to see "live theater" that night, and she'd seemed both frightened and appalled by everyone's boorish behavior. As she walked through the drifts of popcorn she muttered to her date, "Ugh . . . What an offensive waste of food. Just think of all the starving children in Africa." She may have had a point, but I thought it was a little offensive to want to give starving people popcorn touched by vaginas. "Here you go," I could imagine her saying condescendingly to the villagers. "Take some more vagina popcorn. This batch was only on the floor for an hour. You need it more than we do." It seemed insulting, and I felt pretty certain that even starving people would have turned their noses up at it. "No, no. We're fine. *Really.* Please stop with the vagina popcorn." Also, the popcorn was kind of stale and gross, and I know this because I ate some, and then I felt very sick later. Victor pointed out that it was no surprise. I was eating from the same bag of popcorn that I'd thrown at people, and that they'd thrown back, and it would land in my bosom and I'd scoop it out and throw it back at them, and then they'd volley it back, and inevitably some of it was landing in the sack I was eating from, and I'm pretty sure that's how I got swine flu.

The next day we went back to my parents' to set off fireworks for the Fourth of July, and as we finished up the Roman candles my dad said, "Oh! I promised the grandkids we could set off the cannon tonight," and Hailey screamed, "Yay!"

"You promised my preschooler *that she could light a cannon?*" I asked in disbelief.

"No. *Of course not,*" he replied. "I told Tex he could do it." And that seemed much safer, because *Tex was fucking six.* I looked at my sister to see whether she was okay with her kid light-ing a Civil War cannon, but she just kind of shrugged, because she's used to this sort of thing, and had learned to pick her battles.

My parents' backyard. The gas pump is not functional. The cannon and chickens are.

"Are you sure this is safe?" Lisa asked, and Daddy assured us that he was only going to let Tex pack and prep the cannon—which consisted of Tex standing right in front of a *giant fucking loaded cannon*—but my sister was fairly undisturbed, because she knew Daddy probably couldn't get the rusty cannon lit anyway. And she was right. But then Daddy decided he just needed more fire, so he brought out the blowtorch to light the dodgy cannon. This was when I ran for my camera, because I knew no one would ever believe me.

The cannon would undoubtedly be loud and unneighborly obnoxious at that time of night, but then I remembered that the neighbors had been setting off fireworks at midnight all week long, and I thought it would kind of be kick-ass payback if the cannon actually did go off. And it did. And it was awesome, and no one died *or* got blood on them, so we considered it one of the most successful nights that week.

As we walked back inside for our final night at my parents', Victor pointed at a table that had been raised up with chains to the ceiling of the carport. He said there seemed to be a dead bear on it, and I assumed that Victor was drunk, but when we went out to pack the car the next morning I realized Victor was correct. My first thought was that I probably need glasses, because it's probably odd to not notice a dead bear floating on a table in the backyard all week. But then I realized I hadn't actually noticed the cannon at first either, and blamed it on the fact that I was too distracted by everything else. Because that's the kind of backyard they have. One where cannons and floating bears don't stick out.

I stared at the bear and wondered whether Daddy was trying to raise him from the dead, à la Dr. Frankenstein when he hoisted his monster up to the roof to attract the lightning. But then I realized it was probably just a polite way of getting a dead bear out of the way when you had company over, and in a

way it struck me as being kind of ingenious. Like window blinds, but with dead bears.

Victor agreed that it made sense, but then he looked a little shaken and insisted we go home immediately, because whenever all of this starts to seem rational to us that's usually a sign that we need to leave.

Stabbed
by Chicken

A couple of years ago one of my fingers swelled up like an enormous wiener. The kind you get at the ballpark that plumps when you cook it. Not the other kind. That would be weird. I don't even know why I'm clarifying this. You know what? *Let's start again.*

A couple of years ago one of my fingers swelled up like an enormous vagina. *Kidding.* It actually just swelled up like a giant swollen finger. It looked like I was wearing one of those "we're number one!" foam fingers, except that I wasn't. Sometime during the night I had been struck down with a case of lethal finger cancer. Victor rolled his eyes and muttered that I was a chronic hypochondriac, and I glared at him and rubbed my enormous nonfoam finger down his cheek, whispering, "Thinner." Then he made me go to the doctor. Alone. Because apparently he thinks I'm strong enough to handle a finger cancer diagnosis with absolutely no support. Or because he's emotionally shut down and didn't want to consider my own mortality. Or because he thought I'd just injured it again, like the time when our dog stabbed me with a chicken in the finger. Probably the last one.

This is the point where I would go into detail about my finger cancer, but my editor just read this and told me that you can't claim that your dog stabbed you with chicken and not logically explain that. I told her that logic didn't enter into it and she agreed, but probably not for the same reasons. So, *fine.* Here is the prequel to the cancerfingersplosion story, which I pretty much just pulled from my blog because it happened years ago and I only vaguely remember the details. Because I blocked them out. Because my dog tried to kill me. With chicken.

Blog entry: I can barely even type this because my hand is all swollen, but I was just carrying my pug (Barnaby Jones Pickles) into bed when he suddenly did this flip that almost broke my middle finger, and then he ran in between my legs, and I fell so hard that I couldn't even move. And just to make it more festive, the dog was jumping on my head (probably to make it seem like we were just play-wrestling and that he *wasn't* trying to murder me, in case witnesses were watching), but I wasn't falling for it, so I yelled for Victor, who found me lying on my stomach in front of the fridge. He was all, *"What. The fuck. Did you do?"* and I said, "The dog tried to kill me." Then Victor leaned down and raised an unnecessary eyebrow as he said in disbelief, *"Our dog*? Our *tiny* little dog did *this to you*?" and I was all, "HE'S LIKE A NINJA!" Then Victor said, "He's a fucking *pug*. He can't even reach the couch," and I was all, "I'M VULNERABLE, ASSHOLE," and then Victor tried to help me up, and I screamed because I'm pretty sure you're not supposed to move an accident victim, because they could be paralyzed.

Victor agreed to let me just lie on the floor, but only if I would wiggle my feet for him, but at that point I was too afraid that the jostling of my legs might cause my spinal cord to snap, so he picked up the phone and I yelled, "DO *not* CALL AN AMBULANCE," and he sighed, saying, "If you don't move your legs I'm going to call the ambulance. Except that *I'm* probably going to get arrested for domestic battery, because *what the hell happened?!"* And I was all, "Oh my God, there are a *lot* of marbles under the refrigerator. *When did we have marbles in the house?*" Then Victor made that noise that usually accompanies him putting his hand over his face and shaking his head like he can't even believe this is his life, but after a few seconds he paused and said, "Wait. *Where is all this blood coming from?*" And that's when I noticed I had a long, shallow gash on my hand, and I propped myself up on my elbows to look at it, saying, "How the hell *did* that happen?" And that's how we figured out I wasn't paralyzed.

I half suspected that Victor had poured fake blood on me just to distract me into moving, but he almost never has fake blood on him. He's just not that kind of guy. He might have a tape measure or an expired credit card, but if you need a fake arm or a bear claw you're looking at the wrong guy. It was nice, though, to see that I was bleeding, because then I knew that at least Victor would take me more seriously. However, I quickly discovered that the main reason he was freaked out about the blood was that we hadn't sealed the kitchen grout yet, and that this would surely leave a stain. It was a bit uncaring, but I understood his aggravation, because if I ever ended up abducted, this bloodstain could tie him to the murder, but I didn't mention it, because I didn't want to give him any ideas. Also, he may have just been pissed about all the marbles under the fridge. But I brushed off his silly housekeeping concerns because I suddenly realized that I was bleeding BECAUSE I'D BEEN STABBED BY CHICKEN.

Coincidentally, this is also when I realized that no one would ever believe this scenario, and also that Victor was *definitely* going to jail, because *who gets stabbed by chicken?* I do, *apparently.* It was one of those dried, sliced chicken-breast treats that I'd been holding in my hand because I was going to feed it to Barnaby Jones, and it was ~~slightly~~ ~~dangerously~~ *ludicrously* sharp and apparently quite stabbable with enough force. It seemed unbelievable, but it was the kind of thing that could happen to anyone who fell onto a shiv made of poultry. Except that now that I consider it, I'm probably the only person in the world to ever get knifed by a chicken. So *I win*. Or lose. Maybe both.

And then I explained to Victor that it was just that I got stabbed with a chicken, and he started to call the ambulance again, because he assumed I had a concussion. I sighed, tugging on his pant leg to get his attention, and gave him a demonstration by grabbing the chicken shiv and making a stabbing motion with my good hand. And then he stared at me in bafflement and hung up the phone, because he finally understood, or maybe because he thought I was threatening to stab him. Victor explained that he didn't know what he would tell the ambulance drivers anyway, because, *"There's no way anyone would believe that our adorable dog could do this sort of damage,"* and he said it in a *really* condescending and judgmental way, and I think that's why I found myself defensively screaming, "YOU DON'T KNOW WHAT HE'S LIKE WHEN YOU AREN'T HERE." This was when Victor tucked Barnaby Jones under his arm, saying, "Don't listen to Mommy's ravings, Mr. Jones," and carried him to bed so they could watch *Mythbusters* together. I may have yelled from the floor, *"He would have pushed me down the stairs, if we had stairs."* I also may have implied that Barnaby Jones would probably rip out our throats while we slept, now that he'd developed a taste for human blood, and Victor yelled that Barnaby Jones couldn't hear the TV because of all of the shouting, and that he wasn't going to talk to someone who was overreacting on the kitchen floor. I explained that "overreaction" is a common symptom of a person going into shock, and he said that it wasn't, and so I had to go look for my medical dictionary myself, with my broken finger, and I couldn't even find it. I shouldn't even be allowed to type this right now.

I should be wrapped in a warm blanket and not be allowed to go to sleep. Or I should be made to go to sleep. One of those. Or maybe I need a hot toddy. I probably *knew* the correct procedure for this sort of thing before the dog gave me a concussion by trying to kill me with chicken.

P.S. Victor *totally* owes me, because he would have gone to jail automatically because he was wearing only a half-shirt, and if you aren't wearing a whole shirt when the police come, you go to jail. That's how jail works.

P.P.S. Just to clarify, it's a half-shirt in that it's sleeveless. It's not the kind that ends under his nipples. Victor can't really pull that sort of look off. I don't know whether you go to jail for that kind of shirt. Probably so, though, if there's a nipply half-shirt, a dog, and a bunch of human blood involved.

P.P.P.S. How do you know whether your pupils are dilated? What are they supposed to look like normally? Why is WebMD so complicated? Why can't I stop reading about cancer when I'm trying to look up concussions? Great. *Now I have cancer.* Thanks a lot, Barnaby Jones.

Updated: Went to the ER this morning. Explained the situation. They wrote, "Stabbed by chicken," on my chart. Then they asked whether I had any "psych issues," but I thought they said "psychic issues" and I was all, "Like . . . *can I read your thoughts*?" Then they put me in a private room. I think the lesson here is that you should fake mental illness to get faster service. Turns out, though, that it's just a sprain, so I have to wear a splint until it heals, and I also have to keep it elevated. Here's a picture of me driving myself home:

Stop honking at me. I'm disabled, you bastards.

Awesome. The people in my neighborhood are lucky to have me.

P.P.P.P.S. Several of my friends have implied that Barnaby Jones was probably just acting in self-defense, since you're not supposed to give dogs chicken bones, but these are *fancy, filleted, boneless chicken breasts.* Meanwhile, *I'm* eating ramen noodles, and his sweater cost more than my entire outfit. Way to blame the victim, people. *I may never play the ukulele again.*

No one's falling for it, Barnaby Jones.

AND *THAT'S THE END* of the "stabbed by chicken" story. Unless I'm at a party. Then you can't *get me to stop telling that story*, because it never gets old. Unless you're Victor, who says he would prefer that I never mention it again. Probably because he knows he looks like an accomplice. Plus, I think he's embarrassed when I mention all of those grapes I discovered under the fridge, so for his sake I changed them to "marbles" in this book. *You're welcome, Victor.*

Aaaanyway, right now you're probably asking yourself, *"Just how many finger-injury stories can this girl possibly have?"* and the answer is, "Lots." But the only one I'm telling you (aside from the "stabbed by chicken" story) is the one I started with way back at the beginning of this chapter, because I'm saving the rest for book two. But these are totally the best of all my finger stories, so just be forewarned that when book two comes out, *Publishers Weekly* is going to be all, *"If you are expecting more of the same masterful retelling of brilliant finger-damage stories from overnight-sensation and long-suffering saint Jenny Lawson, then think again, because this book is all thumbs."* Or they might say something about how it has "two left feet." It's hard to tell with *Publishers Weekly.* Honestly, they write just horrible reviews. In fact, I bet they're writing a terrible one about this book even as we speak, but probably just because I totally called them out, *and* I just used the review *they* wanted to be able to use, and now they're all, "What the hell are we going to say now? She took all the good lines. I mean, 'All thumbs'? *That's gold, you guys.*" And I'm sorry about that, *Publishers Weekly*, but I'm a writer. *That's what I do. (Editor's note: I quit.)*

So. As we discussed earlier, I'm at the doctor's office, alone with my finger cancer, wondering whether I should have just gone straight to an oncologist instead, but I bravely hold out my swollen finger and the doctor looks at me condescendingly and says, "Oh. You got a boo-boo, huh?" Then I kicked him right in his junk. But only in my head, because doctors are quick to file assault charges, because they can make up their own medical damages. Like, *a doctor* could claim I gave him "popped ball," and no jury in the land would question him, but if *I* insist that I have finger cancer, people stare at me like I'm crazy (in, coincidentally, exactly the same way that the doctor was looking at me right then. Like *I'm* the crazy one). Keep in mind that *he* just sued *me* for something called "popped ball." Except that that only happened in my head too. On second thought, don't keep that in mind. This whole paragraph isn't really doing me any favors.

The doctor quickly dismissed my claims of cancer, but I insisted that he research digital cancer first, because I was pretty sure I was dying of it.

"What's that? You think you have cancer caused by digital exposure?" Dr. Roland asked me over the rims of his glasses.

"*No,*" I replied testily. "I'm pretty sure 'digital' is Latin for 'fingeral,' so finger cancer equals digital cancer. *This is all basic anatomy, Dr. Roland.*" Then Dr. Roland told me that he thought I was overreacting, and that "fingeral" wasn't even a real word. Then I told him that I thought he was *underreacting*, probably because he's embarrassed that he doesn't know how Latin works. Then he claimed that "underreacting" isn't a word either. The man has a terrible bedside manner.

Dr. Roland sort of harrumphed at me, and I pointed my enormous E.T. finger at him, demanding, "*This* doesn't look cancerous to you?!" He assured me it wasn't cancer and was simply a spider bite. A savage, noxious spider that injects the eggs of her young with her venomous bite so that they can fester and feed on the finger flesh of an unsuspecting young writer who probably also has *one hell* of a malpractice case on her (probably cancerous) hands. The doctor didn't actually tell me any of that last part, but I could see it there in his eyes.

When I got home Victor asked what the doctor had said, and I explained, "He sent me home to die."

"*He did what?*"

"I mean, he sent me home with ointment." It was all very anticlimactic.

Turns out, though, that Dr. Roland was very wrong, and after a lot of blood work (and a new doctor), I discovered that I didn't have finger cancer *or* finger spiders, and that instead I had arthritis.

Whenever I tell people I have arthritis they usually say, "*But you seem so young*," which is sort of a backhanded compliment that I never get tired of hating. I will probably only hate the phrase even more when I get to the age when people *stop* saying it, and suddenly begin saying, "Oh, arthritis. Of course you have it." Then I plan to run over them with my wheelchair. I always explain that it's *rheumatoid* arthritis (a.k.a. RA), which can strike even children, and I'm not even sure why it's labeled as arthritis at all, since it's only vaguely related to the osteoarthritis that your great-grandmother complains about. I've considered lobbying the medical field to rename rheumatoid arthritis something sexier, younger, and more exotic. Something like "The Midnight Death," or "Impending Vampirism." Or perhaps to name it after someone famous. Like "Lou Gehrig's disease, part two: THE RECKONING." After all, rheumatoid arthritis is painful enough without the added embarrassment of sounding like something your nana had, so it seems only fair that we should be able to tell people that we had to miss their party because of an unexpected flare-up of "Impending Vampirism."

My new RA doc was very kind, and reassured me that an RA diagnosis was not the death sentence it had once been, and then I found myself hyperventilating a bit because a doctor had just said "death sentence" to me, and he got his nurse to help me put my head between my knees and breathe deeply. Then he said that although there was no cure, there were a lot of experimental treatments that we could "try." Then I passed out, but probably less from the news that I had an incurable disease and more because I tend to pass out whenever I see people in doctors' coats. I have passed out on school field trips to clinics, at the optometrists', during gynecological visits, and once even at the veterinarian's, when I fainted unexpectedly and fell on my cat. (The last one was the most disconcerting, because I came to in the lobby with a lot of dogs and strangers leaning over me as

I realized my shirt was completely unbuttoned as a team of paramedics checked my heart and my cat cowered under a chair while glaring at me accusingly.) When I came to in the RA office, my doctor had me lie down as he explained that it was nothing to panic about, and that although no one knew what caused the disease they suspected it was congenital. I'd been only half listening because I was too busy trying not to throw up, and so I looked at the doctor with wide eyes and said, "I'm sorry. *Genital?*"

"Uh . . . *what?*" the doctor asked.

"Did you say my arthritis is genital?"

"No." He chuckled. "*Con*genital. Or possibly hereditary." I sighed in relief, finding at least a little solace in his answer, and I found myself wondering what an arthritic vagina would even look like. He assured me that my genitals would be just fine, but honestly he looked a tiny bit alarmed. Probably because he'd never thought to research arthritis of the vagina. But they should. So far I've had arthritis in all fingers, my neck, arms, legs, feet, and in one ear. I can only assume vaginal arthritis is lurking right around the corner, waiting to strike when you least suspect it. Which is *always*, really. No one ever expects vaginal arthritis.[1]

My doctor explained that I had a rare form of the disease called polyarthritis, which meant that instead of staying in a single place, the arthritis jumps around from body part to body part on an almost daily basis. One day I'll wake up with an ankle so swollen it looks like I'm wearing a single nude leg warmer stuffed with apples. The next day my ankle will be fine, but I won't be able to move my left shoulder without wanting to stab a kitten. The best way I can describe it is that every night I go to bed knowing that Freddy Krueger will be waiting to beat the shit out of me with a baseball bat, and that I'll wake up with whatever horrific injuries he's inflicted. Except that this isn't a movie about Elm Street and it's my life. Plus, Johnny Depp isn't there. So it sucks in a myriad of ways.

-- -- -- -- -- -- -- --

1. Or the Spanish Inquisition.

The doctor was right about there being a lot of treatment options, but I was disappointed to find that none of them included medically prescribed Segways, or personal monkey butlers to help you open pickle jars. Instead I was given a drug that starts with "meth-" and ends with "your-hair-will-fall-out-and-you-will-never-stop-vomiting-if-you-don't-take-a-daily-antidote," because apparently it's also a chemo drug. Interestingly enough, one of the many side effects of the drug is that even though it's a drug designed to battle cancer, IT FUCKING *CAUSES* CANCER. The doctor explained that the drug-induced cancer happened only in rare cases, but considering that I was just diagnosed with one of the rarest forms of a rare disease to begin with, it seemed like this was exactly the kind of lottery I should be avoiding. He convinced me it was worth the risks, but cautioned me not to panic when the warning label on the medicine would scare the shit out of me. He was right. It said, "Holy *shit*, MOTHERFUCKER. *YOU ARE GOING TO FUCKING DIE.*"[2] I'm just paraphrasing, but that's the gist. Also, in my head it sounded exactly like Samuel L. Jackson, so I was scared, but still entertained.

And what really sucks is that NO ONE EVEN KNOWS WHY THIS DRUG WORKS. They're guessing it *may* work because it fucks up your immune system and keeps cells from growing properly, so your body attacks your immune system instead of your joints. Because who needs a working immune system when you have an autoimmune disease that makes you so sick that your best option is to take a drug *that can kill you*? Basically it's like being stabbed in the neck to take your mind off your stubbed toe. Still, the drugs seem to help somewhat, so I take them and try not to imagine what it would be like without them.

I've had arthritis for years now, and sometimes it's gone, and some-

---

2. Actual warning: "Some side effects may cause death. You should only take this drug to treat life-threatening cancer, or certain other conditions that are very severe and that cannot be treated with other medications."

times I'm bedridden, but either way I'm constantly having to go in for blood work and X-rays, and the best news that the doctor can give me is that my blood has not turned toxic and that there are "no obvious deformities yet." That's how you know you're fucked. When a medical professional tries to give you a high five *because you're not as deformed as they expected.*

I muddled through the first few years, always hoping that I'd suddenly find out that I'd been cured.

"I don't understand," I told my doctor. "I've been taking various treatments for years and I still hurt."

"It's easy to get discouraged," he said gently, "but you have to keep in mind that you have a degenerative disease."

"Yes, but I thought I'd be better by now."

"Ah," said my doctor. "I think maybe you just don't understand what 'degenerative' means."

Awesome. I was not getting cured *and* my vocabulary skills were being questioned.

When my latest blood test came back, the doctor said it was no surprise that I was in a lot of pain, since my results showed an arthritis "double positive." I wasn't sure what that meant, but I suspect it means that my arthritis is an overachiever.

I started taking herbal supplements and giant fish oil pills every day, and when Victor complained that I was just throwing money away, I pointed out that fish oil is supposed to be good for your joints, because fish are . . . well lubricated, I guess? He stared at me, perplexed at my reasoning.

"Well, it can't hurt," I said. "You almost never see a fish with bad ankles. Or . . . you know . . . limping."

"I think someone just sold you a bill of goods. Didn't they used to sell fish oil back in the eighteen hundreds to suckers?"

"No," I answered. "That was *snake* oil. Although I have always wondered how you get oil from a snake. It seems like a lot of trouble to go through

for something that didn't work anyway. Imagine how many people were getting bitten each day trying to oil snakes."

"What are you talking about? You don't *oil* snakes."

"Yeah, you do. I'm pretty sure 'oil' is a verb in this case. You get cow milk by milking a cow, so you get snake oil by oiling a snake. This is all basic commonsense stuff."

This was when Victor asked exactly what sort of herbal supplements I was taking, and insisted that I stop taking the ones that weren't written in English or came in baggies from questionable health stores. He was right, but I was desperate, and it was that fit of desperation that led me to agree to let Victor take me to an acupuncturist.

I'd never gone to an acupuncturist before, but I'd heard enough about them to think that I knew what I was getting myself into. But it turns out that all the people who told me that acupuncture is awesome and doesn't hurt at all *are complete fucking liars.* Or maybe my acupuncturist is just bad, or just really hates white people. Hard to tell.

Regardless, I think it behooves the world for me to tell you what really happens at an acupuncturist so that you won't go in as blindly as I did:

1. The nurse will tell you to take off everything but your underwear. So maybe you should wear underwear. And maybe they should *tell you that* when you make the appointment.

2. Special note to people bringing their small children: What the hell is wrong with you? The "dollhouse" on the waiting room floor isn't a dollhouse. It's a shrine. If you let your son's G.I. Joe "conquer it and claim it in the name of the United States," you are probably going to go to hell. Also, maybe you shouldn't piss off the guy who's about to stab needles into you. Just a suggestion, lady.

3. The acupuncturist will come in and you'll try to explain what hurts, and then he'll shake his head, because he doesn't speak English. He'll call in his nurse and you'll explain about where your rheumatism is, and how long it's hurt, and what drugs you're on, and she'll look at the doctor and yell, "SHE SAYS SHE HURT," and then walk out of the room. Then the doctor will give you a look like "Why are you wasting my time? *Of course you hurt.* Why would perfectly normal people come to have needles stuck in them?" Then he'll make you lie back on the table and start jabbing needles into you.

4. The needles are small and won't hurt at all. In fact, they'll feel good. Ha, ha! Just kidding. They feel like needles. *Because they are.*

5. The doctor will stick one needle into your ear and it will start bleeding. You will be bleeding from your ear. I can't even stress this enough. BLEED-ING FROM THE EAR. Then he'll open an English book about acupunc-ture and make you read a paragraph about how the ear is the shape of an upside-down fetus and so it's good to stick needles in it. I desperately hope that paragraph has lost something in translation, because I'm pretty sure you're not supposed to stab needles in fetuses. I make a mental note to ask my gynecologist. Then I make a mental note not to, because even if I can manage to describe this properly, asking my gynecologist whether it's okay to stick needles in fetuses is just going to make the next Pap smear more awkward.

6. Forty-four needles later. Several of them are bleeding. The other ones actually start to feel a little tingly. The doctor will leave and you'll try to look down at yourself, but you can't because it's making the needles in your neck stick farther into you. At this point you will pass out from shock.

Then the acupuncturist will come back in and smugly claim you fell asleep from all the chi. I agree, if *chi* is Chinese for "massive blood loss."

7. The forty-four needles all come out. You start to leave and the doctor laughs and tells you he's just begun, and that now he has to do "your butt side." Then you say, "My butt side?" and he's all, "No. Your butt side." Then the nurse yells, "YOUR BACKSIDE," from out in the hall, and he's all, "Yes. Your butt side." Awesome.

8. Forty-two more needles. All in my butt side. Two hurt like hell and are bleeding a lot. You start to suspect that the acupuncturist is just mad at you. You try to explain that you were not with the woman in the lobby who let her kid's action figures commandeer his shrine. He totally does not believe you.

9. Forty-two needles all come out. Then he pours some sort of liquid on you that I've decided to call "stink juice." And he kneads it into your pores, so that you smell like a dirty old sock that someone has been storing patchouli and VapoRub in.

10. Then you hear the sound of a lighter, and you suspect that you're about to get your hair set on fire, but then the acupuncturist explains that he's going to do a little "cupping," which I think was what my first boyfriend referred to as second base. It sounded totally inappropriate, and I started to protest, but turns out it's just when a doctor sets fire to the alcohol in a small jar and then places it over the skin so it acts as a vacuum and gives you an enormous hickey. Which, now that I think about it, still sounds kind of inappropriate.

11. Then the acupuncturist will open up a piece of tissue paper filled with a white powder, and will hand it to you, and look at you in expectation. And you'll be like, "Do you want me to . . . *Do I snort this?*" And then he'll shake his head at your idiocy and make you open your mouth so he can pour what looks like the stuff from the inside of a Ped Egg into your mouth. Then he'll laugh at your look of horror, and hand you water and make you keep drinking and swishing it in your mouth until it's all gone. Then he'll say, "Ginseng tea for detox," and you'll be all, *"That's not how you make tea,"* and he'll smile and walk out while you wonder why you just allowed a strange Chinese man to feed you mystery powder wrapped in tissue paper *when he doesn't even know how tea works*. You can just stop wondering now, because there is no fucking good answer to this question.

12. The acupuncturist will leave and you'll get dressed, feeling mildly assaulted and vaguely confused, and then you'll realize that you can actually put on your shirt for the first time all week without screaming in pain. And then you go and make another appointment for next week. Except your husband will vow to never drive you again because he claims that now his car smells like "old dirty hippie."

But here's the deal: Between the herbs, and oil, and acupuncture, and the cancer drugs, and all of the rest of it, you find yourself occasionally having pain-free days. Days that you learn to appreciate simply because no one stuck eighty-six needles in you that morning. Days when you have an impromptu picnic on the lawn because you can bend your knees that day. Days when studies are released showing that booze helps stave off arthritis attacks. Those are the golden days.

And even on days when I'm bedridden and can't move, I'm grateful to have my daughter curl up near me and watch old *Little House on the Prairie* episodes. I try to be appreciative of what I have instead of bitter about what I've lost. I try to accept this disease with grace, and patiently wait for the day when they find a cure. And for when I get my monkey butler.[3]

_____ _____ _____ _____ _____ _____

3. Also, from now on, all the handicapped parking spots really do belong to people in wheelchairs and not just to people who *feel* like they're disabled because they have really bad cramps that day. And also, if you're in a wheelchair you get frontsies in line at the liquor store from now on. And you get free sexy shoes. We need to get this all passed in Congress ~~before I'm disabled because then it'll look like I'm just doing it for me~~ *because that's what Jesus would do.*

It Wasn't Even
My Crack

Not long after I quit my job to become a writer, Victor quit his to be an executive at a medical software company. This was awesome, except for the fact that now both of us worked at home and constantly wanted to murder each other. I took a lot of freelance writing jobs to pay the bills, including one where I was paid to review bad porn. Victor would walk around the house in his Britney Spearsesque hands-free headset, making business deals and screaming things like "BUY! SELL! WE NEED MORE ELEPHANTS ON THIS PROJECT!" Or something like that. Honestly, I wasn't really listening. I just know that nothing is more distracting than a man wandering aimlessly through your home while yelling to himself about spreadsheets and investment returns while you're trying to write a satirical article about the eternal cultural relevancy of *Edward Penishands*.

Inevitably Victor would wander blindly into my office as he walked around the house, looking as if he were screaming about project management to the confused cats hiding under my desk. I'd glare at him, but he would never get the hint, so instead I'd pull up a work-related porn clip from my computer, skip to the money shot, and turn the volume to eleven. Victor would look at me in horrified panic as he'd cover his mouthpiece and run from my office, desperately hitting mute and whisper-screaming to me about being on an important conference call. Then he'd ask—in his professional telephone voice—whether everyone was all right, as it sounded like someone was hurt, and I had to hand it to him, because that was a pretty good recovery. Then he'd come back and explain the importance of silence on his serious conference call, and I would stress the importance of staying in his own damn office. Then he'd stress the importance of my "doing some real work instead of just watching porn at three in the afternoon," and I'd stress that I was not "enjoying" the porn and that I was merely "reviewing" it. FOR RESEARCH. Considering that we spent a majority of our workday in pajamas while porn played in the background, there was a surprising amount of stress in that workplace.

Eventually Victor would stalk off, muttering about ethics and courtesy, and I'd scream down the hall, "THIS IS MY JOB, ASSHOLE. STOP HASSLING ME OR I WILL STAB YOU IN THE EYE," and then he'd put his call on mute again and threaten to poison my coffee. It was a lot like working in a regular office, except that there were cats there, and also you got to say out loud exactly what you would have just said in your head if you worked in an office that had cubicles and security guards.

Before, when we both worked out of the house, we used to come home and bond by complaining about the moronic people in our respective offices who were obviously trying to destroy us, but now we couldn't even have that conversation, because, as we were the only ones there, it was perfectly obvious that the only moronic coworkers now trying to destroy us actually *were us*. After many months of near stabbings, we finally agreed that we needed a house where our offices were farther apart, and we realized that there was nothing tying us to Houston any longer. We were free to move anywhere we wanted. Victor suggested Puerto Rico, but when I looked in my heart I knew where I wanted to move, and no one was more shocked about it than myself, because it went against everything I'd promised myself years earlier when I had Hailey.

When Hailey was born my first thought was that I needed a drink and that hospitals should have bars in them. My second was to assure myself that Hailey would have an *entirely different childhood* than I had had. I looked at her little face, and I promised to never throw large, dead wild animals on the kitchen table, or set cougars loose in the house. Victor seemed confused but agreed, as he assumed that the drugs were still in my system. They were, but it didn't change the fact that I was determined that Hailey'd have a life of ballet lessons and museums, and would never wander into the backyard to look at the caged bobcats, only to find a pet duck whose beak had been eaten off by a wild raccoon.

After Hailey was born, Victor and I had settled into life in the suburbs just out of Houston, and I struggled in vain to fit in. Hailey was almost four now, and she was sheltered, and protected, and slightly pale from lack of sun in her small private school, where she was learning music and dance and how to be exactly like everyone else. We enrolled her in gymnastics, but all the other preschoolers seemed to be practicing for the Olympics, and more than one mom mentioned putting their toddlers on diets, which was just fucking crazy. In the end, we decided to just quit and let her jump on the couch. Still, she was on the perfect path to fitting in beautifully in a normal, pretty life, *and it scared the shit out of me.* Both because I wasn't sure I was actually doing her any favors by protecting her from a life that I found I actually missed, and also because I had to admit that I found myself feeling a little sorry for Hailey. For not being able to go explore the canals, or feed deer in the yard, or have memories of playing with baby raccoons in the house. We had our cats, and she loved our sweet pug, Barnaby Jones Pickles, who was awesome (who was as close to Laura Ingalls's brindle bulldog as we would ever get), but he was no bathtub full of raccoons, and I suspect even he would have agreed with that.

And so that's when I found myself convincing Victor that we should move to the country with a few acres of land, so Hailey could run, and explore, and experience a little of the fucked-up sort of rural life that had made Victor and me able to pretend to be comfortable in many different social circles without ever actually fitting into any of them. We'd both had fond memories of growing up in wide-open places, and I was shocked to suddenly realize that now that I'd seen what it was like to live on the pleasant-but-boring "other side of the tracks," the childhood of country life that I'd wanted to save Hailey from was one that I now treasured. The heat and wild animals and isolation had molded who I was, and I found myself proud of those bumps along the way that had shaped me. It seemed unfair to deprive Hailey of those same experiences, and moving to the country seemed like the perfect answer.

Hailey—discovering the joy of dirt.

West Texas had changed too much to feel like home, but we eventually found a house in the Texas Hill Country, an hour outside Austin. It was in a tiny town, thirty miles from the nearest grocery store, but it was quiet, and nice, and the house sat on a few acres of trees that drifted down to a pretty, open meadow filled with bluebonnets. I felt like I was home. Plus, my office was on the opposite side of the house from Victor's, and both had doors you could actually close.

And there was sun:

As always when we bought a new home, Victor asked the questions about deed restrictions and taxes, while I asked the two questions I was always responsible for: "Has anyone ever died in the house?" and "How many bodies are buried on the property?" I always assume real estate agents are honest on the first question, because legally I think they have to disclose that, but technically I don't think they're required to answer the second. I used to ask whether *anyone* was buried on the property, but I was afraid that real estate agents weren't being honest with me, so I switched it to "*How many* bodies are buried on the property?" because then it makes it sound like I expect there are bodies buried because that's totally normal, and so they'll be relieved and casually let slip that there are only two and a half bodies buried there. Victor says that my asking those questions is actually doing just the opposite, and that I'm making every-one uncomfortable, and then I point out that I'm actually fine with bodies buried on the property, but that I want to know where they are in case of the zombie apocalypse. This is the point when most real estate agents excuse themselves. Probably because it's boring to see couples arguing about the zombie apocalypse all the damn time. I expect this sort of thing is the downside to being a real estate agent.

Eventually, though, we bought the house and began the five stages of moving:

DAY 1: Pack everything nicely with Bubble Wrap. Clean it all first so it's fresh and ready to be unpacked. Label boxes on all sides.

DAY 2: Start intentionally breaking things so you have a reason not to wrap and pack them.

DAY 3: Find eighteen choppers in the kitchen drawers. Demand that Victor stop buying shit from infomercials late at night. Intentionally break seven-teen choppers.

DAY 4: Question why you ever started collecting little glass animals, and who allowed you to have fourteen hundred of them. Also, why do we have three junk drawers? Is that a sign that we've finally "made it," or a sign that we're hoarders? Try to get on Twitter to ask your friends, but then realize that your husband has already packed your computer cords. Feel utterly and completely alone. Cry in the bathroom, but be unable to blow your nose because you can't find the box you packed the toilet paper in.

DAY 5: Set a large bonfire in the living room. Laugh maniacally as you push cardboard boxes into it.

This was all true except for the very last part. In actuality, my father-in-law (Alan) came on day five to help us throw everything into boxes, and to keep me from throwing choppers at Victor, who'd spent all four days "packing" the garage, which I was pretty sure contained absolutely nothing of value, and which I would have sold for twenty dollars on Craigslist if Victor had died. I'm not entirely sure why a man would need two cabinets filled with tools, when *I've* been able to make it through thirty-five years of life with just duct tape and one screwdriver. Victor says it's because "people don't rebuild carburetors with duct tape," but I'm pretty sure that Victor just doesn't know how versatile duct tape is.

After we'd packed up the moving van, we began our long ride to our new home. A few minutes into the drive, Alan cleared his throat and self-consciously pulled a baggie out of his front pocket. "Oh. By the way. I found some . . . uh . . . *crack*, maybe?" he said as he hesitantly handed me the Ziploc bag of crack. My first thought was that it was strange that my very conservative father-in-law would offer me crack, and I wondered whether this was some sort of test. My second thought was that although I'd never seen crack before, I assumed it was expensive, and this seemed to be *a lot* of crack to have at one time. Unless possibly he was selling it, which seemed strange, since Alan was a very successful businessman. Still, I was aware that he'd given up a whole day to come help us, so I tried to be nonjudgmental as I struggled to find a polite way of turning him down, but then I recognized my handwriting on the baggie. I realized with relief that Alan must have found the bag when he was packing and was nice enough to bring it along for the ride. I laughed and explained, "Oh, this is not my crack. It's Hailey's," and he looked a bit more nauseated, and then I explained that what I really meant was that it was Hailey's *and* that it was not crack. It was a powder you can buy that explodes into fake snow when you add water. I explained that Hailey played with it every winter, since we didn't get real snow in Texas, and it was reusable but that when it dehydrates it looks like crack. I threw a small crack rock into an almost empty water bottle, and it instantly filled with snow, and Alan sighed with relief. It was a little insulting that he'd found crack and automatically assumed it was mine, but I considered everyone else who lived in the house and instead gave him credit for knowing me so well.

Soon after we moved in, I started researching the history of the area and found that we now lived on the edge of "The Devil's Backbone," one of the most haunted stretches of land in Texas. I've always been fascinated with ghost stories, so it didn't bother me until a neighbor came over and told me about the bodies buried down the road from us. "The *who* buried *where*?" I asked her. Turns out a family had been buried in what was then their backyard, but the wilderness had grown up around it, and now the graves were all but lost. It bothered me. Not that there was an impromptu cemetery down the road (dead neighbors make quiet neighbors . . . I think Robert Frost said that), but that there was a lost graveyard in our subdivision that no one could find. Had it been built over? Were the graves fresh? I'd been happy that we were so far out in the country and wouldn't be attacked by the hordes of overpopulated city zombies, but it concerned me that if the zombie apocalypse came we might have homemade zombies planted nearby, and we had no idea which direction they might come from. I was concerned. So was Victor, who said he'd appreciate it if I'd stop talking about the zombie apocalypse in front of our neighbors. "She deserves to know," I retorted, and I told Victor that we needed to find these graves, because I wouldn't be able to sleep until I knew where they were.

"No," he said firmly. "We're not going traipsing around the woods, look-ing for bodies in the unlikely event that there is a zombie apocalypse."

"CONSTANT VIGILANCE," I (may have) screamed. *I'm doing this for all of us, asshole."* And I was. We had a zombie garden somewhere nearby, and I wanted to be sure that it was old enough that the zombies would be no threat. We fought about it for a few days, until finally he agreed to find out where the graves were, probably because he finally realized that there are some unpleasant things the protector of the house is responsible for. Or possibly because I continually woke him up every three hours to ask whether he heard something on the back porch that sounded "hungry and shuffling."

Victor found a local guy who claimed to know where the graves were, and he said to just take the road at the end of the street. Except that there

wasn't a road at the end of the street. I pointed at two overgrown tracks in the grass. "I think that's what he's talking about."

"That's not a road," Victor said dismissively, but there was nothing else there.

"I'm pretty sure it's a road," I explained. "You can tell because there's a fire hydrant next to it."

He stared at me in aggravation and clenched his jaw as he turned our car onto the road that wasn't a road. Several minutes (and one dented oil pan later) we reached a dead end and Victor glared at me. Then something ran out from the brush and I screamed, "CHUPACABRA!" And then Victor slammed on the brakes and just stared at me like I'd gone insane. Probably because I'd been so flustered that I'd accidentally shouted, "CHALUPA!" which *I'll admit* is disconcerting to have someone scream at you while you're being attacked by a dangerous creature. In my defense, though, no one could be expected to communicate properly after seeing a vicious

Mexican goat-sucker monster running through the woods. Victor said he'd agree with me completely if the chupacabra hadn't actually just been a small deer. It was disheartening. Not only were we living in a neighborhood littered with chupacabras[1] who were great at impersonating deer, but also we never found the graves. *And* now I wanted a chalupa, and there wasn't a Taco Cabana within sixty miles of us. It was a failure by any standard, but I consoled Victor by reminding him that at least we didn't own any goats that we'd have to worry about getting sucked. Then Victor asked me to stop talking, and he told me (for the first of what would eventually be eight thousand times) that we had made a huge mistake in moving to the country.

I defended our new town and assured him we just needed to readjust, but he was right. Clearly we were in over our heads, and I felt it was just a matter of time until one of us got dysentery or yellow fever. Until then, though, we settled back, safe in the knowledge that in moving we'd somehow cheated death . . . certain that when the end came, it would not be from Victor and me stabbing each other from work-related stress, but more likely from the unchartered wilderness (and possible chupacabra zombies) outside our door. Victor and I were comforted in the knowledge that our offices were now far enough apart that we would be safe from each other, but still we were worried.

And we were right to be.

---

1. Spell-check refuses to recognize the word "chupacabra." Probably because it's racist. Spell-check, I mean. Not chupacabras. Chupacabras are monsters from Mexico that suck blood out of goats. They don't care what race you are. Bizarrely, spell-check is perfectly fine with the word "CHUPACABRA!" in all caps, which makes no sense at all. Unless it's because it recognizes that you'd use that word only while screaming. Touché, spell-check. P.S. Actual words used in this book that spell-check insists are not real words: Velociraptors. Shiv. Chupacabra. Yay. It's like spell-check doesn't even *want* me to write my memoir.

Honestly, I Don't Even Know Where I Got That Machete: A Comic Tragedy in Three ~~Parts~~ Days

Day 1:

The day that Barnaby Jones Pickles died was a difficult one.

We were still getting used to our new house, and we were planning how to build a backyard fence that would keep him in and the scorpions out. Until then, though, we'd simply let him run around the house most of the day, terrorizing the cats, and then put him out on an incredibly long leash/dog run attached to the back-porch banister, so he could run down to the meadow behind our house. But having a dog in the backyard, even for a little bit a day, is risky, and in the country I learned that it was just damned dangerous.

Learn from my mistakes, people.

I convinced myself that he'd be fine, as he had a covered porch to rest under, with several outdoor ceiling fans that ran constantly, plus a sprinkler to run in. I was certain that he was perfectly safe from everything but himself. He'd be frolicking around as I watched from the living room, and then two minutes later I'd look up again to find him with no leash left, having somehow woven an enormous, terribly designed sort of spiderweb with his leash, all of my porch chairs now caught unnaturally inside of it as he looked at me, his little pug head cocked to the side as if to say, ". . . *what the fuck just happened?*" I'd painstakingly untangle him and move the porch chairs around to the front of the house, but by the time that I got back he'd be tied to the barbecue grill, giving me the exact same look.

I started to suspect that in a past life he'd been a small and not very good pirate whose specialty was lashing himself to the mast at the most inopportune times. I could imagine the captain giving him the same pitying but frustrated look when he came up from his nap to find that Barnaby Jones Pirate had lashed himself to the wheel of the ship because he thought he saw a cyclone, which turned out to be some birds. I knew exactly how that captain must have felt, as he undoubtedly sighed and spent another half-hour unwinding the knotted ropes as Barnaby Jones licked him uncontrollably on the face. Or at least, that's what Barnaby Jones Pickles always did to me while I was untangling him. I suspect Barnaby Jones Pirate did it as well. There weren't a lot of girl pirates around, and I'm not going to judge a bunch of pirates and their licking practices. I'm totally pro–same-sex-licking. And pro-pirate. Except for the raping and pillaging parts. I'm anti–raping-and-pillaging. I'm pro–hooks-and-peg-legs. Which I think makes me pirate agnostic.

I never yelled at Barnaby, though, because it's hard to be mad at someone who's so damned happy to see you. "Good old Jones," I'd say gruffly, as I rubbed his ears while he joyfully attempted to gnaw the shoes I was wearing off of my feet. He'd smile in that semi-mindless way that pugs have perfected, and I'd try very hard not to fixate on the furious rabbit hiding in his forehead wrinkles (constantly glaring at me accusingly), both because it seemed to make the dog self-conscious, and also because Victor said that seeing an imaginary angry rabbit on your dog's forehead is probably some sort of Rorschach test that proves some mental illness that we couldn't afford to properly medicate anyway. But it was totally there. See below:

Angry forehead rabbit.

You have to tilt your head to the right & squint to see it but I assure you, it's *totally* there.

I drew in the rabbit face for people with little imagination,
but once you've seen it, it can't be unseen.

And then came the terrible day when I called Barnaby Jones to come inside, only to find him dead in the backyard, his furrowed bunny brow gone forever. His face was swollen, and our vet later said he'd most likely been bitten by a snake. I'd write something darkly comedic here to cut the sadness of the whole experience, but I just can't, because *I loved that damn dog.*

In my head I screamed obscenities at myself for ever leaving him outside, but I had to stay quiet so that Hailey wouldn't notice. I didn't want her to see him that way. Victor was out of town, and the vet's office answering machine said they were closed for the weekend, so I picked Barnaby up and carried him down to the meadow behind our house, and then cried until I couldn't cry anymore. Then, after an hour of backbreaking work digging a hole in ground that was almost entirely rock, I buried him there in the meadow he loved to frolic in. I piled a cairn of rocks on top of the grave to mark it. I did it alone, and it sucked.

When it was done, I told Hailey and hugged her while she cried. We held each other on the couch, and every few hours she'd ask me whether it was just a bad dream. I wished it were. She asked if we could go buy another pug and call him Barnaby Jones and just pretend that he never died. I told her that it wouldn't be fair to do that to Barnaby, but the truth was that I knew I couldn't handle this again, and I resolved then and there, *"I will never own another dog."*

I called Victor to tell him what had happened, and he cried. I told him that I'd buried Barnaby Jones in our meadow, and then Victor got very quiet, because he was perfectly aware of the fact that there's almost no dirt in the meadow. I suspected he was just quiet because he realized what a terrible predicament he'd put me in by not being home, but then he said enigmatically, "Keep an eye out to where you buried him." He said it exactly the same way that the guy in *Pet Sematary* (still purposely misspelled) would say it if you accidentally buried someone you loved in the part of the cemetery that resurrects bodies. I sighed and started crying again, because the last thing I wanted to do was to have to kill my already dead dog again when his soulless body dug itself out of the grave, and then Victor was all, *"What in the hell are you talking about?"* and I said, "You know . . . *SOMETIMES THEY COME BACK?"* Then Victor said he was going to call his parents to come get me, because I was obviously having some sort of nervous breakdown. At the time I thought he was saying that because I was getting all of my Stephen King stories confused in my head, but in retrospect it might have been because I just started ranting about having to murder our already dead dog with no real context. Either way, though, the worst part was over, and I assured Victor that in time I'd be okay.

And I totally would have been. If Barnaby Jones Pickles had not risen from the grave.

Day 2:

My neighbor came over to tell me she'd seen me digging a grave in the meadow yesterday, and thought she'd stop by to see if everything was okay. I was touched, both because she'd come to check on me and also because she'd assumed I was digging a grave but hadn't called the police. *"This,"* I thought to myself, "is *exactly* why I love the country." She also told me that it was likely that a rattlesnake had bitten Barnaby, as that had happened to two of her dogs. *"And this,"* I thought to myself, "is exactly why I *hate* the country."

I called Victor, who was still out of town for the week. "Barnaby Jones Pickles was actually killed by a rattlesnake. Also, apparently they're everywhere here, and they all want to kill your dog. I'm never leaving the house again. How do the guns work?" Victor was freaked out about that series of questions, and refused to give me the combination to the gun safe, because apparently he wanted the rattlesnakes to eat Hailey and me. Then he pointed out that rattlesnakes don't eat people, and that it was just as likely that Barnaby was killed by an allergic reaction from a bee as from a rattlesnake, and that I was probably just fixating on rattlesnakes to keep from having to mourn about Barnaby. Then I hung up on Victor and Googled, "How do I make rattlesnakes leave me alone?"

According to Wikipedia, snakes despise mothballs and will run from them at all costs (which seemed questionable, since snakes don't have legs). I suspected that Wikipedia had confused snakes with moths, but the mothball remedy was repeated on other sites as well, so I bought six economy-size boxes of mothballs and sprinkled them around the perimeter of the house so thickly that it looked like it had hailed in an incredibly fucked-up pattern. It also smelled as if my house were being surrounded by little old ladies, which was unfortunate, but I visualized that they were vicious old grannies who were all armed with snake-chopping battle-axes, and that made it easier to deal with.

I also called an exterminator, who said the mothballs were a good start, and that he'd bring over a giant can of snake repellent to spray around the perimeter to keep the snakes at bay. I asked, "So how do you make sure that the snake isn't already hiding *inside* the perimeter, and will now be trapped in here with me?"

He paused for a second, then replied, "Wow. That's a good question.

How *do* you know?" And I was like, "*This isn't a quiz.* I'm asking *you . . .* how do you know?" Then he said that if the snake wasn't already gone, it would be able to pass over the Snake-A-Way just to get far away from the scent. I asked, "So it's not like when you put a circle of salt around you to keep demons away?" And he was like, *"That works?"* And then I thought that maybe I needed to find a new exterminator.

I went out to do a second line of mothballs, and that was when I noticed that Barnaby Jones's grave had been disturbed. The cairn of stones I'd put on his little tomb had been knocked down, and I saw the tiny, horrifying hint of a paw sticking out. For a brief second I was terrified that Barnaby Jones was actually returning from the grave, and I froze, wondering whether I should help dig him out or call an exorcist. But as I watched, an enormous dark bird swooped down and pulled at the leg. I slowly made my way down the hill toward the meadow as a giant horde of raptors shrieked and took off from the tree they were perched in.

Vultures.

I ran to the garage to grab a machete, but every time I would walk away from Barnaby's grave they would swoop back in. Then I would scream and run at them, waving my machete angrily, and they would take a step back and look at me like I was being ridiculous. "You've left us food," they seemed to be saying. "Please stop trying to whack us in the heads with a machete. It's bad enough that you've *buried* our snack. Honestly, you're embarrassing all of us here."

I felt like Laura Ingalls when she was shooing away locusts from the wheat crop, except that my wheat crop was a dead dog and I didn't have a sunbonnet. I finally came inside and called my mom, and she was very understanding and supportive. She is, however, also a realist, and she suggested that maybe I should leave the house for a few days and just let Barnaby Jones have some sort of accidental Tibetan sky burial. My mom is the worst atheist ever. Also, it's possible that she was less pro–Tibetan-sky-burial and more just unsettled to learn that I own my own machete. It's like my mom has never even met me.

She had a point, though. It *was* the circle of life, but I wasn't okay with Barnaby Jones being an appetizer at that circle. I was also afraid that Hailey would see all the vultures pull Barnaby from his grave. She was already peering at the enormous birds suspiciously, and had asked why they were there. "They're . . . praying," I replied, saying the first thing that came to mind. "They're praying and having a funeral for Barnaby." Luckily, this made perfect sense to a six-year-old raised on illogical Disney movies.

I called Victor again. "Barnaby Jones Pickles was actually killed by a shark."

"What?" he choked out.

"Just kidding. But he *is* rising from the grave."

"I'm *working* here," he whispered, voice strained. "Are you drunk right now?"

"I have never been more sober—*or more in need of a drink*—in my entire life." Then Victor hung up to get back to work, and I considered throwing all of our house cats outside to chase off the vultures, but I was afraid that they'd either get lost, since they'd never been outside before, or that the vultures would simply see them as an easier snack, pick them up, and carry them off. Not only would that be very depressing, but I was also keenly aware that if I accidentally killed all of our pets in a single weekend Victor would never leave me alone again, and would probably take to hiding the machete. Instead I decided to just draw all the curtains and pretend that this was totally not happening.

Day 3:

"Holy fuck," I thought to myself. "This is *totally* happening."

There were now a dozen vultures hovering around Barnaby's grave and knocking off stones. I called a million (a million = fourteen) places to get someone to come disinter my dog—who was already partially disinterred by the horrible vultures that I'd been attacking with a machete—but no one would come, because it was the weekend. Apparently people need to have their dogs' corpses disinterred only Monday through Friday. Then I found a guy on the "services" part of Craigslist who claimed on his listing that he would "do absolutely *any job* for the right price," but when I looked up his e-mail address on the Internet I found that he also ran ads for people looking for prostitutes, so basically he's a pimp, and it felt weird to invite a pimp over when it was just me and Hailey, and this was when I screamed in my head, *"WHY IS VICTOR NOT HOME YET?"*

I called him again. "Barnaby Jones was actually killed by a horde of . . . I don't know. *I don't even have the strength to make shit up.* But I found a pimp who'll come dig him up." Then Victor pointed out that the pimp was probably referring less to jobs that involved digging up dead animals, and more to jobs that involve hands and blow, and I said, "I can't pay him in cocaine. I DON'T EVEN KNOW WHERE TO GET COCAINE." And then Victor told me to just go stay at a hotel, and that he'd take care of everything when he came back in a few days. I was half tempted, but I told Victor that I already felt bad enough for not being there for Barnaby when he'd died, and I was damned if I was going to desert him while he was being eaten. Victor told me to calm down, because I sounded like I was hyperventilating. I pointed out that I was just out of breath because I was outside, swinging the machete at the vultures.

Then Victor realized that I must be using his hands-free headset, and he got all kinds of pissed off that I was "getting it sweaty." And that's when I hung up on him. Because getting a headset sweaty was kind of small potatoes compared to the fact that I was brandishing a machete at large raptors, while considering the pros and cons of hiring a pimp to dig up our dead dog. Victor kept yelling at me, though, since technically I didn't actually know how to hang up a hands-free headset, but I explained that he was wasting his breath, because I'd already hung up the phone in my mind and wasn't listening anymore. Then he got really shouty, so I started singing "Total Eclipse of the Heart" to drown him out, and that's when my neighbor showed up again.

She seemed more concerned this time, possibly because I was belting out Bonnie Tyler and crying while swinging around a machete over a partially disturbed grave. Or possibly it was because she was thinking, "You're totally getting that headset all sweaty." People are weird, and it's hard to guess what's going through their heads. She looked up at the vultures and immediately realized what was going on, and brought over a giant blue plastic tarp to help me cover Barnaby. We put heavy rocks all around the edges of the tarp and the vultures looked pissed, but I was so grateful I cried. Then I went inside and took a very, very long shower. When I came back out I realized that vultures are surprisingly strong, and that the blue plastic tarp had become a kind of vulture Rubik's Cube, each of the birds trying a corner to get it all solved. I was having a nervous breakdown, but at least I was bringing the vulture community together.

My friend Laura (yes, the same one who'd dragged me to wine country) noticed that my Twitter stream was filled with updates about vultures, and machetes, and dead dogs, and how glad I am that Cartoon Network exists, and so she called. I was all, *"I'm fine,"* and she very plaintively said, "Well, you don't *sound* fine. I'm coming over to dig up your dead dog," and I immediately said, *"No!* No one needs to see that. *Especially* you, because you knew him." Then she said, "You sound terrible. We'll be right over. I'm bringing my four-year-old. And a shovel." And she did.

I couldn't let her do it alone, so we put on a video game for Hailey and Harry and told them we were going gardening. Then we both put on gloves, and she put on a bandanna to mask the smell, and we did it. And by "did it" I mean that we dug up my dog and sealed him into an Igloo cooler. Except that *technically* I did it with my eyes mostly closed, because I couldn't bear to look, and so Laura was all, "Okay, lift. Shovel to the left. YOUR OTHER LEFT. HOLY SHIT, DO NOT LOOK. Further . . . further . . . lower into the box . . . *DONE!* HIGH FIVE, TEAM."

And then it was done, and Laura, an Emmy Award–winning cosmopolitan woman who owned shoes that cost more than my wedding, stuck her chin out at the vultures (who were all glaring at us from a few feet away) and muttered menacingly, "That's right, assholes. This shit is *over*." It was surprisingly empowering for both of us.

We sealed the cooler completely and carried it toward the garage, where it could wait in peace until the crematory came to pick up Barnaby Jones on Monday. It seemed both ridiculous and terribly sad, but then Laura looked at me with understanding eyes and said, "*Aw*. We're Barnaby Jones's paw-bearers. Get it? *Laugh now*." And I did. I laughed for the first time in days as I carried my sweet, dead dog from his shallow desecrated little grave. And that's when I realized how incredibly lucky I am to have friends like Laura. Because she took something traumatic and awful and made it . . . *okay*. And also because when I apologized—for the eighteenth time—for getting her into this, she said, "It's totally fine," and waved her hands in dismissal, as if I'd simply spilled my martini on the table. Then she said, "Dude. Your dog is like Jesus. He's rising on the third day." And then I told her she was like "Mary Magdalene, only less whorey," and she was like, "Well, it's not a *contest*." Then we came inside and scrubbed our hands for two hours, and then she told me that she had everything in her purse to make fresh salsa, including beer and a tiny Cuisinart, because she knows I don't own appliances. It was like her purse was magical, and I peered in, asking her where the pony was. *"Ew,"* she said, looking at me with judgment for the first time that whole day. "Who the hell puts *pony* in salsa? You really *are* a terrible cook." And at the end of a week that was so horrific that I didn't think I'd come out the other side again, I somehow ended it feeling something that I would never have expected.

I felt *lucky*.

I was reminded of something my father used to say when I would deplore his taste in friends (who occasionally turned out to be murderers and homeless people). For once I found myself agreeing with his mantra: "A friend is someone who knows where all your bodies are buried. Because they're the ones who helped you put them there."

He was right. And sometimes, if you're really lucky, they help you dig them back up.

EPILOGUE: Hailey and Harry decided they needed to take a picture of Laura and me after we were finished "gardening." It is the single worst *and best* picture I own.

It's like some kinda fucked-up *American Gothic* portrait, but with fewer pitchforks and more rappers. If there was a song for this chapter it would be the *Golden Girls* theme. But less douchey, and with a kick-ass drum solo in the middle. And the lyrics would be like *"You would see the biggest gift would be from me, and the card attached would say, 'Thank you for helping me dig up my dead dog.'"* That shit's Grammy *gold*, y'all.

Shovel, Laura, shovel for dwarves (apparently), me.

Several weeks later, a deliveryman came to the door with a package for me to sign for, and I was so excited because I thought it was a scarf I'd ordered, but then I opened it and realized it was a box of Barnaby Jones Pickles's ashes. You're really never prepared for packages like that. But really, you should be. Some days are good, and some days are bad, and some days are the days you get a dead dog in the mail. They can't all be winners.

Later we disposed of some of Barnaby Jones Pickles's ashes in the Devil's Backbone where we live, because it's apparently very haunted by Indians and Spanish monks, and I'd like to think it would be less horrifying if people drove up on the ghost of a lone Indian, grudgingly accompanied by a smiling pug who was just *so damn happy to see you.*

You're welcome, Texas.

I'm Going to Need
an Old Priest
and a Young Priest

The following is a series of actual events pulled from my journal that led to me believe that our home was possessed by demons and/or built over an Indian burial ground. (Also, please note that the first part of this chapter actually happens just *before* the previous chapter, and the last part of it happens just *after* it. This could be viewed as "clunky and awkward," but I prefer to think of it as "intellectually challenging and chronologically surreal. Like if *Memento* was a book. About dead dogs and vaginas and puppets made of squirrel corpses." You can feel free to use that quote if you're reviewing this chapter, or if you're a student and your teacher asks you, "What was the author trying to say here?" That was it. *That's* what I was trying to say. That and *"Use condoms if you're going to have sex, for God's sake. There are a lot of skanks out there."* That's not really covered in this book, but it's still good advice.)

Let's get started.

- - - - - - -

You know what would suck? If, after you moved, you suddenly remembered that you might have left a cigar box with a ten-year-old joint in your garage, and your husband doesn't remember whether he saw it, and you don't know whether the movers found it and packed it for you, and so now you *may or may not* have illegal drugs somewhere in your house. And you want to hire a drug dog to come sniff it out so that your kid doesn't find the box one day, but you don't know anyone who rents out drug dogs. And you kind of just want to call the cops to have them come find it, and you'll just tell them that they can have it if they find it, but you don't know whether they'll arrest you or not, even though technically you're just trying to rid yourself of illegal drugs. This is all hypothetical. It's also the reason we're losing the war on drugs. Also, is pot illegal if it's expired? And how do you know whether it's expired? These are all questions I'd ask the police if I weren't so afraid to call them.

— — — — — —

Holy shit, y'all. I just looked up and there was a fox in our yard. *A fucking fox.* I know this is no big deal to most people, but it kind of blows my mind that we live so far out in the country that there are actual foxen that live in our hills. Also, spell-check refuses to recognize the legitimacy of "foxen," even though it is *clearly* a word. One ox, *two oxen.* One fox, *two foxen.* This is all basic linguistic stuff here.

— — — — — —

Victor and I are having a huge argument about whether or not to feed the foxen. Victor says yes, because they're adorable and—according to the neighbors—are quite tame. I say no, because we have a fat little pug who likes to frolic outside occasionally and I don't want to see him eaten. I thought we were on the same page about the fox, but then Victor went and threw an apple at it.

Actual fox in my backyard.
Looking for cider, I assume.

And I was all, *"What the fuck? We don't feed the foxen,"* and he said, "I was throwing the apple at it *to chase it away,"* but Victor is a tremendous liar, and he didn't go to pick up the apple, probably because he knows that foxen love apple cider. Also, everything I know about foxen I learned from *Fantastic Mr. Fox,* which was a great movie, but I suspect was not *entirely* fact-driven. This is probably all obvious even without the explanation.

— — — — — —

The foxen have not given up and hang around the backyard like a pack of loitering teenagers who need to get a damn job. I scream, *"Get off my lawn,"* but they just look at me inquisitively and roll over on their backs like they want their tummies scratched. *I am not scratching your tummies, foxen.*

Victor has fallen for their clever ploys and is sneaking food out to the backyard so he can feed them. Because Victor thinks I'm stupid. He goes through the fridge and carefully pulls out perfectly good sausages and eggs and loudly exclaims that they've gone bad, and then he throws them out the back door and watches for movement. He says he's "composting," but I've called him on his bullshit. *"You can't feed them,"* I explain again. "That's like chumming for foxen. I'm not going to *bait the hole* and then put Barnaby Jones Pickles out there. We'll come out to see a fox chewing on the end of an empty leash."

"BUT I WANT TO SEE ONE UP CLOSE," Victor yells.

"They look like cats," I say. "Like grayish, plotting cats." He refused to believe me, so the next day we drove past a buzzard eating one on the side of the road, and I was all, "LOOK! FOX!" Then I smugly said, *"There. Now* you've seen one. Not that exciting, is it?" And Victor pointed out that the dead animal was a cat, and I was like, *"Exactly.* THAT'S HOW ALIKE THEY LOOK." Also, it might have actually been a cat. It's hard to tell what buzzards are eating when you drive past them at sixty miles an hour.

- - - - - -

The foxen have got to go. Barnaby Jones Pickles seems to think they're friendly kitties and keeps trying to run over to them to play. Luckily his dog run goes only so far, so the foxen just stand beyond his grasp and stare at him patiently, like he's someone's child who needs to be running along now. They ignore him and don't seem to be a threat, but at this point I'm a little embarrassed at Barnaby's exuberance and desperately obvious desire to play with foxen, who clearly think they're better than him. Those foxen are being assholes and I will not stand for their attitude.

My friend Karen told me that when they have a fox problem in England, the man of the house just pees all around the perimeter, because there's something in male urine that scares the shit out of foxes for some reason. It seems legit, so I tell Victor that I need him to pee in a circle around our house to protect the dog. Victor walks out of the room and locks himself in his office. I can almost *hear* him shaking his head through the door. In retrospect, I probably could have started with more context.

- - - - - -

I was just reading this chapter to a friend and she stopped me and said, "Wait. Didn't Barnaby die in the last chapter? I'm so confused. Why are you trying to protect your dead dog?" So I'm going to pop in here again to point out (*again*) that this part all happened before Barnaby died. I wasn't trying to protect my dead zombie dog from judgmental, loitering foxen. *Because that would be crazy.*

- - - - - -

It's been days and the foxen seem to love sleeping just out of reach of Barnaby. Victor says this just shows how tame they are, but I'm pretty sure they're just trying to give him some sort of airborne fox disease. "JUST GO

PEE!" I scream desperately at Victor. *"If you loved Barnaby Jones you would be peeing all OVER him right now."*

Victor looked up. "Do you ever even listen to the things you say out loud?"

"Well, *I try not to*," I admitted. "But in this case? *I'm right.* You need to go pee all over the backyard. And possibly the front yard. And on the dog."

Victor shook his head. "I'm not peeing in the yard. We don't have a fence. *That's how you get arrested.* I don't even *have* that much pee."

"YOU KNOW WHAT?" I said, my arms crossed angrily. *"FINE. I'm* trying to save our dog, and *you're* hoarding pee. PEE HOARDER."

"I'm not *HOARDING* pee," Victor yelled. "I'm flushing it down the toilet. WHERE IT BELONGS."

"You're WASTING IT."

"You're *supposed* to waste it. THAT'S WHY IT'S CALLED '*WASTE.*'"

"Great," I answered. "I'm sure Barnaby Jones will be very comforted knowing that he died of fox disease *because of semantics.*"

- - - - - - -

I called my mom to ask whether Daddy could drive a few hours to come pee around my house for protection, but she said he couldn't, because it's a really busy season for taxidermy. But she said if I "really needed it" she could probably mail me some. I considered it, but then said no, because first of all, *that is a package I don't ever want to sign for*, and second, because I can already predict that Victor will be all pissed off (no pun intended) that I asked my father for help protecting us from foxen, and then Victor will be all, *"I* AM THE ALPHA MALE IN THIS HOUSE AND NO ONE IS PEEING ON IT BUT ME." Then the next time my dad comes over they'll end up in a pissing contest. *Literally.* Except Victor is too competitive and he'd probably push it too far and would be like, "Oh, yeah? Forget pee; *I'll throw up everywhere!*" and I'll be all, "Your overachievement is gross." We never had these problems when we lived in the suburbs.

Last week Barnaby Jones died valiantly of a wasp sting/snakebite/shark attack. It was awful and I still can't write about it without crying. *I loved that damn dog.* The foxen have been cleared of any suspicion of involvement in his death. By Victor. Who I think might be biased, since he seems set on taming them and creating a fox circus. *This will not stand.* Honestly, I know the foxen aren't responsible for Barnaby's death, but I suspect that if Victor weren't feeding them all the time, they would have been hungry enough to eat the wasp/snake/shark that killed Barnaby. I have forbidden Victor to throw food in the backyard. He says I'm crazy and that he stopped doing that a long time ago. Three hours later I saw a fox walk by the bedroom window eating a leftover hamburger. *Mother. Fucker.*

Our house seems to be infested with scorpions. *Awesome.* They're not the fatal kind, but they hurt like hell if they sting you, and they're creepy and were made by Satan. Fortunately, cats are immune to scorpion venom (fun fact!), so they're safe. *Unfortunately,* the cats don't understand that I am not immune to scorpion venom, and so instead of killing them they just bat them toward my bare feet while I'm watching TV. Probably because they want me to join in the fun. Or because these cats are assholes. I'm leaning toward the latter, because these same cats just murdered Hailey's pet frogs today. It was a goddamn massacre. First snakes, then the frogs, then a plague of scorpions. I'm starting to suspect we've reached the end of days, or have built our home on an Indian graveyard. I keep searching for the dead bodies supposedly buried in my neighborhood, but if I don't find them soon I'm going to just have to assume someone built this house over them.

The exterminators have come to spray for scorpions four times in the last month, and it's not working. I read online that chickens eat scorpions, so I consider buying some, until Victor reminds me of the foxen. So, basically I can't get chickens to take care of the scorpion infestation, because the chickens will be eaten by the fox infestation. I think I need a lion to eat the foxen. Except we can't *have* a lion, because of deed restrictions.

Frankly, I'm not even sure what the point was of moving out to the country if you aren't allowed to have lions.

— — — — — —

The exterminator says the scorpions are probably all coming from the attic, because that's where scorpions like to live, so I went on an Internet chat room for advice.

INTERNET GUY: You need to buy some ducks. Ducks eat the shit out of scorpions.

ME: But the scorpions are in my attic.

INTERNET GUY: You get about five hundred ducks up there and you're not gonna have to worry about any more scorpions left in your attic.

ME: Yeah . . . I guess. But then I'll have five hundred ducks in my attic.

INTERNET GUY: You got a gun?

And that's exactly why you shouldn't ask for advice on the Internet.

— — — — — —

Victor bought a giant bag of *diatomaceous earth* that he's going to use to kill all the scorpions. Apparently, it's dirt that makes scorpions commit suicide, and it sounds like something wizards would sell you.

"Did they teach you how to pronounce *'Avada Kedavra'* when you bought it?" I ask. Victor just stares at me. Probably because he's never read any of the Harry Potter books. "Sorry," I explain. "It's just that I'm pretty sure you just bought something made up by sorcerers. Were they all out of magic beans?"

"It's not magic. It's just ground-up shells," Victor says. "Scorpions really hate it, apparently."

"Ah," I say. "Well, that explains why you never see scorpions vacationing by the seaside."

– – – – – – –

The scorpions have all left the attic. For the house. I'm ordering a flamethrower to keep beside the bed. Just a small one, though, because I'm aware of fire safety. I bought the kind you use to make the top of crème brûlée crunchy. And a lot of lighter fluid. I still shoo spiders and moths out of the house with plastic cups, but these scorpions are going to die painfully.

Neighbors advised that we should place the feet of our beds in mason jars to keep the scorpions from crawling into bed with us at night, as glass is the only surface they're unable to climb. I consider how much it would cost to cover everything in the house with a layer of glass, but Victor convinces me the glass couch would leave questionable marks on sweaty summer days. I add "have glass shoes made" to my to-do list so that I can keep scorpions from crawling up me when I stand in one place for too long. I suspect Cinderella had an undisclosed problem with scorpion infestation in her home too. Although knowing her, she was probably breeding them. That's what *I'd* do if I were forced to be a slave in my own house. Plus, she made the rats and mice and pigeons design clothes for her, so she probably taught the scorpions to do tricks too. Maybe to hold hand mirrors for her with their pincers. Or to punish the lazier mice who would rather look for cheese than make a sash. Cinderella was kind of a bitch, now that I think about it.

Today the exterminator came out to spray for scorpions *again*, and he left a note saying that he found an enormous snakeskin next to our house. Then I screamed, "EVERYTHING IN THE COUNTRY WANTS TO KILL YOU," and Victor told me to go lie down. But then I went to go look at the snakeskin, and I was all, "This is a used paper towel." Then Victor said, "Dude. That's totally a snakeskin that's been shed. Look at the diamond scale pattern," and I was all, "That's a textured diamond weave to absorb more wetness. You can tell it's a paper towel because snakeskins aren't square. Or perforated." And I spread it out on the ground and then he was all, "Huh. That is a fucking paper towel. I think we need a new exterminator."

We're probably not going to survive the year.

My foot. My welcome mat. My uninvited guest.
(A mostly dead poisonous centipede.)
I also found four scorpions that same day.
I'm probably going to die here.

I'm still focused on finding the family cemetery in our subdivision, and I've taken to wandering in the empty fields, looking for headstones. A neighbor I hadn't met yet pulled up to introduce herself and told me to be careful hiking because of all the snakes. I thanked her, but explained that I'm not a hiker and was just looking around for dead bodies. Victor says I'm not allowed to talk to the neighbors without him anymore.

– – – – – – –

Last night Victor was out of town, so there was no one to keep me from freaking out when something large started violently knocking on my bedroom wall at midnight. I called the exterminator to complain that something very loud was hurling itself at my bedroom wall. He said it was probably a field mouse trapped in the wall, and I said, "No. It sounds crazy-dangerous and *huge*. It sounds like a demon is throwing a bear into the wall. Or a chupacabra . . . with a handgun." And the pest guy was all, "A chewpa-*what?*" Because HE'D NEVER HEARD OF A CHUPACABRA. Then I was like, "Wait . . . *seriously? Are you new?*" Because that's exactly the kind of shit I expect my pest control guy to know. Then I called Victor and I was all, "Okay, our pest control guy *doesn't know what a chupacabra is*," and he said, "*Really?* We live in Texas. *That shit should be on the exam*," and I was like, "*EXACTLY.*" This whole week is being a tremendous asshole.

– – – – – – –

My bedroom smells terrible. It's been a week since all those awful sounds stopped, and it's become obvious that the chupacabra has died in the wall. The exterminator crawled up in the attic and said he thinks it was a squirrel that fell into a hole in between the walls, and that he was going to try to "hook him" from the attic. After twenty minutes he said he just couldn't reach him, so he gave up. He also told me there's a bunch of dirt in the attic we might want to check out.

Then the next day another dead-squirrel fisherman from the same company came by, because he'd heard about it and *he* wanted to try to hook it. So basically my house is like a giant claw-crane game, and the prize is a dead squirrel. After about thirty minutes I started to suspect that he'd been murdered by the remaining chupacabras, but turns out that he'd just given up and dumped a bottle of Rat Sorb into the wall. That's a real thing, y'all. *Rat Sorb.* To absorb the smell of dead animals. That's on the label. So apparently I just live with a dead squirrel in my bedroom wall for the rest of my life. The exterminator says this is very common and that *all* houses have desiccated dead animals in their walls. On the positive side, the next time I feel intimidated at a fancy dinner party I can remind myself that there are probably dead animals all over the place. It's like when you have to speak in front of a group and so you imagine them all naked. Except that the dead animals in the wall aren't imaginary and are actually naked. I can't tell whether that makes it better or worse.

– – – – – –

It's been a week since the Rat Sorb, and the smell has finally dissipated, but a few minutes ago I heard something shuffling around in the walls. I can't go through this again, so I decided to scare it out by screaming, and growling, and pounding on the walls like I was a vicious predator. But then I turned around and both of the cats were just staring at me disgustedly, like, *"You're embarrassing us all here,"* and I was all, "Oh, *fuck you*, cats. At least *I'm* trying." And that was when I noticed that our mailman was staring at me through the glass of the front door. I explained that I was trying to scare away the possible chupacabra that seemed to be making a home in my wall, and the mailman said, *"Oh.* It's probably W. C. Fields," and then I just stood there, because usually I'm the weird one in the conversation, and I wanted to appreciate the moment. Turns out, though, that there's actually an escaped angry spider monkey named W. C. Fields who is stalking our area, and who just attacked a woman and trapped her in her garage for an hour. All of this is true, y'all.[1]

I looked up "spider monkey" on the Internet and apparently they're afraid of pumas, so all this morning I've been playing the sounds of pumas screaming (on a loop) on my computer, and so far I haven't heard any more noises coming from the walls, which I think pretty much confirms that we totally have a spider monkey in there. Victor says it just confirms that it's impossible to hear anything when the house is filled with screaming pumas. Then he yelled at me about the kitchen being a wreck, but it was easy to tune him out because of all the pumas. Which? *Kind of a bonus.* Screaming pumas are my new sound track.

P.S. Actual MSNBC quote about W. C. Fields, the escaped spider monkey: *"Don't go outside. Don't try to pet him. Do not befriend him."* Holy crap. The spider monkey has just become the hero from *The Running Man.*

- - - - - - -

You know what's awesome? When you move into a new (to you) house and you smell something musty in your bathroom, and so you call someone to look at what you *really* hope isn't black mold, and they're all, "Shit, lady. *You're fucked.*" And then a scientist comes out to take lab samples and says, "You haven't been sleeping near this room, have you?" And they seal the whole section of that house off and put a zipper in it so that the mold spores don't escape into the rest of the house. Then they get dressed up in the exact same outfits that the FBI people wore when they accidentally almost killed E.T., and they rip out Sheetrock and cabinets, and you want to take pictures but they won't let you in unless you're dressed in protective gear, and then they're all, *"No, ma'am, feetie pajamas are not going*

---

1. Actual title from MSNBC: "Escaped Spider Monkey Roaming San Antonio: 'W. C. Fields' Escaped from Primate Reserve After Storms Damaged His Pen."

to cut it." You try to sneak into the bathroom to get your toothpaste, but you trip over the opening, because it's almost impossible to walk into a room that has a zipper for a door, and when you fall it hurts so much that you forget that you aren't supposed to breathe, and so you take a breath of what will probably kill you. Then you start to feel sick, but you remind yourself that you've been showering in that room for months, so you probably already have tuberculosis anyway, and you're not going to have enough money for hospitalization, because you're spending all your money on air samples, and lab techs, and supporting the people who probably killed E.T. And then you go lie down and cry for a minute, and the mold guys are all, "You know, you really shouldn't use this room."

Yeah. That's awesome.

P.S. By "awesome" I mean, "I'd like to go hide under the house but I suspect that's where all the scorpions are living now that the chupacabras have taken over the attic." Also, yes, of course I have pictures:

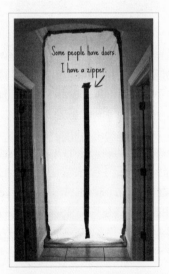

It's like living in a camping tent—
if the tent were filled with spores
that could kill you.

This is what the mold guys look like when you sneak up on them. Also, they might hit you with a board. But not on purpose. Just reflexes, probably.

"I just killed your alien and stuffed him in this bag. I'll leave you alone with him so you can cry and bring him back to life. Also I just ruined E.T. for you. Spoiler alert."

Eventually they fixed everything and I was very relieved, until they told me that when they cut a hole in the wall a bunch of dead scorpions fell out. I'm never going to sleep again. Probably because of the combination of fear, concussion, and tuberculosis.

Victor is out of town and I keep hearing weird noises in and out of the house. Rationally, I realize it's probably just the house settling, but

I'm pretty sure we're all going to die here, and *I suspect we need an exorcist. In the last six months we've had scorpions, mold, murdered pets, and possible chupacabras in the walls. I suspect the house was built on an Indian graveyard. I wonder how much an exorcism costs, and whether it's more expensive if I'm not Catholic. Is there a coupon code I can use? This is probably exactly the sort of thing they teach you in catechism.*

The Internet recommended "smudging," a Native American practice of burning sage in order to purify things, and so I burned a bowl of dried sage and I walked around the house with it, chanting biblical phrases I'd heard in *The Exorcist*, and wafting the sage smoke around. I also told the spirits that I wanted them to leave, but perhaps they should go check out Hawaii, because I heard it was awesome. Then I did some Gregorian-style chants, but I didn't know the lyrics so instead I just substituted the words *"You don't have to go home, but you can't stay here."* Suddenly there was a deafening screeching, and I screamed and thanked God that Hailey was spending the night with my in-laws, because I suspected the walls would start dripping with blood next, but then I realized that the noise was just the fire alarm going off. It was pretty much the same thing that happened in our last house, except that this time it was caused by angry spirits rather than me catching towels on fire.

I called my mom to ask her how to turn off fire alarms, but it was so loud she could barely hear me. You sound silly when you tell someone that you're burning sage inside your house to appease the Indian burial ground that might be under your house, but you sound *fucking ridiculous* when you're screaming the exact same thing over the sound of fire alarms. I tried to explain that a poltergeist was the only logical conclusion in light of all the crap that had happened lately. She said that it was more likely a series of tragic but common events that just coincidentally hit at the same time. I countered that it didn't seem "common" to have to protect your dead dog by going after a vulture with a machete. My mom said, "Don't be ridiculous.

Where would a vulture get a machete?" Not because she was stupid, mind you . . . simply because she didn't see this emergency as important enough for me to start using sloppy sentence construction.

Then my mom pointed out that Native Americans revered vultures, so if there *was* an Indian graveyard under my house I'd probably really pissed them off, and she suggested I make an offering to the vultures, and I totally would have if Victor hadn't given all of our hamburgers to the foxen. She told me how to disconnect the fire alarms, but it seemed very complicated, so I just nodded until she stopped talking and then got a broom and hit it like a piñata until it stopped, which was a relief for me (and probably for our neighbors, considering it was eleven o'clock at night).

The next day Victor came home and saw the wires hanging from the shattered fire alarm, and I admitted that I'd tried to smoke out the ghosts and that I suspected the alarms were a sign that the spirits were appeased. He stared at me and told me that it was more likely a sign that the smoke detector was working properly until I murdered it after intentionally filling the house with smoke. It sounded much worse when Victor broke it out like that.

- - - - - - - -

This afternoon I sauntered into Victor's office and said smugly, "So, *apparently* my *'craazy'* plan for setting off the fire alarm to appease the ghosts worked, because guess who just found the dead bodies I've been searching for? *ME, MOTHERFUCKER. I found the dead bodies*." Then I held up my hand for the inevitable high five, but instead he just hit the mute button on his office phone and dropped his head into his hands. Which was disappointing for both of us. And, *granted*, this probably would have been better received if I'd realized he was on an important conference call at the time, but really, it's not my fault Victor doesn't know how to use a mute button properly.

Victor finally looked up, and then he told me to put my hand down, because he was not going to high-five me for digging up dead bodies, and that was when I started to think that Victor was a very strange man, because *why in the hell would I dig up dead bodies?* I explained that what I meant was that I'd finally stumbled on the lost cemetery I'd been searching for since we'd first moved in, and that the graves were so old that the bodies would no longer be a threat during the zombie apocalypse. He didn't seem as relieved as I was, so I decided to be relieved for both of us.

Our extremely quiet neighbors.

Then I told him that I wanted to buy the land the cemetery was on so that we could purposely *not* build over it, and that way if we *were* accidentally living in a house built over graves, this would sort of make it all cosmically even. Victor was unconvinced, but I put an offer in on the land, which was promptly declined, because it was apparently owned by the family of the people buried there, and they weren't interested in selling their dead relatives. Which was awesome, because I didn't have to spend money on land that I wouldn't build anything on anyway, plus I got karmic credit for trying. Victor said that's not how karma works, but then a few seconds later he mentioned that he'd found something that morning that he assumed was mine and pulled out the missing cigar box that contained the ten-year-old joint. I screamed, "OH, HELL, YEAH. *I have been looking everywhere for this!*" and Victor glared at me and I said, ". . . to throw out, I mean. I'm getting rid of this right now." He still glared at me rather harshly for having a ten-year-old joint in a cigar box, and so I said,

"'From you, Dad. *I LEARN IT FROM WATCHING YOU*,'" and he just looked at me quizzically, because he apparently didn't watch a lot of TV in the eighties.

The whole week had been a relief, and I felt that things were finally starting to look up. I took the cigar box containing the ancient joint and walked outside with it thoughtfully. I considered throwing it away, but after a moment I changed my mind and lit it, leaving it to smolder in the same glass pot I'd used to burn the sage in. I hoped that this would be the final, perfect peace-pipe offering to the vulture-loving Native Americans who may or may not have been throwing scorpions at us.

As the final ember burned out, I thought about our new life here. We'd lost our beloved dog, but had rescued a mischievous kitten who seemed gifted at finding scorpions. We'd struggled to fend off hordes of insects, but we'd adopted a pack of foxen, and had spent many nights watching dozens of deer walk noiselessly past our porch. We'd left old friends behind and made new ones along the way. We'd found a quiet happiness as we watched Hailey dance through the meadow, a flaming sunset stretching forever around our new home. Without even knowing it we'd followed in the footsteps of Laura Ingalls and found a bit of the simple but hard-fought contentment she'd written of a hundred years ago. I took a deep breath and thought, *"I'm home."*

Then Victor walked outside and said, "Why do I smell pot? *Are you smoking a ten-year-old joint? WHAT THE HELL IS WRONG WITH YOU?"* He may have ruined a bit of the romance of the moment, but I suppose he created one that was more fitting for us, and I laughed and assured him that the Indians were the only ones smoking out in the backyard. He didn't understand, but I didn't bother to explain, both because I felt it would be impossible to describe this Native American version of pouring out a forty-ounce for your fallen homies without making it sound ridiculous, and also because I suspected I might have gotten a small contact high. Either way, I smiled gently and patted the chair beside me as Victor paused and then settled down on the porch with me to watch the hummingbirds buzz around the wild morning glories as we listened to the wind and understood why no one would ever want to leave here . . . even if given the chance to go to Hawaii.

Home. The view makes up for the scorpions. Sort of.

And That's Why You Should Learn to Pick Your Battles

This morning I had a fight with Victor about towels. I can't tell you the details, because it wasn't interesting enough to document at the time, but it was basically me telling Victor I needed to buy new bath towels, and Victor insisting that I NOT buy towels because I *"just bought new towels."* Then I pointed out that the last towels I'd bought were hot-pink beach towels, and he was all, "EXACTLY," and then I hit my head against the wall for an hour.

Then Laura came to pick me up so we could go to the discount outlet together, and as Victor gave me a kiss good-bye he lovingly whispered, *"You are not allowed to bring any more goddamn towels in this house or I will strangle you."* And that was exactly what I was still echoing through my head an hour later, when Laura and I stopped our shopping carts and stared up in confused, silent awe at a display of *enormous* metal chickens made from rusted oil drums.

LAURA: I think you *need* one of those.

ME: You're joking, but they're kind of horrifically awesome.

LAURA: *I'm not joking.* We need to buy you one.

ME: The five-foot-tall one was three hundred dollars, marked down to a hundred. That's like two hundred dollars' worth of chicken *for free.*

LAURA: You'd be crazy *not* to buy that. I mean, look at it. IT'S FULL OF WHIMSY.

ME: Victor'd be pissed.

LAURA: Yup.

ME: But on the plus side? It's not towels.

LAURA: Yup.

ME: We will name him Henry. Or Charlie. Or O'Shaughnessy.

LAURA: Or Beyoncé.

Insert inappropriate cock joke here.

ME: *Or Beyoncé.* Yes. And when our friends are sad we can leave him at their front door to cheer them up.

LAURA: *Exactly.* It'll be like, *"You thought yesterday was bad? Well, now you have an enormous metal chicken to deal with. Perspective. Now you have it."*

Then we flagged down a salesman, and we were all, "What can you tell us about these chickens?" as if we were in an art gallery, and not in a store that specializes in last year's bath mats. He didn't know anything about them, but he said that they'd sold only one and it was to a really drunk lady, and then Laura and I were all, "*SOLD*. All this chicken belongs to us now."

So he loaded it onto a trolley, but Beyoncé was surprisingly unstable, and the giant five-foot metal chicken crashed over onto the floor. And Laura and I were all, "CHICKEN DOWN! CLEANUP IN AISLE THREE," but he didn't laugh. Then the manager came to see what was causing all the commotion, and that's when he found the very conservative salesman unhappily struggling to right an enthusiastically pointy chicken that was almost as tall as he was. The salesman was having a hard time, and he told everyone to stand back "because this chicken *will cut you*," and at first I thought he meant it as a threat, like "That chicken has a shiv," but turns out he just meant that all the chickens' ends were sharp and rusty. It was awesome, and Laura and I agreed that even if we got tetanus, this chicken had already paid for itself even before we got it in her truck.

Then we got to my house and quietly snuck the chicken up to my front door, rang the doorbell, and hid around the corner.

"Knock-knock, motherfucker."

Victor opened the door and looked at the chicken in stunned silence for about three seconds. Then he sighed, closed the door, *and walked away.*

LAURA: What the fuck? *That's it? That's the only reaction we get?*

ME: That's it. He's a hard man to rattle.

Victor was surprisingly pissed that I'd "wasted money" on an enormous chicken, because apparently he couldn't appreciate the hysterical value of a five-foot chicken ringing the doorbell. Then I said, "Well, at least it's not *towels*," and apparently that was the wrong thing to say, because that was when Victor screamed and stormed off, but I knew he was locked in his office, because I could hear him punching things in there. Then I yelled through his door, "*It's an anniversary gift for you, asshole.* Two whole weeks early. FIFTEEN YEARS IS BIG METAL CHICKENS."

Then he yelled that he wanted it gone, but I couldn't move it myself, so instead I said okay and went to watch TV. Then when the UPS guy came I hid, but he was all, "Dude. Nice chicken," and Victor yelled, "IT IS *NOT* A NICE CHICKEN." Which was probably very confusing to the UPS guy, *who was just trying to be polite, Victor.* Victor seemed more disgruntled than usual, so I finally dragged the chicken into the backyard and wedged it into a clump of trees so that it could scare the snakes away. Then I came in and Victor angrily pulled me into his office so that I could see that I'd stationed Beyoncé directly in front of his only window. And I was all, "*Exactly.* YOU'RE WELCOME." I told him that he could move Beyoncé if he wanted to, but he totally hasn't. Probably because of all of the giant rocks I piled on Beyoncé's feet to dissuade burglars. Or possibly because Beyoncé is growing on him. Still, I can't help thinking that we wouldn't even be *having* this argument if Beyoncé was towels. Honestly, this whole chicken is really a lesson in picking your battles more carefully. Plus, he's awesome and I can't stop giggling every time I look at him. Beyoncé, that is.

Best. Fifteenth anniversary. *Ever.*

Hairless Rats:
Free for Kids Only

This morning Victor and I followed our usual routine. We got up, drove Hailey to kindergarten, and stopped into the local gas station for coffee and local gossip. On the way out we stopped in front of the public bulletin board that serves as our small town's newspaper. It's always filled with invitations to neighborhood barbecues, and ads selling broken tractor parts or requesting clean dirt (which seems like an oxymoron), but today we found that the same person who had fascinated us with bizarre ads last year was back. They were the kind of ads that made you question exactly what was going on in his home, and also your own sanity. They were ads like:

"FLYING SQUIRRELS: CHEAP. FREE DELIVERY."

A month later that ad was replaced by another:

"REGULAR SQUIRRELS—FREE TO GOOD HOME. *NOT FOR EATING.*"

I tipped my hat to his ethical disclaimer, but it was puzzling. Had the flying squirrels been "regular" the whole time? Had it taken the seller a month to realize they didn't have wings? How many squirrels had been dropped from the roof before he finally gave up and realized they weren't faking it? Were these regular squirrels free only because they all now suffered from post-traumatic stress disorder and vertigo?

I imagined a horde of squirrels, all hunkered close to the ground as they stared in horror at their former friends who easily jumped from branch to branch. "YOU'RE GOING TO GET KILLED!" the squirrel would yell, and his former buddies would shake their tiny heads in pity, wondering what horrors their friend had seen to change him so. In my head, it was as if the squirrels were damaged Vietnam vets, shell-shocked and unable to cope with real life after the terrible things they'd had to witness.

Victor said I was being ridiculous, but I pointed out that it was also pretty ridiculous to give away squirrels that you could just set free, and he admitted he had no real answer to that.

The ads kept coming over the summer, and then very abruptly stopped. Most likely (Victor and I speculated) it was because the (probably very well-intentioned) man was eventually murdered by his own squirrels. But this morning, almost a year from the time since we'd seen his first ad, a new sign was up with the same distinctive handwriting. He was alive and the world was a better place for it:

I censored the phone number to protect them from prank calls.
And because I want to keep all the sugar gliders for myself.
Sugar gliders who, I half suspect, might actually
just be mice with flabby underarms, and who
have survived being thrown off the roof.

VICTOR: Wow. I don't think I want to know of the situation you have to be in where you need a rat delivered so desperately *that it can't wait until morning.*

ME: Ooh, I would.

VICTOR: Well, *of course you would.*

ME: Who *wouldn't* want to know about an emergency rat situation where the emergency is that you NEED a rat. It's like the exact opposite of every regular emergency rat situation ever. It sounds fascinating. We should call this guy just to see what his deal is. I bet he has great stories. I mean, who gives hairless rats to children? He's like the bizarro-world Candy Man.

VICTOR: So call him. Pretend to apply for a free squirrel and see what his story is.

ME: I wonder what the application process is on that? It would be really depressing to get turned down for free squirrels.

VICTOR: True. *"I'm sorry. We're going to have to decline you. Your home isn't even fit for squirrels."*

ME: Our home is pretty messy, but I think it's *at least* fit for squirrels. I'd be like, "But *our* squirrels seem quite happy." I'd totally appeal that ruling.

VICTOR: "I'm sorry, but your references didn't check out."

ME: "But our references *were squirrels.*"

VICTOR: "Right. *And they're not happy.* Plus, there have been some reports of hate speech."

ME: *"What?"*

VICTOR: "Last week you dropped a fork and yelled, 'Rats.' Then in January you complained that your computer wasn't working properly and was acting 'all squirrelly.' We have people on the inside, you know."

ME: "Hang on. *Are those people the squirrels who live in my attic?* Because they're all high and they don't know what they're saying. *Those squirrels are junkies and they are not to be trusted.*"

VICTOR: "Ma'am, *that was slander.* You'll be contacted by the squirrel civil liberties union for a statement. Plus, you need to stop referring to squirrels as *'those people.'* Please get your shit together."

ME: *Wow.* We sound . . . *totally unfit to have squirrels.* Now I don't even want to call the guy, because I'm all nervous about being judged. I don't even think I could pass the interview.

VICTOR: We probably shouldn't apply for more squirrels if we can't even manage to keep ours off the horse.

ME: ?

VICTOR: It's another word for heroin.

ME: Yeah, *I know what "off the horse" means.* I just can't remember how we got to the point where I'm defending myself against the imaginary accusations of a man who gives hairless rats to neighborhood children, and who apparently trusts the nonexistent squirrel junkies in the attic.

VICTOR: True. I don't remember ever having these conversations before we moved to the country.

ME: Me either. Also, I just realized that I just went to a gas station in my pajamas to buy coffee. I just became a giant warning sign to others. I can't decide whether this is a problem, or I'm just more comfortable here than I was in the city. Can it be both?

VICTOR: I dunno. *What the hell happened to us?*

ME: [after a few seconds of silence] Growth?

VICTOR: [nodding slowly] *Growth.*

And Then I Snuck
a Dead Cuban Alligator
on an Airplane

November 2009:
He was my first. He was big, with a wide neck like an NFL player and a smile that said, "There you are! I've been looking for you everywhere." Victor stared at me as if I had lost my mind, and pointed out that he was losing his hair and was missing several important teeth, but it didn't matter. *I was in love.*

"Pay whatever it takes," I said to Victor. "James Garfield WILL BE MINE."

It was frightening, both for Victor and myself, this sudden lust I had to possess the dusty, taxidermied wild boar's head hanging from the cracked wall of the estate sale we'd wandered into.

Victor refused to pay money for something he saw as hideous, but there was something in that toothy smile that screamed, "I AM SO DAMN HAPPY TO SEE YOU," and when we left without him I was positively bereft. I spent the next week looking at the blank spot on the wall where James Garfield would have smiled at me. Whenever Victor would try to cheer me up with a joke or with videos of people hurting themselves, I would force myself to smile and then sigh, saying, "James Garfield would have loved that."

Eventually the melancholy got too strong and Victor angrily gave up and drove me back to the estate sale, where he was totally unsurprised to find that James Garfield had not been sold. He'd made me stay in the car, because he said my look of intense longing would affect his ability to negotiate, and offered the guy in charge of the sale twenty-five dollars for him. The man sneered and said that he could just rip out the tusks and sell them on eBay for that, and Victor came back to the car to tell me how negotiations had broken down. *"THEY'RE GOING TO DISMEMBER JAMES GARFIELD?"* I screamed. "STOP THEM. PAY ANYTHING. *HE IS A MEMBER OF OUR FAMILY.*" Victor stared at me in bafflement. "I'd do it for you," I explained. "I'd pay the terrorists anything to get you back." Victor sighed and laid his head on the steering wheel.

A tense twenty minutes later he came back to the car, lugging the beautiful head of James Garfield like some kinda goddamn American hero. I cried a little, and Hailey clapped her tiny hands in delight. "You will be my best friend," she said to him as she petted his snout.

Victor looked at both of us like we were mad, and then stared straight ahead as he made me swear this would not be the start of some sort of wild-boar-head collection. "You're being ridiculous," I said. "James Garfield is one of a kind."

When my parents came to visit a few weeks later, my mother shook her head in bewilderment. I'd expected my father to feel at least slightly vindicated that his love of taxidermy hadn't skipped a generation after all, but he seemed just as baffled as Victor. He peered quizzically at the mangy fur shedding from James Garfield, and told me he could make me a much nicer boar head, if that was what I was into. "No," I said. "This is it." I was not a fan of taxidermy and never would be. Having one dead animal in the house is eclectic and artistic. More than one reeks of serial killer. There really is a fine line there.

APRIL 2010:

Half of a squirrel arrived in the mail today. It was the front part, almost down to the belly button, and it was mounted on a tiny wooden plaque.

It was odd. Both because I was not expecting any squirrel parts, and because the squirrel was dressed in full cowboy regalia. He was holding a tiny pistol out, threateningly trained at the viewer (presumably to defend the miniature marked cards in his other tiny hand), and his eyes followed you from room to room, like one of those 3-D pictures of Jesus from the seventies.

"*Hey, Victor?*" I yelled from the living room. "*Did you buy me a half of a squirrel?*"

Victor walked out of his office and stopped short as he stared at the tiny bandito pointing a gun at him. "*What have you done?*" he asked.

"Ruined Christmas?" I guessed. I found it hard to feel guilty about ruining his surprise, though, since the box *was* addressed to me, but then I saw the note on the package and realized it was actually from a girl who read my blog, and who had agreed that Victor was totally in the wrong last month when he'd refused to buy me the taxidermied squirrel paddling a canoe[1] that I'd found in an antique shop.

---

1. I'd planned on naming her "Pocahontas Wikipedia," but Victor said that the cats would chew the hands off, but then I pointed out that even if that happened I'd love her even more, because then she couldn't paddle *and* she'd be up a creek without hands, which seemed more and more like a metaphor for my life.

"Oh, never mind," I said. "Apparently this half squirrel is a present from someone *who understands fine art*."

"You can't possibly be serious."

"It would be rude NOT to hang it up," I explained to Victor. "I will name him Grover Cleveland." Victor stared at me, wondering how his life choices had taken him here.

"Didn't you once tell me that more than one dead animal in the house borders on serial-killer territory?" he asked.

"Yes, but this one is wearing a hat," I explained drily. He couldn't argue with that kind of logic. No one could.

JANUARY 2011:

"I am a moderately successful writer, and if I want to buy an ethically taxidermied mouse I should not have to justify it to anyone."

This was what I was screaming as Victor glared at me, dripping rainwater all over our foyer. In truth, we weren't really arguing about whether I was *allowed* to spend money. We were arguing about the fact that the taxidermied mouse I'd bought had been lost. The delivery website said it was left on the porch, but it was nowhere to be seen. I suspected burglars, but even imagining the small compensation of their mystified faces as they opened the box containing a dead mouse wasn't enough to make me feel less upset. Then I'd noticed that the tracking page had transposed my street number, and so I sent Victor out into the dark and rainy night to go find the neighbor who was probably very confused about who had mailed him a dead mouse. Victor had been a bit flabbergasted at my request, but after yelling for a bit about . . . *I don't know; I wasn't really paying attention. Budgets, maybe?* . . . he finally threw on a coat and went out in search of the mouse. He returned twenty minutes later and told me that the address didn't even exist, and that he'd asked the people at the houses near where the address would have been and none of them had seen any packages. He was wet and frustrated, and I assumed that accounted for how irrational he was being as I pushed him back out the door to check with all the neighbors on the block.

"You didn't even tell me you'd bought a taxidermied mouse," Victor yelled, and I said, "Because you were asleep when I found it online, and it was so cheap I knew it would be gone if I didn't buy it immediately. I didn't want to tiptoe into our bedroom at three a.m. to whisper, *'Hey, honey? I got a great deal on a stuffed mouse that died of natural causes. Can I have your credit card number?'* because that would be CRAZY. And that's why I used *my* credit card. *Because I respect your sleep patterns.* But then I forgot to tell you about it, because I bought it at three a.m., when I was drunk and vulnerable. Just like *you* with all those choppers you keep buying on infomercials. Except that this is better, because I'll actually *use* a taxidermied mouse. That is, I *would have* . . . until—*crap*—until he went missing," I ended in a whisper.

"Are you . . . are you *crying*?" Victor asked, stunned.

I wiped at my eyes. "A little. I just hate to think of him out there in the rain. All alone." My voice trembled, and Victor closed his eyes. And rubbed his temples. And sighed deeply before staring at me and walking back out into the rain. Forty minutes later he walked in with a tiny wet box and a look that said, "I will disable your computer when I go to bed from now on." But I rushed up and gave him a dozen kisses, which he gruffly accepted as he dried off with the towel I handed him.

"It was at the abandoned house at the end of the block," he said. "Apparently someone just dumped everything that didn't have a proper address there. There must've been twenty-five packages lying on that porch."

But I wasn't paying attention, as I was too busy pulling Hamlet von Schnitzel from his watertight baggie.

"What. *The fuck.* Is *that*?" Victor asked.

It was pretty obvious what it was. It was a mouse dressed as Hamlet. His Shakespearean ruff collar held up his wee velvet cape, and he seemed to be addressing the bleached mouse skull held nobly in his tiny paw. I held it up to Victor, squeaking, "Alas, poor Yorick! I knew him well."

Victor looked at me worriedly. *"You have a problem."*

"I *DON'T* HAVE A PROBLEM."

"That's exactly what people with problems say. Denial is the first sign of having a problem."

"It's also the first sign of *not* having a problem," I countered.

"I'm pretty sure defensiveness is the second sign."

I placed Hamlet von Schnitzel in a glass bell jar to protect his little ears from Victor's hurtful accusations. But I had to admit that I didn't completely understand my recent obsession with odd taxidermy either. It worried me. I still didn't understand my father's fascination with dead animals, and I refused to buy any that weren't terribly old or didn't die of natural causes. I still shooed spiders and geckos out of the house with a magazine and a helpful suggestion of "Perhaps you'd like some fresh air." I considered myself an animal lover, donated to shelters, and never wore real fur, but it clashed with the other side of my personality, which was continually browsing through shops, always on the lookout for beavers in prairie dresses, or a diorama of the Last Supper made entirely with otters. Victor was right: I needed to stop. I told myself that I was finished and I vowed that I would not end up like my father, surrounded by the soulless, unblinking eyes of dead things. And with a little willpower I vowed to conquer my curious and terrible obsession.

APRIL 2011:

I just bought a fifty-year-old Cuban alligator dressed as a pirate.

This is *so* not my fault. Victor broke his arm by falling down some stairs in Mexico, so I went with him on a business trip to North Carolina so I could help him. The trip was uneventful, until we stopped at a little shop on the way to the airport. While Victor went to use the restroom, I stumbled upon the small, badly aged baby alligator, which was fully dressed and standing on his hind legs. He was wearing a moth-eaten felt outfit, a beret and a belt. He was missing one hand, and he was nineteen dollars. His tiny belt hung sadly, and I appreciated the irony of an alligator wearing a belt that was not made of alligator. His mouth was open in a wide grin, as if he'd been waiting for me for a very long time. I remembered my vow to not buy any more taxidermied animals and feverishly searched for loopholes while Victor looked through the aisles for me. I contemplated stapling a strap to the alligator's shoulders, putting my lipstick in his mouth, and calling him an alligator purse, but it was too late. *He had me at the beret.*

I could hear Victor shuffling around on the other side of the aisle, and I sheepishly poked the tiny alligator over the top. *"Hello, mon ami! I am Jean Louise,"* I said in a daring French accent. *"I have never been on zee plane before and would love an adventure!"*

"Oh," said the confused elderly woman on the other side of the aisle. "Well, good luck to you?"

Victor tapped me on the shoulder and I screamed in surprise, and he looked at me and Jean Louise with disgust. "Don't judge us," I said meekly, as I hugged the alligator protectively. "We're all we have."

Victor shook his head but said nothing as he silently walked up to the cash register to pay. Jean Louise leaned forward and whispered, *"Enabler,"* but Victor still held out his credit card to the baffled cashier. Luckily Victor doesn't speak French.

"I'll need to make him a tiny hook for his missing hand," I said as we walked out. He was far too brittle to go in my suitcase, so I put him in my purse, and Victor insisted there was no way they were going to let me get on the plane with a dead alligator. I disagreed, pointing out that he was quite literally "unarmed," but his tiny gleaming teeth said otherwise, as I remembered the fingernail clippers we'd been forced to throw out at security once before. I turned to the experts (everyone following me on Twitter).

To make a long story short, if you ask people on Twitter whether it's legal to carry a smallish sort of taxidermied alligator onto a plane with you, most of them will say, "Um, *no*. You can't even bring breast milk on a plane." Then you'll point out that the alligator is at least fifty years old, is wearing clothes, and is missing a hand, and some of them will change their mind, but most will still say he'll be considered a weapon. Then you'll write, "I can't imagine anyone *seriously* thinking I'd try to take over a plane using only a tiny clothed alligator as a weapon," and everyone on Twitter will be like, "*Really?* Have you met you? Because that *totally* sounds like something you'd do." And they had a point.

But I wasn't truly concerned until we were already in line at security, and then I suddenly wondered whether someone had once used this alligator to smuggle cocaine in fifty years ago but then forgot to take it out, and now *I'm* gonna get arrested in the airport for alligator-stomach cocaine that's older than me. I quietly asked Victor whether you could tell if cocaine was expired, or if it just stays fresh forever, and he was all, "*CAN WE NOT TALK ABOUT THIS IN SECURITY?*" and I was like, "It's not for me. *I'm asking because of the alligator,*" and he kind of glared at me. I took a deep breath and calmed myself, imagining myself saying to the security officer, "Oh, this? That's old cocaine. It probably expired, like, forty years ago. It's not mine. It's the alligator's. I can't be responsible for the wild lifestyle an alligator had before I was even born. Besides, he doesn't know your rules. He's from Cuba." I felt sure they'd understand. Besides, these are the risks you take when you bring a dead alligator on a plane trip.

Of course, Jean Louise and I got through just fine, and no one even blinked at the alligator on the security conveyor belt. Victor was stopped for a full body search. Probably because he was sweating, and the vein on his forehead was popping out. In the confusion, Jean Louise and I calmly walked through with no problem. Victor could learn a lot from that alligator.

When we finally got settled in I pulled down Victor's tray table and perched Jean Louise on it so that he could see outside. "Take that goddamn thing off my tray," Victor whispered between clenched teeth.

"But he's never been on a plane before," I explained.

"Voulez-vous les window seat?" Jean Louise asked pleasantly.

Victor glared at me. "I'm not kidding. We're going to get kicked off the plane. *Put it away.*"

"You're being *ridiculous*," I said. The man sitting across the aisle was staring at Jean Louise, so I swung him toward his face. *"Votre chemise est mooey bueno,"* Jean Louise said confidently. The man stared at Jean Louise with a slightly open mouth.

"He says he likes your shirt," I explained matter-of-factly.

Victor put his head in his hands. "If I lose my SkyMiles because of this I will murder you."

Just then the flight attendant walked by, a businesslike woman who looked as if she needed a cocktail. I gestured at her and smiled widely as she walked near me, Jean Louise on my lap. "Excuse me, my son would like to see the cockpit."

She hesitated for a moment as she looked at Jean Louise, and then said, "Oh. We don't do that anymore," before briskly walking off.

"These people are racist," I said to Victor, who was pretending to be engrossed in the SkyMall catalog.

"Mmm," he said, noncommittally.

"When we get home I'm going to buy Jean Louise a tiny ruffled pirate shirt. And a hook for his missing hand. And a saucy little ponytail."

Victor put down his magazine and glowered at the dead alligator, whom he seemed to be viewing as a veritable money pit. "That's it," he said. "You've done it. You've managed to become your father."

"Don't be ridiculous," I said flippantly, as I contemplated how many

Barbies I'd have to scalp to make a serviceable alligator wig. "My father has no taste at all when it comes to alligator pirate attire. I'm *nothing* like my father. Honestly, when it comes right down to it, I'm not really like *anyone*."

Victor looked at me and Jean Louise, and slowly his gaze softened. "You know what? You have no idea how true that is."

I stared back at Victor, and then rested my head on his shoulder as I moved Jean Louis to the empty seat beside us. And, as I wasn't quite sure whether I should say thank-you or be insulted, I simply closed my eyes and drifted off to sleep while wondering whether anyone made tiny pocket watches for alligators anymore.

You Can't Go Home Again (Unless You Want to Get Mauled by Wild Dogs)

S o," my sister says, as she leans back in the wooden chair on our parents' front porch, "Victor told me you were mauled by a pack of wild dogs last time you were here." She says it pleasantly, more like a statement than a question, in the same impassive way someone might say, "So, you decided to let your hair grow out again."

"Mmm . . . *sort of*. It's a long story." I drowsily sit back in the matching chair and put my feet up on the authentic child-size chuck wagon my dad had built. In the Christmas months my dad hitches it to a taxidermied pygmy deer with a giant elk horn tied with a red bow to its head, in a strange homage to *The Grinch Who Stole Christmas*, but the rest of the year it stands ownerless, as if abandoned after a 1970s dog food commercial.

"And I have somewhere to go?" Lisa asks.

She has a point. We were both in town to visit our parents for the week. Lisa now lives in California with her husband and a beautiful litter of children, but each year she'll drive down to spend a few weeks in Texas, and I'll bring my family, and we'll have a disorganized family reunion. One where our kids gleefully ride the family goats, where our husbands complain that they are slowly suffocating from the heat and the lack of Wi-Fi access, and where my sister and I shake our heads in disbelief at their soft, sheltered ways, remembering days of bread-sack shoes and of pulling our mattresses out onto the porch so the whole family could sleep there on the hottest summer nights.

"So was it really an all-out *mauling*, or did the dogs just lick you violently?" she asks.

"It was less of an all-out maul and more of a prelude to a maul," I answer. "Like when Julia Roberts got molested by George Costanza in *Pretty Woman*." She looked at me expectantly, and so I told her the story.

When you cross over into our old hometown, you can pretty much guarantee that something fucked up is going to happen, but you're really never prepared for what it is. You may come in knowing that you're probably going to get a little blood on you, but you never think it's going to be your own.

The morning of the day when I was partially mauled, Hailey and I walked outside my parents' back door to see a stranger in a black hat and a bloody rubber apron, who was missing only a mask made of human skin and a chain saw to bring his whole outfit together. He apparently worked for my father, and he'd strung up a buck that he was in the process of skinning. He smiled naturally at Hailey and me, while he seemed to be digging his hands deep into the deer's pockets, as if he were looking for his keys. Turned out, though, that deer don't even have pockets, and he'd simply lost a glove in the deer. These are the things you come in expecting when you're in Wall, and so you aren't *completely* surprised when a stranger cheerfully yells at your preschooler to come over and help him "undress Mr. Reindeer because that'll be a hootload of fun!" And when he tells her she can swing on the deer's skin to help him get it all off, you'll already have one arm on her sleeve pulling her back toward you, because this is the sort of thing you come prepared for. (Side note for nonnatives—"This'll be a hootload of fun," coming from a taxidermist's assistant translates to: "This will cost thousands in psychoanalysis and will probably ruin your dress.") Personally I prefer to avoid any activity that ends with a strange man offering to "hose the blood off of ye afterward, mate." It's just a rule I have. Because I'm picky. Also, when did my father hire a pirate to do taxidermy? The whole thing was weird.

Lisa agreed that it was unusual, but felt it fell short of being all-out "weird." "Take yesterday, for example," she explained. "Yesterday Victor walked into that swampy puddle behind the house and he was all, 'Ew, is this from the septic tank?' and I was like, 'Where do you think you are? *Beverly Hills?* That's leftover skull-boiling water.' He looked ill, but I thought he should know. Comparatively, deer pockets are really pretty humdrum."

She had a point, but it still struck me as odd. Here's a picture of it, but it might gross you out, so use your discretion:

My dad, dinner for weeks,
random drifter/cowboy/pirate/taxidermist.

I know. I'm sorry. But in my defense, I did warn you.

Anyway, I expect a lot of odd things in a town known for armadillo races, and bobcat urine collections, and high school bovine fertility rituals, but one thing I did *not* expect was to be attacked by a pack of wild dogs. And yes, perhaps *technically* they weren't "wild" so much as they were "excitable," and maybe I wasn't attacked by a *pack* of dogs as much as it was one jumpy dog and one bitey dog, but I can honestly say that the dog that bit me was probably infused with radioactive spider juice and had diesel-fueled vampire fangs. And adamantium claws. Also, he was part bear and his whiskers were made of scorpions.

Lisa laughed, and so I pulled out my phone and showed her the pictures of me after getting out of the hospital the next day. I'd added some text to make things more clear:

"Holy crap," she said. "That looks disgusting. Okay, I apologize, because I was really sure this was blown out of proportion."

"Apology accepted," I replied magnanimously.

"So, where did you even *find* wild dogs?" she asked.

"Oh," I said hesitantly. "Well, *'wild'* is perhaps a strong term."

She raised an eyebrow. *"Out with it."*

I explained that Mom, Hailey, and I had gone to our uncle Larry's house so I could meet his new wife, who was sweet and adorable, and who had pet dogs that were ginormous.

"Oh, yeah. I've met them," Lisa said. "Cute dogs."

"Yes, well, apparently they've been trained to *look* very cute and tail-waggingly giddy to see you in order to lull you into coming outside with them so they can chew your bones off."

"You got attacked by Theresa's *pet dogs*? *Aren't they like collies or something?*" she asked in disbelief.

"They're *animals. Literally*," I assured her.

She looked at the pictures again doubtfully.

"After eating dinner, I carried Hailey out to the backyard, because she wanted to see the dogs. It was pitch dark, but Uncle Larry was feeding them, so I thought they'd be distracted and Hailey could just look at them. But then one of them jumped up, in an 'I'm-a-big-dog-and-I-want-to-smell-the-top-of-your-head' kind of way, and Hailey was squealing in an 'I'm-a-crazily-excited-and-slightly-freaked-three-year-old' kind of way, and then I'm suddenly wondering why I'm outside in a 'These-motherfuckers-are-the-size-of-polar-bears' kind of way. Larry heard the barking, and settled the one dog down as I was backing off toward the door. But then another dog must've thought I was an attacker, because it jumped up and bit me in the arm that I was holding Hailey with. (In an 'I-would-like-to-pull-you-to-the-ground-so-I-can-chew-your-nose-off' kind of way.) I knew I'd been bitten, but I also knew that if I screamed for help Hailey would freak out and I might lose my grip on her, so I bit my lip and turned around so my back was to the dog and Hailey was blocked from him. Then I felt another bite on my arm as I slid open the back door and pushed Hailey through. I was afraid that the dog was trying to get at her, since she was squealing with excitement, so I blocked the door with my body to give her time to get farther in, and that's when the dog bit me in the back. He latched on and yanked, and for a second I thought I was going to fall to the ground, and in my mind flashed all of those news stories about women killed in freak dog accidents. I put my leg back to steady myself and made sure Hailey was safely in, then pulled hard to rip my back out of the dog's mouth and slammed the door behind me."

Lisa looked at me in silence for a moment. "*Dude.* Was everybody freaked out?" she asked.

"No. No one even realized it had happened. I swooped Hailey up and checked her out all over, looking for blood and bites that I knew she *must* have gotten, but she didn't have a scratch on her. It was weird. Then Mom assured me that I was overreacting and that everything was fine, and then she saw the blood and realized that I'd been bitten. Uncle Larry hadn't even realized what had happened, because I'd been so quiet when it happened. The two bites on my arm were so deep that you could see a bit of fat poking out of them, and on my back you could see the dog's teeth marks, like some sort of doggie dental impression. I spent the rest of the evening in the emergency room being stitched up, getting a tetanus shot, and wishing I'd had my camera with me so I could send pictures to Victor to show him what he was missing while he entertained clients with lobster dinners."

"So, what did they do with the dogs?" she asked.

"Nothing. I'm sure if I'd asked them to, Larry and Theresa would have put the dogs down, but they've been around Theresa's kids for ten years with no problem. I think they saw a large, screaming, unfamiliar object approaching their master in the dark and were trying to protect him. Besides, it kind of felt like I'd asked for it. Taking your three-year-old out in the dark to see giant strange dogs while they are eating is bewilderingly stupid.

"Oh, and we'd just eaten, so I probably smelled like KFC.

"Plus, *I'm kind of delicious*. It was like I was wearing a perfume designed to get me mauled. But in a bad way."

Lisa nodded slowly. "That's gotta be in, like, our top-ten worst family stories ever."

I raised an eyebrow.

"Okay," she admitted. "Top fifty."

"It wasn't that bad, really." I explained: "It was kind of a learning experience."

"Right," she agreed. "And the lesson was, 'Dogs eat meat. *People are made of meat*. You do the math.'"

"Okay, that's not a lesson. That's a word problem. A really bad one. No, I learned that I could put someone else's life before mine. I always thought that I would, of course, give my life for Hailey, but in the back of my mind was always a sneaking doubt that if the time came I wouldn't be able to physically force myself to go into the burning building for her, or step in front of an angry dog to save her, but that day I found out that I could. It was scary as hell, but in a way it's reassuring to know I could do it if I had to."

"Aw," Lisa replied. "That's pretty profound for a dog bite."

"I *also* learned that seeing your own fat poke out of you is disgusting and is good motivation not to eat that third drumstick," I added. "Oh, and that when a hot doctor comes in to tell you he really wants to 'irrigate your holes,' you shouldn't laugh, because apparently that's a real thing and not some sexual innuendo. Oh! And when they did it *they found a tooth in my back.*"

"Because it was from your silent twin," Lisa said conspiratorially.

"EXACTLY!" I exclaimed. "Except not at all. It was just a tooth from the dog, because he was so old. But I did immediately tell the doctor that maybe it was a twin that I'd ingested before birth, and I asked him to feel around in my back hole for any human hair or a skull, since I was already numb, but he acted like I was crazy. Probably because I'd laughed at his sexual innuendo."

"Yeah, doctors hate that," she added.

"I guess the good thing about getting attacked by the dog is realizing that I'm a little less selfish than I thought I was. Before, the most selfless thing I had done was give all my wishes to Hailey. I see a falling star or blow out my candles and I wish for something for her, but it feels selfish. Knowing that she's happy is going to make me happy anyway, so it feels like cheating, like wishing for more wishes. Also, it's not much to give up, considering that every wish prior to having Hailey involved my seeing a unicorn." I half hesitated in even telling Lisa that part, knowing that once you tell someone your wish it doesn't come true, but the chances of my seeing a unicorn are slim. Especially since they appear only to virgins, according to unicorn lore. I imagine that if I ever see a unicorn it'll be one that's mostly senile and sort of skanky, purposely showing up disheveled and unshowered just to fuck with the other unicorns, who wish that that unicorn would stop embarrassing them all like this. Harold would be his name, probably, and he'd be a smoker. So I wasn't giving up much. But getting attacked by wild dogs to protect my child? It was like a nod from the universe. A subtle recognition that *yes*, you *are* a good mother. It was one I was just as surprised to receive as the universe was surprised to give, and I sat there in the hospital room thinking that if I had to give some sort of acceptance speech I would be earnestly shocked and humbled, and I would probably cry the ugly cry, and not just because I was having large gashes sewn up at the moment. I would thank my mother for teaching me to put others first, and my father for unintentionally preparing me to not panic when attacked by large unknown animals. I would thank Victor for not being surprised that I'd sacrificed myself for our daughter, and I would thank Hailey for mindlessly trusting that she was okay in my arms. And then I would nod silently to the disheveled unicorn at the back of the room as he caught my eye and tipped his head at my awesomeness.

"And that was what I was thinking. And also that I needed to find out what kind of drugs they'd given me, because anything that makes you hallucinate proud but chaotic unicorns watching your acceptance speech for being mauled by dogs is okay by me."

"Wow," my sister said as I realized I'd been saying all of this out loud. "That's . . . *totally messed up*. But," she admitted, "I've given up my birthday wishes for my kids too. I guess it's a sign of being a grown-up. God, imagine what our lives would have been like without Mom wishing good things for us on *her* birthdays. We'd probably be dead by now."

"Probably," I agreed. "Although, now that I think about it, maybe Mom wished for our lives to end up just like this. It's no magical unicorn, but it brought us here, and I can't think of anyplace I'd rather be. Unless it was the exact same place with an air conditioner."

Lisa nodded. "I'd fist-bump to that, but it's too hot to move. So what do you wish for Hailey when you blow out your candles?"

"Can't tell you or it won't come true. But I suppose it's the same sort of wishes all parents wish for their kids. I wish for her to have love, and just enough heartbreak to appreciate it. I wish for her to have a life as blessed as mine. With her own dead magical-squirrel puppet, and getting arms stuck up a cow's vagina, and to know the pride that comes with choosing to be mauled by a dog to save someone else. I guess those would be the things I'd wish for Hailey."

Lisa looked at me quizzically. "Yeah, I don't think anybody wishes for their kids to get mauled and stuck in a cow vagina."

"I just mean *metaphorically*," I added.

Lisa nodded and closed her eyes as she rested her head on the porch chair. "Well, that's good," she said absently as she stretched her legs out to bask in the sun. "Because in real life that's the sort of shit that haunts you forever. Those are the kinds of memories that get seared into your mind for good."

I looked over at her and mimicked her pose, feeling the sun bake into my bones as I let her words run through my mind. I smiled gently to myself as I closed my eyes and thought, *"My God. I certainly hope so."*

Epilogue

Fifteen years of marriage and one beautiful daughter later, Victor and I are still as mismatched as ever. We fight. We make up. We occasionally threaten to put cobras in the mailbox for the other person to find. And that's okay. Because after fifteen years, I know that when I call Victor from the emergency room to tell him that I was attacked by dogs when visiting my parents, he'll take a deep breath and remind himself that this is our life.

I watch Victor almost in wonderment at the man he's become, now completely unfazed when my father asks him to pull over so he can peel a dead skunk off the road because he "might know someone who could use it." I see Hailey slip easily between the world of ballet classes and helping her grandfather build a moonshine still.

I see how we've changed to create a "normal" that no sane person would ever consider "normal," but that works for us. A *new* normal. I see us becoming comfortable with our own brand of dysfunctional functionality, our own unique way of measuring successes.

But most important, I see me . . . or rather, *the me I've become*. Because I can finally see that all the terrible parts of my life, the embarrassing parts, the incidents I wanted to pretend never happened, and the things that make me "weird" and "different," were actually the most important parts of my life. They were the parts that made me *me*. And this was the very reason I decided to tell this story . . . to celebrate the strange, to give thanks for the bizarre, and to one day help my daughter understand that the reason her mother appeared mostly naked on Fox News (that's in book two, *sorry*) is probably the same reason her grandfather occasionally brings his pet donkey into bars: Because you are defined *not* by life's imperfect moments, but by your reaction to them. Because there is joy in embracing— *rather than running screaming from*—the utter absurdity of life. And because it's illegal to leave an unattended donkey in your car, even if you do live in Texas.

And when I see another couple, who seem normal and conventional and who *aren't* having a loud, recurring argument in the park about whether Jesus was a zombie, I don't feel envious. I feel contentment and pride as Victor and I pause our shouting to share a smug, knowing smile with each other as we pass the baffled couple, who move to give us room on the sidewalk. Then I lean in to rest my head on Victor's shoulder as he laughs quietly and lovingly whispers to me, *"Fucking amateurs."*

The End

(Sort of)

Hi.

You're still here, which means that you are probably the kind of person who forces your angrily impatient spouse to sit through the credits of the movie on the off chance that there might be some sort of bonus scene at the end, even though *they're* the kind of person who jumps up three minutes before the movie even ends so that they can be the first person out of the parking lot, because *apparently* that's more important than finding out that "Rosebud" is the name of the sled, or that *Dude, Where's My Car?* is (spoiler alert) a terrible, terrible movie. Or perhaps you're still reading because you think that this can't *possibly* be the end of the book, because there's *no way* it was worth forty-five dollars,* and you're hoping that if you keep reading you'll find something here that actually makes the price of the book worthwhile. Well, congratulations, tenacious and demanding malcontents, *because there totally is.*

If you're anything like me, there is probably at least one well-known fact that you insist is basic common knowledge, but your disbelieving family scoffs at you whenever you bring it up. And so you Google it to prove them wrong, but somehow in the time that it took you to argue that "actually, *yes*, some squirrels *can* breathe underwater," they've managed to somehow rewrite the entire Internet so that it looks as if water squirrels never even existed. And then, after that, whenever you disagree with them about anything at all they automatically dismiss you with a patronizing chuckle, saying to one another, "*Yeah*. This coming from the same person who thought squirrels could breathe underwater," and then they shake their heads with pity and refuse to even *consider* your theory about why Jesus is technically a zombie. That totally sucks. But you're in luck, because the last page of this book will fix all of that.

Just get a pen and write in whatever fact you want to prove in the space provided, and then casually show it to your detractors in a mature and mildly condescending manner. I suggest something like "So I was just doing some light, squirrel-based reading, and *apparently* some squirrels *can* breathe underwater. I can see how you might doubt it, but it must be true BECAUSE IT'S IN A FUCKING BOOK, YOU SKEPTICAL ASSHOLE."

You're welcome. I'm pretty sure that alone is worth forty-five dollars.*

---

*My editor just pointed out that this book will not cost forty-five dollars, and I do realize that, but when people read that the book is forty-five dollars after *they* paid only thirty-five dollars for it they'll feel really good about what a great deal they got, even though technically they paid full price. This is how marketing works.**

My editor just argued that "that's not how marketing works at all," that the book wouldn't cost thirty-five dollars either, and that when people hand this book to their detractors, they'll probably just look at the cover and realize immediately that this is not a squirrel-based book at all. I explained that she was not looking at the big picture, and that we are going to have to charge thirty-five dollars in order to cover the costs of the removable dustcover identifying this book as *Squirrel-Based Facts for the Intellectually Elite. Volume 2: The Elusive Aqua Squirrel*. She then claimed that if we did that, the only people who would actually buy this book would be "the three soon-to-be-disappointed squirrel enthusiasts searching for books about squirrels *that don't even exist.*" I reminded my publisher that squirrel researchers are an untapped market, and I pointed out that I am pretty damn sure that aqua squirrels *do* indeed exist because (1) I've actually seen one, and (2) *their existence is documented in a fucking book.* Then she asked which book I was referring to, and I was all, *"THIS ONE."* I'm pretty sure this proves my point on all counts.*

***My editor says that "there is no way in hell they are going to print a book with a fake dustcover about *'water squirrels'* just so that you can win an argument with your husband." So I called my mom (since she was there when I was swimming with my sister in the nearby creek and witnessed an entire family of water squirrels), and she told me that she *did* remember it, but that she and my father simply hadn't had the heart to tell an enthusiastic eight-year-old (flush with the giddy excitement of discovering the existence of water squirrels) that she was swimming with a nest of dead squirrels who were floating down the stream after having most likely drowned in the previous day's flash flood. *Awesome.* It's like my whole life was based on a lie. Plus, I'm pretty sure that's how you get cholera.

True Facts

- Milk has no discernible smell . . . at all. . . .

- "Problemly" is a real word. (Definition: Something that will probably be a problem.) It is unchallengeable in Scrabble.

- "Flustrated" is not a real word, and regular use of it will result in your genitals' falling off. Problemly . . .

- Some squirrels have gills, although this is typically noticed only by the truly observant and highly intelligent.

- _____

- _____

WARNING: In an effort to save the environment, this book was made from the recycled tissues of tuberculosis patients, and should NOT be handled by persons lacking current tuberculosis vaccinations. Also, some of them had the flu. And problemly dysentery.

james garfield and i love you.

This is the actual holiday card we send out each year,
and it's also a special thank-you to you for listening to my story.
P.S. This counts as me sending you a Christmas/Hanukkah card.
You are welcome.

Acknowledgments

A HUGE thank-you goes out to all of my grandparents, assorted awesome family members, friends who've loaned me money for booze, and everyone who has ever said a kind word to me, or who has (intentionally or accidentally) not kicked me. I also want to thank everyone who ever read anything of mine and enjoyed it, or at least pretended to for the sake of getting to third base with that girl who tried to convince you that I'm hilarious. Thank you, and I apologize for the chlamydia.

A very special thank-you goes out to my wonderful and supportive readers, and to the people who helped make this book possible. This includes Neeti Madan, Amy Einhorn, Laura Mayes, Karen Walrond, Maile Wilson, Katherine Center, Brene Brown, Jen Lancaster, Neil Gaiman, Stephanie Wilder-Tayler, Nancy W. Kappes, Donnell Epperson, Laurie Smithwick, the Bir clan, Bonnie and Alan Davis, Wil Wheaton, everyone on Twitter who helped me write this book, Maggie Mason, Tanya Svoboda, Stephen Paroli, Alice and Eden, Evany Thomas, Heather Armstrong, Debbie Gorman, Jeanie M., Mrs. Gilly, the Menger Hotel, Diana Vilibert, the Gruene Mansion, and you. Yes, *you*. You thought I'd forget you, didn't you? You have so little faith in me. But it's fine. *I forgive you.*

And my deepest thanks and love go out to Mom and Dad, who taught me everything I know about compassion and bobcats, and to my sister, for laughing both with me *and* at me. And most especially to my daughter, Hailey, who saves my life every day, and to my husband, Victor, whom I love even more than I want to strangle. *Thank you for giving me a life worth writing about.*

Family portrait ~ 2005.

About the Author

Author Jenny Lawson relaxes at home. Her husband glares off camera and asks whether that's his toothbrush. Her husband should probably get his priorities straight. And go get her a margarita. Even if it's three a.m. Seriously, Victor, go get me a margarita. Also, the people who published this book probably shouldn't have let the author write her own biography. Poor planning on their part, I'd say.